BECOMING WISE

ALSO BY KRISTA TIPPETT

Speaking of Faith

Einstein's God

BECOMING WISE

*An Inquiry into the Mystery
and Art of Living*

KRISTA TIPPETT

PENGUIN PRESS
New York
2016

PENGUIN PRESS
An imprint of Penguin Random House LLC
375 Hudson Street
New York, New York 10014
penguin.com

ISBN 9781594206801

Printed in the United States of America
7   9   10   8   6

Designed by Michelle McMillian

For Aly and Sebastian
My Darlings, and Most Beloved Teachers

AUTHOR'S NOTE

This book was many years in the making, and has been held and made possible by a life-giving ecosystem of friends, family, colleagues, and conversation partners near and far. I must begin with the elegant and erudite Sarah Chalfant of the Wylie Agency, who kept this project alive across years when I did not believe I could do it. She is the best champion a writer could have, and at pivotal moments she provided precisely the insight—and friendship—I needed to move forward. Scott Moyers and Ann Godoff saw potential in this manuscript when it was still messy and largely unformed. I will always be grateful for that and for Scott's sensitive editorial intelligence. Thanks also to the whole team at Penguin Press, especially Sarah Hutson, Meghan White, and Matt Boyd, and to Jacqueline Ko at Wylie. Eli Horowitz provided helpful "writer whispering" at an early, difficult stage of this writing.

I was helped in carving out time and mental space by a few people and places. Nell Hillsley has been a friend and source of courage and inspiration from the very beginning of my adventures in radio and writing, and once again she and Van Lawrence provided a beautiful, hospitable space for me to write. Susan Boren and Steve King also offered respite and friendship in their lovely world. Will Rosenzweig opened his fantastic home/garden/salon, the IdeaGarden. I found an early muse while at Ghost Ranch in New Mexico. The magical Ragdale Foundation's writers' retreat outside Chicago took me in at blessedly short notice. The exquisite Mesa Refuge writers' retreat in Point Reyes, California, was the place I finally found the voice, my voice, for this manuscript. Across these years, I found restoration again and again at Rancho La Puerta in Tecate, Mexico, and I was fortunate to retreat there for a last, cathartic edit. The Birchwood Café in Minneapolis is my enduring place of local, momentary retreat, and many of the words in here have spent time there with beautiful local food, wine, coffee, and company.

My incredible and beloved team of comrades at *On Being* is a source of everyday joy and inspiration. Our move to independent enterprise in 2013 delayed and complicated the writing of this book, but it ultimately unleashed a creativity, joy, and integrity that I had not known in my working life before. Trent Gilliss has been my partner in crime now for a dozen years, and it is such an honor and pleasure to work with a person who is not only brilliant and prodigiously creative and productive, but always growing, always searching, always deepening. Lily Percy has brought a genius and an incredible spirit of excellence and fun to leading our production process and in so doing literally freed me to be able to write and do so much else. Chris Heagle is a creative master of the art and craft of radio, of the wonders of audio, and he has become such an essential partner and friend in helping me grow more winsomely into my own craft. I cannot believe my good fortune each and every day when I begin work with these three along with the amazing team—at this writing—of Mariah Helgeson, Maia Tarrell, Annie Parsons, Marie Sambilay, Aseel Zahran, Bethanie Kloecker, and Michelle Keeley. Parker

Palmer, Omid Safi, Courtney Martin, and Sharon Salzberg are part of the *On Being* team through the fabulous voice they bring weekly to our blog, and they are accompanied by others too numerous to name, "spiritual geniuses" of the everyday. Graham Griffith has been a tremendous friend and colleague of my work in these years, as has Padraig O'Tuama of the Corrymeela Community and the one and only Seth Godin. Our wonderful board members are Julie Zelle, Jay Cowles, and Jeffrey Walker. I am constantly amazed by our design colleagues at Pentagram, especially Emily Oberman and Elliott Walker, and I'm beyond grateful for their beautiful imagining of the jacket of this book.

A world of generous and gracious funding partnership underpins *On Being* and has made my life of conversation possible. It includes the Ford Foundation, the Henry Luce Foundation, the Fetzer Institute, the John Templeton Foundation, Bill and Penny George, Bill and Bonnie Clarke of the Osprey Foundation, Kalliopeia Foundation, and in earlier years the Lilly Endowment, the Corporation for Public Broadcasting, the NEH, and the Pew Charitable Trusts. I am privileged to be part of these networks of companionship, support, and inspiration, and also of the remarkable network of community and goodness that is public radio. I was fortunate to be able to create the show at Minnesota Public Radio/American Public Media. Public radio stations around the United States were the place all of the conversations in this book were initially welcomed and hosted. Our friends at StoryCorps and The Moth, especially Dave Isay and Catherine Burns, are exemplars of the best public service tradition of public radio, and provided special comradeship for the spirit and some of the passages in this book.

Webs of friendship and chosen family have held me—especially Kathy Crowley and her crew, Laurisa Sellers, Arnie Shore, Kerri Miller, Chris Cohen, Betsy Hodges, Larry Jacobs, Julie Shumacher, Pauline Boss, Dudley Riggs, Irene Dunkley, Ulrich Koestlin, Beate Herbig, Candace Eck, fellow hockey moms Shelley Berven and Wendy Tully, and my childhood best friend and anchor Karen Fluke and her parents, Nita and the late John Fluke. I once listed my dear, spectacular friend Serene Jones as my "spiritual adviser," and she is that and so much more. Our impassioned conversations across the last six years, and through travel and adventures together and apart, have shaped this writing in a thousand ways and flow all the way through it. And my actual family, especially my wise mother, Charlotte Lankard, together with Gene Rainbolt, who has become so important to me, has been enduringly loving and supportive. A shout out also to J. T. Weedman, Jayna Oakley Haney, and Bart Weedman. This book could only be dedicated, as it is, to my utterly delightful and admirable children, the people with whom I am privileged to share life and to continue, myself, to grow up.

My gratitude goes, finally, to our far-flung universe of listeners and digital community—who defy every prognosis of human decline or cultural malaise and keep me going every day—and of course to my conversation partners across the years. A few of them appear by name in these pages, but this is not a "best of." It is a slice that illuminates—a slice that lent itself to translation on the printed page at this moment in time. Each of their names is listed in the back of this book. They have all contributed to the fabric of my thoughts and my being in the world, and to whatever wisdom I am able to muster.

CONTENTS

BECOMING WISE

ONE

·· ·—|————————|— · ··

INTRODUCTION
The Age of Us

I'm a person who listens for a living. I listen for wisdom, and beauty, and for voices not shouting to be heard. This book chronicles some of what I've learned in what has become a conversation across time and generations, across disciplines and denominations.

This adventure began as the century turned and has grown and evolved along with it. My interest in these pages is on qualities of the art of living that have taken me by surprise, uprooting my assumptions. I've tried, in what follows, to show how my ideas have emerged conversationally, through a back and forth with graceful minds and lives. I've come to understand the cumulative dialogue of my work as a kind of cartography of wisdom about our emerging world. This book is a map in words to important territory we all are on now together. It's a collection of pointers that treat the margins as seriously as the noisy center. For change has always happened in the margins, across human history, and it's happening there now. Seismic shifts in common life, as in geophysical reality, begin in spaces and cracks.

This daunting and wondrous century is throwing open basic questions the twentieth century thought it had answered. Our questions are intimate and civilizational all at once—definitions of when life begins and when death happens; of the meaning of marriage and family and identity; of our relationship to the natural world; of our relationship to technology and our relationships *through* technology. The Internet in its infancy is upending the nature of making and leading and learning and belonging. It's sending us into a new Reformation, but this time of all of our institutions at once—political, educational, economic, and religious. The interesting and challenging thing about this moment is that we know the old forms aren't working. But we can't yet see what the new forms will be. We are making them up in "real time"; we're even re-imagining time.

Humanity first looked inside with global sweep in what is sometimes called the Axial Age—a handful of centuries midmillennium before the Common Era. In utterly disconnected cultures in another world of upheaval, Confucius was born in China, the Buddha sought enlightenment, Plato and Aristotle examined life and mind and soul, and the Hebrew prophets began to pen a people of God into being. The cultivation of inner life arose in interplay with the startling proposition that the well-being of others beyond kin and tribe—the stranger, the orphan, the outcast—was linked to one's own. Humanity gave voice to the questions that have animated religion and philosophy ever since: What does it mean to be human? What matters in a life? What matters in a death? How to be of service to each other and the world?

These questions are being reborn, reframed, in our age of interdependence with far-flung strangers. The question of what it means to be human is now inextricable from the question of who we are to each other. We have riches of knowledge and insight, of tools both tangible and spiritual, to rise to this calling. We watch our technologies becoming more intelligent, and speculate imaginatively about their potential to become conscious. All the while, we have it in us to become wise. Wisdom leavens intelligence, and ennobles consciousness, and advances evolution itself.

Religious and spiritual traditions have borne wisdom across time, though in charged cultural spaces they can become parodies of themselves. When I speak of these things, I'm speaking of places where we pay essential humanity an attention unmatched in our other disciplines—our capacities to love and take joy, our capacities to damage and deceive, the inevitability of failure and finitude, the longing to be of service. I love the deep savvy about hope that religion tends, its reverence for the undervalued virtue of beauty, its seriousness about the common human experience of mystery. Our spiritual lives are where we reckon head-on with the mystery of ourselves, and the mystery of each other.

We tried to retire mystery in the West in the last few hundred years and enshrined reality's sharp edges instead—solutions and plans and ideologies; communism and fascism and imperialism, with capitalism shape shifting among them. In our somewhat chastened age, we're circling back to the underlying reality that was there all along: the human condition, in all its mess and glory, remains the ground on which all of our ambitions flourish or crash. The adage that "he who does not know history is doomed to repeat it" doesn't go far enough. History always repeats itself until we honestly and searchingly know ourselves. Now the chaos of global economies points at human agency. So, increasingly, does the chaos of the weather. Terrorism, the only "ism" left swaggering in the post–cold war world, hinges on raw human despair all around.

I think a great deal about a moral equation Einstein made that is as radical in its way as his mathematical equations, if far less famous. He began his life with a profound faith in the social good of the scientific enterprise—a community of cosmic endeavor that should transcend tribal rivalries and national boundaries. Then he watched German science hand itself over to fascism. He watched chemists and physicists become creators of weapons of mass destruction. He said that science in his generation had become like a razor blade in the hands of a three-year-old. He began to see figures such as Gandhi and Moses, Jesus and Buddha and St. Francis of Assisi, as "geniuses in the art of living." He proposed that their qualities of "spiritual genius" were more necessary to the future of human dignity, security, and joy than objective knowledge.

My work has shown me that spiritual geniuses of the everyday are everywhere. They are in the margins and do not have publicists. They are below the radar, which is broken. The discourse of our common life inclines towards despair. In my field of journalism, where we presume to write the first draft of history, we summon our deepest critical capacities for investigating what is inadequate, corrupt, catastrophic, and failing. The "news" is defined as the extraordinary events of the day, but it is most often translated as the extraordinarily terrible events of the day. And in an immersive 24/7 news cycle, we internalize the deluge of bad news as the norm—the real truth of who we are and what we're up against as a species.

But our world is abundant with beauty and courage and grace. I'm aware of a growing aspiration to attend, with all the tools we have at hand, to the human change that makes social change possible. The digital world, though a new Wild West in many ways, is on some basic level simply another screen on which we project the excesses and possibilities of life in flesh and blood. Spiritual life is evolving, and its sources of nourishment are becoming more broadly accessible. Science is yielding knowledge of our bodies and brains that is an everyday form of power for softening the gap between who we are and who we want to be, as individuals and as a species. Across social and medical disciplines, we are gathering a radical new understanding of the nature of human vitality and wholeness.

We create transformative, resilient new realities by becoming transformed, resilient people. This is about the lover as well as the beloved, the citizen as well as the politician, the social entrepreneur as well as the person in need. It means me, and it means you.

Listening is about being present, not just about being quiet. I meet others with the life I've lived, not just with my questions. I've learned along the way to be grateful for the unlikely trajectory my life has taken, the perspective it's granted. It's given me intimate familiarity with some margins that are in fact the heartbeat of a society and access to places where power is exercised—the power of idea, and the power of action. I have been afforded a sense of long arcs of history that infuse what we perceive to be crises of the moment—where we came from, and how we got here from there.

I was born in the wee hours of the night as the 1960 election returns came in and John F. Kennedy was elected president. I grew up in Shawnee, Oklahoma, a small town in a young state in the middle of the middle of America, where people had come to forget the past and leave their ancestral demons behind. My mother's ancestors drove their covered wagons into the former Indian Territory to create their lives from scratch in the unforgiving Oklahoma dust. My father had been adopted by the people I knew as my grandparents at the age of three. History was one thin, tenuous layer deep—him, and now us.

I grew up full of longing but unsure of its object, and without much sense of the world beyond Oklahoma and Texas. The backdrop of social life was the Southern Baptist church, in which my maternal grandfather was a preacher. The only serious reading I had to work with was the Bible, and I was prone to late night wrestling with the large questions it raised as well as those it seemed willfully not to resolve. Then I spent the summer of my junior year in high school at a debate camp in Chicago and made friends who opened my sense of the secular possible. The most wonderful of these wanted nothing more than to go to Brown University, about which I had never heard, and so I applied there too. Going to Brown, for me, was like moving to Mars. I arrived to find the son of the long-ago-slain president living upstairs in my freshman dorm. Life on other planets, parallel universes, scenarios I always adored in science fiction and which physicists now take seriously—so much about the leap between Shawnee and Providence felt tantamount to that for me.

Great leaps, however exhilarating, are hard on mortal creatures. At the bottom of a dark place I now recognize as my first depression, early in my second year at college, I was overwhelmed by all the books I hadn't read, the places I hadn't traveled. I felt I would never catch up with my peers in that rarefied world. But I would throw myself into the chances that were now coming my way. I learned German, backpacked around Europe, and went to Mars again: I spent a semester in an improbable exchange program in the Communist East German city of Rostock on the Baltic Sea.

In Rostock, I was captured—intellectually and emotionally—by the division of Germany in particular and the world in general into communism and capitalism, geopolitical Good and geopolitical Evil. I internalized the message of the mid-twentieth century that politics was where all the important questions resided and all of the valid solutions too. I stopped thinking about God and threw myself into saving the world respectably, by way of journalism and politics.

After college I studied in the sleepy West German capital of Bonn and then went on to divided Berlin as a *New York Times* stringer. I had no promise of a living wage or a byline. But those were busy years in central Europe and I filed stories by teletype from East Germany and through the brave new modem technology from the West. After eighteen months, I was offered a job with the State Department, which was essentially an arm of government in the four-power postwar arrangement that applied until the Wall came down. I had my finger on a pulse of relationships growing across the Berlin Wall, and I was hired to keep it there. There were human bonds proliferating across the "inner-German border" throughout the eighties: environmental activists waking up together to the effect of human interaction with the natural world they shared; art and church and politics meshing in fantastic, subversive ways; young people coming of age in a world that imbibed Communist propaganda by day and Western television at night, culturally schizophrenic and restless beyond measure.

I had thrilling jobs in the West, eventually as chief aide to the young American ambassador, a nuclear arms expert. This career I was building was my calling card. I learned so much in Berlin that flows directly into the very different career I have made now. I scarcely had any conversations in those years about religion or spirit or meaning beyond politics. But geopolitical drama, in that time and place, was existential. Coming from my childhood, I was captivated by this intensity. German history was so many layers deep, so consuming for the most ordinary person, with terrible, unshakable heft. Its demons were in every room, named and confronted incessantly.

More riveting to me in the end than the politics of Berlin was the vast social experiment its division had become. One people, one language and history and culture, were split into two radically opposing worldviews and realities, decades entrenched by the time I arrived. I loved people on both sides of the Wall that wound through the heart of the city. But I found myself drawn again and again, almost for sanity's sake, to the East, where so much more was at stake, and life and mind felt more passionate and vital. This realization unsettled my sense of personal progress and education: it was possible to have freedom and plenty in the West and craft an empty life; it was possible to "have nothing" in the East and create a life of intimacy and dignity and beauty.

Until the Wall actually broke open on November 9, 1989—my

twenty-ninth birthday—no one imagined that it could fall or the Iron Curtain crumble. We err when we confine our telling of those events to the calculus of diplomacy and missiles, the charisma of Reagan or Gorbachev. Each of them played a pivotal role in that drama, to be sure, as did the diplomats and strategists around them. But they only brought things so far. The Wall finally collapsed with a whimper, not a bang, as fear lifted all at once from an entire nation. I had driven or walked through Checkpoint Charlie hundreds of times, respecting its absurdity as authority. On the night the Wall fell, after a bumbling bureaucrat misspoke at a press conference, the entire city walked joyfully through it. The border guards joined them. It was truly nearly that simple. There are places in human experience that politics cannot analyze or address, and they hold more possibility for change than we can begin to imagine.

My time in Berlin began to point me to the kinds of questions I've asked ever since. How to give voice to those raw, essential, heartbreaking and life-giving places in us, so that we may know them more consciously, live what they teach us, and mine their wisdom for our life together?

Theology, which I began to ponder in my thirties, offered up vocabulary and resources to pose these kinds of questions. As much as theology's public face has been equated across time with abstractions about God, and fights about God, I cherish its robust tradition of wrestling with the maddening complexity of human nature, human action, human being. It has insisted on the cultivation of qualities that would have sounded suspect, laudable but idealistic, to my ambitious younger self: wholeness beyond progress; hope beyond pragmatism; love beyond realpolitik.

I'm accompanied, in the pages that follow, by voices and lives that see such possibility for the change we are living through now. There is a great deal of poetry here, because it is beautiful and necessary and for other, deeper reasons that I will explore. There is a great deal of science here too. My life of conversation is enriched with the insights of physicists, neuroscientists, and biologists who are posing questions, and making discoveries, that shed light on the questions of meaning and moral action once reserved for theology and philosophy.

The connective tissue of these pages is the language of virtue—an old-fashioned word, perhaps, but one that I find is magnetic to new generations, who instinctively grasp the need for practical disciplines to translate aspiration into action. Our spiritual traditions have carried virtues across time. They are not the stuff of saints and heroes, but tools for the art of living. They are pieces of intelligence about human behavior that neuroscience is now exploring with new words and images: what we practice, we become. What's true of playing the piano or throwing a ball also holds for our capacity to move through the world mindlessly and destructively or generously and gracefully. I've come to think of virtues and rituals as spiritual technologies for being our best selves in flesh and blood, time and space.

There are superstar virtues that come most readily to mind and can be the work of a day or a lifetime—love, compassion, forgiveness. And there are gentle shifts of mind and habit that make those possible, working patiently through the raw materials of our lives.

I've organized my reflections around five of these raw materials, basic aspects of the human everyday, which I've come to see as breeding grounds for wisdom. My own understanding and experience of these things have been utterly transformed.

The first is words. We have outlived our faith in facts to tell us the whole story or even to tell us the truth about the world and ourselves. So many of us feel excluded and dismayed by what passes for discourse in our common life. But the words we have for virtue are also endangered by overuse and cliché. I explore the real-world power of "words that shimmer," in the language of the poet Elizabeth Alexander. I know it is possible to speak about our deepest passions and convictions in a way that opens imaginations rather than shuts them down. I share what I've learned about the virtue of asking better questions. The world right now needs the most vivid, transformative universe of words that you and I can muster. And we can begin immediately to start having the conversations we want to be hearing, and telling the story of our time anew.

The second is the body. The body is where every virtue lives or dies, but this statement has a vastly different meaning for me than it did in the religious world of my childhood. The cutting edge of science is yielding a vision of human healing and restoration that is realizable as never before. Our physical selves, as we're learning, are so much more than merely physical. They carry trauma and joy and memory and our capacity for opening or closing to life and one another. There are deep connections between beauty and pleasure and wisdom, and we are relearning these with practical effect, beginning with the food we eat. I've come to believe that our capacity to reach beyond ourselves—experiencing mystery or being present to others—is dependent on how fully we are planted in our bodies in all their flaws and their grace.

The third is love. Love is the only aspiration big enough for the immensity of human community and challenge in the twenty-first century. *Love* is another word that is a bit (or a lot) ruined—something we routinely speak of as something to fall into and fall out of. But as a piece of intelligence about what makes us human, and what we are capable of, it is a virtue and way of being we have scarcely begun to mine. People who have turned the world on its axis across history have called humanity to love. It's time to dare this more bravely in our midst, and dare learning together how love can be practical, creative, and sustained as a social good, not merely a private good. Everything is no longer political, as the old saying goes, but nearly everything now holds civic importance. I hear the word *love* surfacing as a longing for our public life everywhere I turn. I share what I'm hearing about what love might look like as we grapple with crises of racial and economic well-being. Our unfolding knowledge of the brain is part of this picture too—a fantastic new companion in stepping out of fear and into care, and realizing our natural belonging one to another.

The fourth is faith. I began my life of conversation with the theme of faith, and my questioning has evolved as faith has evolved in the early years of this century. The spiritual wisdom of the ages is openly accessible as never before, and we are free to craft our own spiritual lives. This is leading, counterintuitively, to rediscoveries of the depths of tradition, for the sake of the world. My own musings and questions are richly informed by my conversations with physicists and with the growing sphere of the new nonreligious. Paradoxical connections intrigue me—the way our technologies are reopening a sense that literal reality is not all there is; the robust vocabulary scientists and mathematicians have of beauty and of mystery. I believe that mystery is a common human experience, like being born and falling in love and dying. A new openness to the language of mystery—and the kindred virtue of wondering—across boundaries of belief and nonbelief, science and faith, is helping us inhabit our own truths and gifts exuberantly while honoring the reality of the other. I have no idea what religion will look like a century from now; but the evolution of faith will change us all.

The fifth is hope. My life of conversation leads me to reimagine the very meaning of hope. I define hope as distinct from optimism or idealism. It has nothing to do with wishing. It references reality at every turn and reveres truth. It lives open eyed and wholeheartedly with the darkness that is woven ineluctably into the light of life and sometimes seems to overcome it. Hope, like every virtue, is a choice that becomes a habit that becomes spiritual muscle memory. It's a renewable resource for moving through life as it is, not as we wish it to be. I describe some of the luminous faces and voices and stories I see as part of the story of our time, pointing to what we're capable of as much as every narrative of danger and decay.

The Jesuit paleontologist Pierre Teilhard de Chardin is a beacon for this book, and especially in my reflections on hope. In life, he joined intellectual rigor, scientific discovery, and an adventurous, expansive view of the human spirit. "An interpretation of the universe," he wrote, "remains unsatisfying unless it covers the interior as well as the exterior of things; mind as well as matter." While he was excavating the primitive "Peking man" fossil in China, he imagined future humanity excavating the modern human psyche and spirit—and seeing it revealed as primitive. He foresaw that we would overlay the biosphere with the noosphere—the realm of human intelligence, information, and action. He predicted, that is, something like the Internet. He believed that the noosphere would drive the next stage of evolution—an evolution of spirit and consciousness. This is a grand and exciting vision for imagining the long-term stakes of what we might be fermenting now.

But Teilhard thought in slow, deep, geologic time, and so must we. A long view of time can replenish our sense of ourselves and the world. We are in the adolescence of our species, not by any measure in full possession of our powers. The twenty-first-century globe resembles the understanding we now have of the teenage brain: dramatically uneven; immensely powerful and creative at times and in places, reckless and destructive in others.

In America, many features of national public life are also better suited to adolescence than to adulthood. We don't do things adults learn to do, like calm ourselves, and become less narcissistic. Much of politics and media sends us in the opposite, infantilizing direction. We reduce great questions of meaning and morality to "issues" and simplify them to two sides, allowing pundits and partisans to frame them in irreconcilable extremes. But most of us don't see the world this way, and it's not the way the world actually works. I'm not sure there's such a thing as the cultural "center," or that it's very interesting if it exists. But left of center and right of center, in the expansive middle and heart of our life together, most of us have some questions left alongside our answers, some curiosity alongside our convictions. This book is for people who want to take up the great questions of our time with imagination and courage, to nurture new realities in the spaces we inhabit, and to do so expectantly and with joy.

I have yet to meet a wise person who doesn't know how to find some joy even in the midst of what is hard, and to smile and laugh easily, including at oneself. A sense of humor is high on my list of virtues, in interplay with humility and compassion and a capacity to change when that is the right thing to do. It's one of those virtues that softens us for all the others. Desmond Tutu, whom I found impossible to doubt, says that God has a sense of humor. There is science helping us to see a sense of humor in the brain as an expression of creativity, making unlikely connections and leaning into them with joy. So I hope and trust that a smile in the voice may sometimes rise from these pages. And I do bring many voices along with me here, snatches of conversation completing and informing my thoughts, as they do all the time in my life and work.

I'm not surprised by the fact that inexplicable and terrible things happen in a cosmos as complicated as ours, with sentient beings like us running the show. But I am emboldened by the fact that surprise is the only constant. We are never really running the show, never really in control, and nothing will go quite as we imagined it. Our highest ambitions will be off, but so will our worst prognostications. I am emboldened by the puzzling, redemptive truth to which each and every one of my conversations has added nuance, that we are made by what would break us. Birth itself is a triumph through a bloody, treacherous process. We only learn to walk when we risk falling down, and this equation holds—with commensurately more complex dynamics—our whole lives long. I have heard endless variations on this theme—the battle with illness that saves the life that follows; the childhood pain that leads to vocation; the disability that opens into wholeness and a presence to the hidden wholeness of others. You have your own stories, the dramatic and more ordinary moments where what has gone wrong becomes an opening to more of yourself and part of your gift to the world. This is the beginning of wisdom.

And what is true for individuals is true for peoples. Our problems are not more harrowing than the ravaging depressions and wars of a century ago. But our economic, demographic, and ecological challenges are in fact existential. I think we sense this in our bones, though it's not a story with commonly agreed-upon contours. Our global crises, the magnitude of the stakes for which we are playing, could signal the end of civilization as we've known it. Or they might be precisely the impetus human beings perversely need to do the real work at hand: to directly and wisely address the human condition and begin to grow it up.

TWO

WORDS
The Poetry of Creatures

I take it as an elemental truth of life that words matter. This is so plain that we can ignore it a thousand times a day. The words we use shape how we understand ourselves, how we interpret the world, how we treat others. From Genesis to the aboriginal songlines of Australia, human beings have forever perceived that naming brings the essence of things into being. The ancient rabbis understood books, texts, the very letters of certain words as living, breathing entities. Words make worlds.

We chose too small a word in the decade of my birth—*tolerance*—to make the world we want to live in now. We opened to the racial difference that had been there all along, separate but equal, and to a new infusion of religions, ethnicities, and values. But tolerance doesn't welcome. It allows, endures, indulges. In the medical lexicon, it is about the limits of thriving in an unfavorable environment. Tolerance was a baby step to make pluralism possible, and pluralism, like every ism, holds an illusion of control. It doesn't ask us to care for the stranger. It doesn't even invite us to know each other, to be curious, to be open to be moved or surprised by each other.

Here are some words I love, words that describe presence rather than means towards an end: *nourishing, edifying, redemptive; courageous, generous, winsome; adventurous, curious, tender.* I began my professional life as a journalist dealing in words the twentieth century favored: *crisis, containment, realpolitik.* Along the way in that era and beyond it, we reserved some of the other words we need the most for sidebars to the news. They fell into disrepair and cliché. *Peace* is strangely divisive. *Justice* is somehow partisan. I'm unmoved when we "celebrate diversity" by putting it up on a pedestal and avoiding its messiness and its depths. I intermingle the language of *common life* with *public life* because in recent generations we've collapsed our imagination about public life to be too narrowly about *political* life. I always rush to add qualifiers when I use the word *civility*—words like *muscular* or *adventurous*—because it can otherwise sound too nice, polite, and tame.

Of course all words are just containers on some level, but that is really the point. The connection between words and meanings resembles the symbiosis between religion and spirituality. Words are crafted by human beings, wielded by human beings. They take on all of our flaws and frailties. They diminish or embolden the truths they arose to carry. We drop and break them sometimes. We renew them, again and again.

> Here's what we crave. We crave truth tellers. We crave real truth. There is so much baloney all the time. You know, the performance of political speech, of speeches you see on the news, doesn't it often feel to you like there should be a thought bubble over it that says, "what I really would say if I could say it is . . ."

Elizabeth Alexander was the poet of the first Obama inauguration, and she is one of my favorite thinkers about the failure of "official language and discourse." The poem she wrote and read on the Washington Mall in January 2009 was about the mundane, miraculous interwovenness of words with reality. I called her up for a conversation two years later, in the midst of a political season of language grown feral. Then the congresswoman Gabrielle Giffords was shot and wounded, and several others killed, at a civic gathering in front of an Arizona grocery store. I worried that a show with a poet in a week of national tragedy might seem beside the point at best, callous at worst. Instead, there was an outpouring of the same wild gratitude I know in myself when poetry intrudes and demands I let it take up space in me.

We are starved, and ready, for fresh language to approach each other; this is what Elizabeth Alexander names.

> I learn so much every day from being a mother. My sons are 11 and 12, and you see the way children know when they're being bamboozled. And they also are drawn towards language that shimmers, individual words with power. They will stop you and ask you to repeat a shimmering word if they're hearing it for the first time. You can see it in their faces.

I have a young son too—can you think of one of those words?

> Well, actually, if they were right here, they would love *hoodwinked* and *bamboozled*. People sometimes ask me when they read poems that have an "I" in them that seems to be autobiographical—people are interested in the details. Oh, did that really happen to you? Is that from you? What I try to explain is, even if I am drawing on personal experience, the truth of a poem is actually much deeper than whether or not something

really happened. What matters is an undergirding truth that I think is the power of poetry.

As you're talking, I'm thinking of your poem "Ars Poetica #100: I Believe," *especially these lines:*

Poetry is what you find
in the dirt in the corner,

overhear on the bus, God
in the details, the only way

to get from here to there.
Poetry (and now my voice is rising)

is not all love, love, love,
and I'm sorry the dog died.

Poetry (here I hear myself loudest)
is the human voice,

and are we not of interest to each other?

So I think that the truth of that poem is not about true things or things that happened, but rather in the question are we not of interest to each other? Which to me isn't about, I like her shoes or, oh, he has a fascinating job. It's much deeper than that. Are we human beings who are in community, do we call to each other? Do we heed each other? Do we want to know each other? To reach across what can be a huge void between human beings. I look at my children and I think, as deeply as I know you I do not know what's inside your heads. But I crave knowing them that deeply. And so it's most intense with one's beloveds, but I think it's a way to move in the world. And if we don't do that with language that's very, very, very precise— not prissy, but precise—then are we knowing each other truly?

I began to learn an art of conversation about undergirding truths from the Benedictine monks of St. John's Abbey of Collegeville when I moved to Minnesota by way of one of life's odd, unplanned trajectories in the mid-1990s. Religious stridency in American life had reached a fever pitch of toxicity, spurred on by a media appetite for voices that delivered entertainment. I was fresh from my study of theology, and intensely aware that we were working with a very limited vocabulary and skillset to discuss things that matter in public. These Benedictines had founded a quiet but mighty institute for "ecumenical and cultural research" in the 1960s, when the notion of Catholics and Protestants in relationship was a now unimaginably daring move. It became a seedbed of cross-religious ferment for the latter half of the twentieth century.

One of the ecumenical institute's founding visionaries was developing Alzheimer's disease. Others were simply growing old. And so they sent me off to gather an oral history of what had happened, and how, in this place. Far-flung lives had come quietly into relationship here and in turn informed the way their denomination entered into relationship with the religious other. They were Roman Catholic and Eastern Orthodox, Presbyterian and Nazarene Holiness and Pentecostal. Among them were a leading Evangelical seminary president and a Paulist priest, Tom Stransky, who had been Pope John XXIII's liaison with non-Catholic observers at Vatican II and now was running the Tantur Ecumenical Institute, a place of Christian, Jewish, and Muslim encounter on the road between Jerusalem and Bethlehem.

The friendship between these former religious strangers was in itself remarkable. It was their corollary to my experience in Berlin that there is more change possible in our lifetimes than we can foresee. They all remained as distinct and impassioned on their spectrum of belief as ever. And yet the delight, curiosity, and esteem they had acquired for each other's minds and journeys changed everyone profoundly. It humanized doctrine. It invigorated their sense of their own tradition, and simultaneously imparted them with a grateful sense of mystery about what other traditions bring into the world. They took these new ways of seeing and being back into their lives in their own communities. The great religious historian Martin Marty has said that America's transition from a Protestant majority nation was one of the most graceful handoffs in history. There are many chapters in that story, and what happened in Collegeville is one of them.

Father Kilian McDonnell, the monk of St. John's Abbey who founded the ecumenical institute, had become a globe-trotting theological ambassador after growing up in the backwoods of South Dakota. "It wasn't the end of the world," he liked to say of the little town where he grew up, "but you could see it from there." A decade after I came to know him, when he was in his seventies, he became a fairly successful published poet himself. My favorite of his poems goes like this:

Perfection, Perfection

I have had it with perfection.
I have packed my bags,
I am out of here.
Gone.

As certain as rain
will make you wet,

perfection will do you
in.

It droppeth not as dew
upon the summer grass
to give liberty and green
joy.

Perfection straineth out
the quality of mercy,
withers rapture at its
birth.

Before the battle is half begun,
cold probity thinks
it can't be won, concedes the
war.

I've handed in my notice,
given back my keys,
signed my severance check, I
quit.

Hints I could have taken:
Even the perfect chiseled form of
Michelangelo's radiant David
squints,

the Venus de Milo
has no arms,
the Liberty Bell is
cracked.

Father Kilian and his community taught me the magic of rooting words about meaning in the color and complexity, the imperfect raw materials, of life. Profound truth, like the vocabulary of virtue, eludes formulation. It quickly becomes rigid, gives way to abstraction or cliché. But put a spiritual insight to a story, an experience, a face; describe where it anchors in the ground of your being; and it will change you in the telling and others in the listening.

In Collegeville, discussion about a large, meaty, theological subject began by framing it as a question, and then asking everyone around the table to begin to answer that question through the story of their lives: Who is God? What is prayer? How to approach the problem of evil? What is the content of Christian hope? I can disagree with your opinion, it turns out, but I can't disagree with your experience. And once I have a sense of your experience, you and I are in relationship, acknowledging the complexity in each other's position, listening less guardedly. The difference in our opinions will probably remain intact, but it no longer defines what is possible between us.

At St. John's, we had hours to tell our own stories and listen to others, days to unfold the "why" and "what next" and "so what" questions that followed—and take them up together. I've found it possible to preserve the core wisdom of this approach and condense it in other times and places. I walk with people back and forth across the intersection of what they know and who they are, what they believe and how they live—and what that might have to do with all the rest of us. My usual opening inquiry—whether I'm with a theologian or a physicist, a parent or a poet, atheist or devout—is this: was there a religious or spiritual background to your childhood, however you define that now? To be clear, this is radically different from the more obvious, unnerving question I would never ask: tell me about your spiritual life now. This part of us is as intimate as anything we attempt to put words around, and it ultimately defies them. The wise Quaker author and teacher Parker Palmer, my beloved mentor and friend, likens the human soul to a wild animal in the backwoods of the psyche, sure to run away if cross-examined.

The word *soul* is one of those overused words of which some of us are understandably wary. But almost everyone, I've learned, has a story to tell about the spiritual background of her childhood. This simple inquiry invites an open-hearted recollection that honors all the nuance and improvisation and clarity we've gathered around whatever *soul* or *spirit* means. It stirs a part of us where certainties are leavened by experiences, by hopes, and by fears. It's a place that remembers questions as vividly as answers—questions we may have followed our whole lives long and which, with the right encouragement, we might take up with different others. Just as importantly, this question plants the entire conversation to come in a stance that is softer and more searching than we usually present as adults to the world. And it leads organically, along straight or meandering paths, into the roots of the curiosity that becomes, in adulthood, passion and vocation.

I've heard answers that are captured in one word, and take off from there—"love," and "loneliness." Much of the way people talk about the religious background of their childhood has to do with absence as much as presence—the mother, for example, who would take the family to church while the father stayed home and read the paper. The newspaper-reading father is etched into the fabric of subsequent spiritual wonderings as much as any ritual inside walls of faith. I've spoken with many, many scientists who describe their discovery that mathematics could explain the colors on the surface of an oil slick, not to mention the motions of stars, and how this realization thrilled them with a sense of purpose transcendent in its way: that it was possible to explore how the world works and our place in it. I've spoken with a neuropsychologist who as a young volunteer with the Special Olympics began puzzling over the question of what makes a mind original and beautiful. I've met a French-born Tibetan Buddhist monk and passionate photographer who started his life as an atheist molecular biologist and whose life was upended by photos he came across of the faces of monks—pictures that revealed an unexpected template for radiant, integrated life.

There are pleasurable, primal, life-giving reasons we are rediscovering the power of personal story everywhere in media and culture. The art of conversation I'm describing here is related, but it is something subtly and directionally different—sharing our stories in the service of probing together who we are and who we want to be. To me, every great story opens into an equally galvanizing exchange we can have together: So what? How does this change the way you see and live? How might it inform the way I see and live? I believe we can push ourselves further, and use words more powerfully and tell and make the story of our time anew.

One of my most beloved examples of this is an early conversation I had with a wise woman and physician, Rachel Naomi Remen. Her words did shift the way I move through the world ever after. She first began to challenge the nature of cancer treatment—and later the content of medical education—with her realization that every illness has a story attached. A person is given a diagnosis of cancer or diabetes or heart disease, but the details of a person's life make every cancer or diabetes or heart disease different and every course of healing unique. In ruminating about the spiritual roots of her life, she told me about her Hasidic rabbi grandfather, and the Birthday of the World—the story behind the evocative, demanding Jewish teaching to "repair the world."

> This was my fourth birthday present, this story. In the beginning there was only the holy darkness, the Ein Sof, the source of life. In the course of history, at a moment in time, this world, the world of a thousand thousand things, emerged from the heart of the holy darkness as a great ray of light. And then, perhaps because this is a Jewish story, there was an accident,

and the vessels containing the light of the world, the whole-ness of the world, broke. The wholeness of the world, the light of the world, was scattered into a thousand thousand frag-ments of light. And they fell into all events and all people, where they remain deeply hidden until this very day.

Now, according to my grandfather, the whole human race is a response to this accident. We are here because we are born with the capacity to find the hidden light in all events and all people, to lift it up and make it visible once again and thereby to restore the innate wholeness of the world. It's a very impor-tant story for our times. This task is called *tikkun olam* in He-brew. It's the restoration of the world.

And this is, of course, a collective task. It involves all peo-ple who have ever been born, all people presently alive, all people yet to be born. We are all healers of the world. That story opens a sense of possibility. It's not about healing the world by making a huge difference. It's about healing the world that touches you, that's around you.

The world to which you have proximity.

That's where our power is. Yeah. Many people feel powerless in today's situations.

Right. But when you use a phrase like that just out of nowhere, "heal the world," it sounds like a dream, a nice ideal, completely impossible.

It's a very old story, comes from the 14th century, and it's a different way of looking at our power. I suspect it has a key for us in our present situation, a very important key. I'm not a person who is political in the usual sense of that word, but I think that we all feel that we're not enough to make a difference, that we need to be more somehow, wealthier or more educated or otherwise different than the people we are. And according to this story, we are exactly what's needed. And to just wonder about that a little: what if we were exactly what's needed? What then? How would I live if I was exactly what's needed to heal the world?

I told my son, who's seven, this story about the beginning of the universe and about the sparks and the holy flying out. He listened to me so raptly, and he said, "I like that."

I was told this story, let's see, 63 years ago. And my response to it was exactly the same. That's very important about stories. They touch something that is human in us and is probably unchanging. Perhaps this is why the important knowledge is passed through stories. It's what holds a culture together. Culture has a story, and every person in it participates in that story. The world is made up of stories; it's not made up of facts.

Although we tell ourselves facts to piece together the story.

Well, the facts are the bones of the story, if you want to think of it that way. I mean, the facts are, for example, that I have had Crohn's disease for 52 years. I've had eight major surgeries. But that doesn't tell you about my journey and what's happened to me because of that, and what it means to live with an illness like this and discover the power of being a human being. And whenever there's a crisis, like 9/11, do you notice how the whole of the United States turned towards the stories? Where I was, what happened, what happened in those buildings, what happened to the people who were connected to the people in those buildings. Because that is the only way we can make sense out of life, through the stories. The facts are a certain number of people died there. The stories are about the greatness of being a human being and the vulnerability of being a human being.

I think you make such an interesting contrast also with the fact that we live with all kinds of stories in our culture, forms of entertainment as well as information, but that those stories always have beginnings and endings. And you say that the stories of our lives, stories as they function in life, take time. Real stories take time.

There's a powerful saying that sometimes we need a story more than food in order to live. They tell us about who we are, what is possible for us, what we might call upon. They also remind us we're not alone with whatever faces us. When I say a story doesn't have an ending, for example, part of my story is you telling your little boy the story of the birthday of the world. That's also part of my grandfather's story, right? And your little boy has never met my grandfather, but perhaps my grandfather will be woven into his life in some way. It may be a very small way or it may not, I don't know, but in that sense no one's story is ever finished.

The thing about the raw materials of the life of the spirit is that they are always changing. What you see in the past is dependent on what you are able to see now. I've done a lot of writing before this in which I would have started my answer to the question of the spiritual background of my life with a story about my Southern Baptist preacher grandfather and his effect on me. There will be much about him in these pages. But at this point in my life, I'm as acutely aware of how my father's lost sense of history and family was the spiritual background to his childhood and a great black hole in the middle of mine. It's a good analogy: time and space had collapsed in on themselves. No light could enter or escape. He'd been dropped off for adoption one day without warning, along with an older sister and a baby brother. I don't know what his first years were like before that; I suspect the worst. My father professed to have no curiosity at all about his sister or brother or mother, though I believe he remembered their names. When he was a bit older, his mother briefly tried to kidnap him back. He shared this story matter-of-factly. But he sometimes had terrible screaming nightmares, which lent a perilous air to my nights, that his mother was coming to get him.

By day in my family, we scarcely spoke of these things. Questions flourished in our midst, unaskable. And of course, those unnamed realities, those unasked questions, shaped us all from the inside out in ways it would take me decades to begin to apprehend. Only in the writing of this book have I come to trace the intensity of my insistence on talking about what matters—now in the world writ large—to the beginnings of my own story. This is ironic, and wonderful in its way. Conversation after conversation, year after year, I've coaxed others to trace the intersection of their grandest aspirations and surest wisdom with real life and time and place, past to present, wound to gift. Now, in the act of offering what I've learned to others, I receive it for the first time, fully, for myself.

At risk of stretching my analogy too far, I find myself drawn to black holes in common life—painful, complicated, shameful things we can scarcely talk about at all, alongside the arguments we replay ad nauseam, with the same polar opposites defining, winning, or losing depending on which side you're on, with predictable dead-end results. The art of starting new kinds of conversations, of creating new departure points and new outcomes in our common grappling, is not rocket science. But it does require that we nuance or retire some habits so ingrained that they feel like the only way it can be done. We've all been trained to be advocates for what we care about. This has its place and its value in civil society, but it can get in the way of the axial move of deciding to care about each other.

Listening is an everyday social art, but it's an art we have neglected and must learn anew. Listening is more than being quiet while the other person speaks until you can say what you have to say. I like the language Rachel Naomi Remen uses with young doctors to describe what they should practice: "generous listening." Generous listening is powered by curiosity, a virtue we can invite and nurture in ourselves to render it instinctive. It involves a kind of vulnerability—a willingness to be surprised, to let go of assumptions and take in ambiguity. The listener wants to understand the humanity behind the words of the other, and patiently summons one's own best self and one's own best words and questions.

Generous listening in fact yields better questions. It's not true what they taught us in school; there is such a thing as a bad question. In American life, we trade mostly in answers—competing answers—and in questions that corner, incite, or entertain. In journalism we have a love affair with the "tough" question, which is often an assumption masked as an inquiry and looking for a fight. I edited the "spiritual background of your life" question out of our produced show for years, for fear that it sounded soft, though I knew how it shaped everything that followed. My only measure of the strength of a question now is in the honesty and eloquence it elicits.

If I've learned nothing else, I've learned this: a question is a powerful thing, a mighty use of words. Questions elicit answers in their likeness. Answers mirror the questions they rise, or fall, to meet. So while a simple question can be precisely what's needed to drive to the heart of the matter, it's hard to meet a *simplistic* question with anything but a simplistic answer. It's hard to transcend a combative question. But it's hard to resist a generous question. We all have it in us to formulate questions that invite honesty, dignity, and revelation. There is something redemptive and life-giving about asking a better question.

Here's another quality of generous questions, questions as social art and civic tools: they may not want answers, or not immediately. They might be raised in order to be pondered, dwelt on, instead. The intimate and civilizational questions we are living with in our time are not going to be answered with answers we can all make peace with any time soon.

The poet Rainer Maria Rilke, who became my friend across time and space all those years ago in Berlin, spoke of holding questions, living questions:

> Love the questions themselves as if they were locked rooms or books written in a very foreign language. Don't search for the answers, which could not be given to you now, because you would not be able to live them. And the point is to live everything. Live the questions now. Perhaps then, someday far in the future, you will gradually, without even noticing it, live your way into the answer.

I wish I could throw Elizabeth Alexander's question by way of poetry, "Are we not of interest to each other?" into town hall meetings, the halls of Congress, and let it roll around for a while.

Our cultural mode of debating issues by way of competing certainties comes with a drive to resolution. We want others to acknowledge that our answers are right. We call the debate or get on the same page or take a vote and move on. The alternative involves a different orientation to the point of conversing in the first place: to invite searching—not on who is right and who is wrong and the arguments on every side; not on whether we can agree; but on what is at stake in human terms for us all. There is value in learning to speak together honestly and relate to each other with dignity, without rushing to common ground that would leave all the hard questions hanging.

I have experienced that even with the most intractable lightning-rod discussions that have ripped our families and some of our institutions apart, reframing the animating questions can start whole new conversations. We can reject the predictable posturing and the inevitable stalemate. Frances Kissling is best known as a pro-choice advocate, the longtime head of Catholics for Choice. Less famously, when she retired from Catholics for Choice a decade ago, she decided to give herself over to learning what it would mean to be in real relationship with her political opposites. I once engaged her and the Evangelical social ethicist David Gushee in a conversation about abortion. Our framing question was to explore what is at stake in human terms in all the things we approach when we approach abortion and what makes this subject so exquisitely fraught and divisive. We nearly succeeded in avoiding the language of "pro-choice" and "pro-life" altogether. The conversation was big and messy in a whole new way. It was uncomfortable and also thrilling because it opened provocative territory we hadn't charted before we began—whether the sexual revolution was good for us, and how to rehumanize and deepen our relationship to sexuality in public as well as private spheres. There was a realization in a room full of people that we long to ponder these things, but they had been obscured by the predictable, well-worn debates.

Sometimes one wise voice that has been in the world for a while and evolved, lived the same human drama from a few different angles, can provide more nuance than any two-sided debate. Frances Kissling is one of those voices for me. She's steeped in the particular context of reproductive rights, but what she's learned applies to every sphere. She's also stopped using some of the comforting words we understandably reflexively leap to as a basis for dialogue, like identifying common ground in the midst of deep differences. She says:

> I think that common ground can be found between people who do not have deep, deep differences. And in politics you can find compromise. Politics is the art of the possible. But to think that you are going to take the National Conference of Catholic Bishops and the National Organization of Women and they are going to find common ground on abortion is not practical, it's not gonna happen. And we could extend that. But I do think that when people who disagree with each other come together with a goal of gaining a better understanding of why the other believes what they do, good things come of that. But the pressure of coming to agreement works against really understanding each other. And we don't understand each other.
>
> The polarization that exists on the abortion issue, in which people have called each other names and demonized each other for decades, definitely speaks against any level of trust that enables people to come to some commonality. So you really have to start with this first idea, that there are some people—not all—who see some benefit in learning why the other thinks the way that they do. Some of it's the simple stuff of humanization—that the person becomes a real person, not an extremist, not evilly motivated; that perhaps for some you can overcome the epithets that we have charged each other with. And that, I'm a very strong believer in.
>
> I have learned—I have changed my views on some aspects of abortion over the last 10 years, based upon having a deeper understanding of the values and concerns of people who disagree with me. As a result, I have an interest in trying to find

a way that I can honor some of their values without giving up mine. That's, for me, what has happened.

And that is, again, different from this rush that I think we make in this culture, a parallel to finding common ground, to getting on the same page, right? You're not talking about getting on the same page.

No, no. But, you know, Sidney Callahan, who is against legal abortion generally speaking, a long time ago said that the hallmark of a civil debate is when you can acknowledge that which is good in the position of the person you disagree with.

I want to read you something that you wrote. You were listing a couple of qualities that you thought were necessary to bring constructive, forward thinking approaches to a difficult issue. One of them that really struck me was "the courage to be vulnerable in front of those we passionately disagree with."

I think that's the hardest thing to do. It is very hard for all of us in these situations to acknowledge, for example, that we just don't have the answers to this problem. I don't think we have the answers to the problem of abortion in our society, whether it's the problem of abortion itself or the problem of how we're going to mediate our differences about abortion.

And a willingness to admit that is very, very difficult. What is it in your own position that gives you trouble? What is it in the position of the other that you are attracted to? Where do you have doubts? I've said this to somebody recently: I don't understand how you can work on an issue for 35 years as complicated as this and never change your mind at all about anything. What we've been doing hasn't been working. I think that you become more willing to be vulnerable at a moment when you recognize that what you have done has not gotten you where you want to be. So an element of vulnerability is some modicum of helplessness. And if you don't think you need any help and you think everything is just hunky-dory, well, then, there's absolutely no reason to be vulnerable.

What do you think you've learned about how social change happens? What would progress look like now in these years ahead?

That's a very difficult question. What have I learned? The need to approach others positively and with enthusiasm for difference is absolutely critical to any change. There is no way to change somebody. I'm the toughest of fighters, let's be very clear. My reputation for being devastating in debate is legendary, and I love a good fight and I love to win. But what I have learned is that, you know, the simplistic way of putting it is that you can catch more flies with honey than vinegar. That's a very wise saying.

And I have learned that people in the center are not going to be the big change makers. You've got to put yourself at the margins and be willing to risk in order to make change. More importantly, you have got to approach differences with this notion that there is good in the other. That's it. And that if we can't figure out how to do that, and if there isn't the crack in the middle where there's some people on both sides who absolutely refuse to see the other as evil, this is going to continue. There's a lot of pressure, and it's much easier, to preach to the choir versus listening to people who disagree with you. But the choir is already there; the choir doesn't need us.

. . .

The crack in the middle where people on both sides absolutely refuse to see the other as evil—this is where I want to live and what I want to widen.

There's no more pressing realm where words are more starkly a cause of division, and more softly a source of healing, than in our reckoning with the natural world. There are fewer and fewer people alive on any continent who do not have a direct experience of environmental volatility. Yet our only sustained public discourse is a pitched battle around "climate change"—a battle that has real consequences but which is, nevertheless, a distraction. It heaps antagonism and dismay upon the already overwhelming deluge of environmental bad news. It deflects from the practical spiritual nature of reckoning with our global ecological future. For this, as clearly as any challenge, brings home the axial question: can human beings come to understand their own well-being as linked to that of others, in wider and wider circles, beyond family and tribe? The natural world is the source and surrounding of our lives, and it is becoming unrecognizable. The work of nurturing and restoring it points at near universal, life-giving experiences like eating, raising children, loving the place one comes from, and discovering magnanimity in the presence of beauty. This is the kind of language I hear from people who are getting on with the work to be done, in the world they can see and touch. It is language that reframes behavior—taking a sense of necessary actions out of the realm of guilt and into good.

Many, many of these people are religious. In conservative Christian circles, there is a fascinating story unfolding in vivid contrast to the strident voices who make the news. It is very much a story of shifts in words that hasten and accompany changes of mind and heart. There has been repentance over words that have done damage—a turning away from classic biblical language that was internalized in an overly linear, literal way and that shaped Western civilization's encounter with nature near and far. The King James Version's translation of God's blessing on humankind in Genesis was taken up as a sacred rallying cry by Christian colonizers and industrialists and explorers: "Be fruitful and multiply, and fill the earth and subdue it; and have dominion over the fish of the sea and over the birds of the air and over every living thing that moves upon the earth."

In our time, those same lines are being interpreted and enacted anew. At Yale Divinity School in the 1990s, I studied the Hebrew Bible with a professor named Ellen Davis, who pointed out language about care for the land in nearly every text. A decade later, she tells me how unprepared she was for that experience, and how it transformed her life and scholarship ever after.

> I was lecturing my way all the way through the Hebrew Bible, the Old Testament, for the first time. And I think at the end of the first semester, one of my doctoral student teaching assistants said, when we were making up the final exam, "You need to ask a question about land." And I said, "Why?" And he said, "Because you talk about it all the time." I was not conscious of doing that; I was simply aware of talking my way through each book of the Bible. I would now say it's obvious that I would be talking about land all the time because you can't go more than a few chapters without seeing some reference to land, water, its health, its lack of health, the absence of fertile soil and water. But at the time, that came as a surprise to me.
>
> At the same time, I had made a trip back to California and to a part of California not so far from where I'd grown up, but far enough that I hadn't been there in a number of years. I was shocked at the changes that had taken place within my mem-

ory. And I began to recognize that there was a huge gap between the kind of exquisite attention that the biblical writers are giving to the fragile land on which they live and the kind of obliviousness that characterizes our culture, or did at that time, in respect to our use of land. California and Israel are very comparable landscapes. They're both fragile, both semi-arid. So I found time collapsing in a certain sense. But there was an odious comparison between that care of land which is at least held up as an ideal in the Bible and the disregard of it that I was seeing in my own place.

And now I continue to find that even reading chapters, passages, that I've written on before, that I've lectured on countless times, when I read them from the perspective of what they have to say about the land on which our life depends and its health, things pop out at me that I had simply overlooked before. Things make sense to me that I had never tried to make sense of.

So how do you step back from the Genesis language of subduing and especially "dominion"—what do you see that is not clear in the way we have translated and used this text?

The Hebrew word is a strong word, and I render it "exercise skilled mastery amongst the creatures." The notion of skilled mastery suggests something like a craft, an art of being human, without taking away the fact that humans do, from the perspective of almost all the biblical writers—not every single one but almost all—humans occupy a very special place of power and privilege and responsibility in the world. But the condition for our exercise of skilled mastery is set by the prior blessing, in previous verses, of the creatures of sea and sky.

They too are to be fruitful and multiply. So whatever it means for us to exercise skilled mastery, it cannot undo that prior blessing. I think that's pretty convicting for us in the sixth great age of species extinction.

It's so important that, as you say, Genesis 1 is a liturgical poem. How would that inform our reading of what it's saying to us and how it's saying it to us?

Poetry is language that speaks to our hearts. And I'm using the biblical word *heart*. I think the closest equivalent to that in 21st-century language is our *imaginations*. The heart, in biblical physiology, is the center of our emotions, but also of our intellect. Those two things cannot be separated. And poetic language is precise. It is detailed, it's realistic, but it is not the discursive language of mere fact. So it's important that in different ways, the first and second chapters of the Bible are telling us about our place in the world, telling us about the web of relationships into which we are born as a species. We are placed creatures. We're placed within an order. That's a quite different way of thinking about ourselves than what we often take to be a literal reading of the Bible—in my view, a cruder way of reading the Bible.

Over the years as you've delved into this, you've worked and written together with Wendell Berry. You've written about the poetry of loss and care as "the poetry of creatures."

A starting point for me in thinking about ourselves as creatures is the observation of Rowan Williams, the former Archbishop of Canterbury, that "now the art of being creatures is almost a lost art." That notion that we need to learn, we need to be skilled, we need to be wise, in order to be the creatures. That, in fact, we are creatures. We think of creatures as anyone who's not human.

It's that dominion that we have over the creatures.

And it's why I like the translation, "the exercise of skilled mastery," rather than "dominion" because it suggests an artfulness in being human. Often you can read an instructional manual or a textbook or whatever, without paying all that much attention. You skim your way through it to get to the heart of the matter. But you can't read poetry that way. Poetry slows you down. And anything in our world now that slows us down is to be valued and maybe as a gift and even a calling from God.

Ellen helped introduce me to a parallel universe of religious environmentalism that I'd not known to exist. One of its icons, Cal DeWitt, is a biologist and zoologist who has been creating and living in a sustainable community in the rural wetlands of Dunn, Wisconsin, for three decades. He's also a lifelong Evangelical Christian.

When you started doing this, you and your community, your town in Wisconsin, more than thirty years ago, you must have been seen as kind of radical.

Very definitely. We were looked at as being odd because there wasn't really any crisis, although I think you could discover it if you worked to find it. But what we did is we studied our town. We did an inventory of all of the things that were present there—farms and marshes and springs and historic sites,

Indian trails, buildings, our tobacco farms included. And what happened after we did this very careful and very extensive inventory is, we fell in love with the place. Most of us didn't know where we lived. We had just moved in and out rather oblivious to the beauty of things.

I like Cal DeWitt's definition of religion: "The passion to live rightly on earth and to spread right living." There are seventy species of plants on his lawn alone, which he describes with delight as "a multi-textured environment for vibrant plant and animal life." He recounts how one year during migration, three thousand robins descended on his lawn to eat earthworms "because I am producing so many, not by trying, but because that's what happens." Cal DeWitt helped galvanize critical Evangelical support for the Endangered Species Act of 1996. The Au Sable Institute of Environmental Studies, which he founded and ran for twenty-five years, creates curricula for Christian colleges and universities. He begins to open my imagination about human ecosystems below the radar of rancor, seeding towards vibrancy just like that visitation of robins on his lawn. He points to the core value of *conversion* as a theological virtue that Evangelical Christianity possesses towards nimble, real-world social change.

In the Evangelical world, there's a great distrust in human authority, and the teaching in the Bible is our source of life, of work, and of practice. So if the reading of the scriptures shows that caring for creation is a vital part of the human task and we have been neglecting that, then that calls for a conversion. And Evangelicals are very used to the idea of taking about-faces, which is really what conversion is about. I was able to observe this in the early to mid-1970s on world-hunger issues. Bread for the World was formed by Christians and other hunger-relief organizations. It was remarkable—and much like what's happening at places like Vineyard Boise right now, the Vineyard church in Idaho. It is Pentecostal. Vineyard Boise's pastor, Tri Robinson, has a daughter who had been taking environmental studies courses and was encouraging her dad to say something about the environment. Tri Robinson is a conservative Republican rancher. What he did, thanks to his daughter, was discover that he should do something about that. It took him about six months of Bible study to find out how he would say this biblically. Then with some fear and a lot of prayer, he gave a sermon on caring for creation. And remarkably, for the first time ever, the congregation stood up and gave him a standing ovation.

Now they have regular programs to eliminate invasive species, recycle materials, and take people high in the mountains to restore trails. They have a food pantry that functions not only as their own food pantry, but also supplies twenty-three other food pantries. The place is absolutely vibrant and alive. And, of course, the church's membership is growing tremendously because there are all sorts of disenfranchised environmental types who have been waiting for the church to do something, and here it is. It's happening. So watch out.

Cal DeWitt uncovers "stewardship" and "service" in the roots of the word the King James Bible rendered as "dominion." Like Ellen Davis, and the world of conversion of which he is a part, he's let the words he uses change him. He's also spent some time provocatively looking behind the word *environment*. It grew, he tells me, from Chaucer's coining of the word *environing*. This word had the imaginative force of positing borders between us and the natural world and each other, a move the language of "creation" couldn't make. Linguistically, we had created, through Chaucer, a way of separating ourselves. "So what's important about the revitalization of words like *creation* and *creation care* and *caring for creation*," he says, "is that it brings these two together again."

In 2002, together with a British physicist, Sir John Houghton, De-Witt organized a watershed forum to expose conservative Evangelical leaders to the hard science of climate change. The then chief representative in Washington, D.C., of the National Association of Evangelicals, Richard Cizik, has said that he was "converted" to the science of climate change at that meeting. Cizik and others went on to raise awareness of such issues in churches across the country. This initiative coincided with the emergence of a younger generation of the faithful for whom care for the natural world was a self-evident calling. In the searching conversation that continues to unfold in those communities, what happened at the Vineyard Boise church has happened in other places. Children have challenged their pastors and parents, Bibles have been pulled out and reexamined. There is reflection—and action—on the generative responsibilities of a belief in creation. The term *creation care* has become an animating form of words, of practical urgency—even for some who resist scientific diagnoses of the problems at hand. "Jesus's teaching, 'Behold the lilies of the field, behold the birds of the air,' is really well taken here," Cal DeWitt says of his marsh, "and beholding is so much different than just checking off species on a life list."

It would be easy to mishear *creation care* as a version of *creationism*, which is quite the opposite move. And indeed, this language is dismissed at one pole of the pitched cultural battle, just as climate change is derided at the other. In the crack in the middle, where people on both sides absolutely refuse to see each other as evil, we rediscover the power of words to move us towards each other and away. We simultaneously circle back to the necessity of virtue to hold us to a care with our words— the intention we bring to what we speak; the trustworthiness and generosity we impart to the spaces in which we share our lives. The point of learning to speak together differently is learning to live together differently. It's a dance of words with arts of living.

END NOTES

Marie Howe

Poetry is Marie Howe's exuberant and openhearted way into the words and the silences we live by. She works and plays with a Catholic upbringing, the universal drama of family, and the ordinary rituals that sustain us. She's perhaps best known for her poetry collection *What the Living Do,* about her brother John's death at age twenty-eight of AIDS.

> I didn't know one could be a poet and live. As a child I would read the old Harvard Classics. We had them in our living room. I would pore through these dusty books and try to find language that was adequate to experience, or try to find language that could somehow hold the unsayable. And some of the Mass did that. Some of the parables do that, you know. I love the parables and the stories of Noah, and Abraham and Isaac, and all those great old stories. They've struck me as poems. They hold so much mystery and complexity. A story is all there, but we know that the story, the real story, is inarticulate. And I love that. I love the spaces in between what happens.

And because you came to poetry as a profession a little bit later in life, I wonder how you experienced and thought about what it is about poetry that we can't do with other kinds of language, and what need it is salving in us?

Well, poetry holds what can't be said. It can't be paraphrased. It can't be translated. The great poetry I love holds the mystery of being alive. It holds a kind of basket of words that feels inevitable. There's great, great, great prose, you know, gorgeous prose. You and I could probably quote some right now. But poetry has a kind of trancelike quality. It has the quality of a spell. My daughter came home one day and she did this whole snappy thing. "Don't make me snap my fingers in a Z formation/explanation/talk to the hand, talk to the wrist/ Ooh, girl, you just got dissed." It was like a counter spell for a mean girl. I thought, this is what we all need to walk around with, a handful of counter spells. And poetry, when you think of its roots, is that.

Making magic with words.

Absolutely. I mean maybe the first poem was a lullaby a woman sang to her child, the incantatory, *Everything is OK, everything is OK, everything is OK. I'm here, go to sleep.* Or we prayed for rain, or we thanked the gods for the corn, or we sang to the deer we were going to catch. It's incantatory. It feels as if its roots can never wholly be pulled out from sacred ground.

I really love these last lines in a poem of yours, "The Meadow": ". . . bedeviled, / human, your plight, in waking, is to choose from the words / that even now sleep on your tongue, and to know that tangled / among them and terribly new is the sentence that could change your life." What a wonderful way to think about the power of language and the mystery of it, where it comes from in us.

Well, language is almost all we have left of action in the modern world. For many of us, at least, action has become what we say: the moral life is lived out in what we say more often than what we do.

John Paul Lederach

For more than three decades, John Paul Lederach spent four to five months a year on the road, mediating crises of life and death in more than twenty-five countries and five continents. He's one of the most esteemed global mediators in the world today, a professor at Notre Dame, and a lifelong Mennonite— an icon of this tradition of a lived commitment to peace building.

I've gotten very interested in the connection between poetry and peace-building over the last years. One of those insights and one of those areas of personal discipline for me was both discovering and working with a kind of a haiku understanding of complexity. Which is, as I see it, an ability to not simplify the complex. To some degree the haikuist is constantly trying to capture the full complexity of a human experience, but in the fewest words possible. And that discipline is a very interesting one. I'm an especially big fan, going back into haiku's origins in schools of Japanese poets. Their understanding of what they were doing was about a way of being in a context, particularly the context of nature. They made the link between the human experience and the experience of the richness of nature in a way that could fully capture the moment, the season, the human experience, but in this very short five syllable– seven syllable–five syllable format. Oliver Wendell Holmes once wrote, "I would not give a fig for the simplicity on this side of complexity, but I would give my life for the simplicity on the other side of complexity."

I love that.

And that is what the haikuist is after. So I do a variety of things. One is that I've become much more respectful of the link between appreciating being in and feeling nature—and noticing things that we're involved in when we're in settings of violence. For me it's a recuperation of sorts. The other is that as I travel in work, I listen for haiku in people's conversation. What I find is that quite often when people say something and we all have a kind of an aha moment around what was said, it often is a capturing of that simplicity on the other side of complexity. And it often comes out very close to, if not actually in the form of, a haiku. I could give you one or two of those if you want.

Yes.

I refer to them as conversational haikus or poetry in conversation.

Seven years after the signing of the Good Friday Agreement, I was sitting in a seminar in Northern Ireland. People, while still happy that the agreement had held, felt that Northern Ireland had fossilized in its sectarian relations. That things were simply not changing, and it might not get much better. In a dinner conversation, one of the colleagues from Northern Ireland I was sitting with said this, which I placed into a haiku. I don't always title my haikus, but this one's called "Rainbow's End?"

Maybe, he says, this
is as good as it will get
Peaceful bigotry.

Another. I've worked on occasion with a group of people
from Burma. They call them ethnic minorities even though
they're the majority. That means they're not Burmese. And
many of them have armed fronts, which have been fighting,
some of them for decades and decades, against the current re-
gime. I worked primarily with a small group of people who for
one reason or another were brought into being shuttle mediators, attempting to open up, discuss, or move some kind of a
negotiation between people in the Burmese government and
various armed ethnic groups. There were small sets of people
from each of the seven or eight ethnic groups. In 2003, I spent
the better part of a week simply listening to their stories. They
were, from a mediator's standpoint, some of the hardest stories
I've ever heard.

I can remember one group who lived very close to the Ban-
gladeshi border with Burma, who needed to carry a message
across the border to the commander of an armed movement
that was just on the other side. But they could not pass directly
through the border to that area. They needed to travel all the
way to the capital city of Yangon and get a passport—and
every passport has to be turned in after each visit. Then fly to
a third country in order to convey one message. And then all
the way back again to bring it forward, many times sitting
with local commanders or groups who would arrest them and
keep them imprisoned for weeks on end, until they sorted
through whether they were legitimate.

The perspective that you have in these situations is so unbelievable about the kind of difficulties that they're facing. The group that I was meeting with referred to themselves as "The Mediators Fellowship." So I wrote a little haiku when I was leaving Yangon, titled "Advice from the Mediators Fellowship."

Don't ask the mountain
to move, just take a pebble
each time you visit.

You want one more?

Yes!

Tajikistan. This was translated back from Tajikian to English, and the way it rang in the translation came out almost as a perfect haiku. They have very odd borders in Central Asia, which were created by Stalin and which have separated small portions of each major group. So every country has a minority of every other country's majority. And some of the most significant cultural cities of one group are located in a country where they don't live. This was the haiku that came out:

Gods and men love maps
they draw borders with pens that
split lives like an ax.

Ann Hamilton

The philosopher Simone Weil defined prayer as "absolutely unmixed attention." The artist Ann Hamilton embodies this notion in her sweeping works of art that bring all the senses together and meet a longing many of us share, as she puts it, to be "alone together."

A friend of mine who's a wonderful poet, Susan Stewart, said that hearing is how we touch at a distance. Isn't that beautiful? I think that's also how I start projects in some ways: I just try to listen for what something needs to become. Or to find the right question. Listening is obviously a very specific thing in a conversation, but it's also a practice for me as I respond to spaces. The felt quality of the architecture of a space already has all this information in it. You're listening to the space.

I think listening is something we really have to practice, because our everyday spaces are not set up for listening.

Or we're plugged in. It's very hard for me to wear headphones at all or sunglasses because then I feel like I'm not where I am, wherever that is. I'm not here. There's some filter going on. But the question is also, how do you listen to yourself?

You do like this language of being a "maker" . . . as much or maybe more than being called an "artist." And it's just occurring to me that this language lends itself to the rest of us too. Being an artist is specialized, but making is something we all do, each in our own ways, including in our family lives.

And there are so many forms for making. I love reading the dictionary. The *Oxford English Dictionary* has I don't know how many pages devoted to "make," and "making," and all of its possibilities. It's the same as making a list of all the materials that exist in the world that you might transform in some way. That can just keep you busy forever. We get blinded to the possibilities that we actually have. So I have these little tricks that I play with myself to see those. Everybody should try that one.

I'm pretty intrigued by the idea of reading the dictionary. I never thought of that.

Oh, it's so beautiful. Just as materials obviously carry histories of the animal or the technologies that made them, or where they came from in the earth, words also carry all of those histories. There's a reason certain words work, and it's because of the histories they carry for us. So, lifting that to the surface of recognition is important.

Vincent Harding

I was privileged to interview, and come to know, Vincent Harding, who died in 2014 at the age of eighty-two. He and his wife, Rosemarie, helped Martin Luther King Jr. develop the theory and practice of nonviolence through the Mennonite Center of Atlanta, and he helped King write his controversial Vietnam War speech. Vincent Harding spent the decades until the end of his life bringing young people into creative contact with elders, civil rights veterans—offering experiences of them, as he said, not as figures in history books but "as living and lively and magnificent."

I'm interested in the fullness of moral imagination and spiritual imagination that has emerged from all your experiences, including, of course, the civil rights movement. The words civil *and* civility *are getting tossed around a lot in America right now. You've stated very emphatically that to reduce to "civil rights" that transformation that you were part of in the 1960s is not correct, and that* civility *is not big enough language. What I'm hearing these days is that a lot of people feel that* civility *is not a big enough word for us right now either.*

Interestingly enough, I hadn't quite made the connection that you are making now with my own thought, but that's wonderful. That's why we need each other. I have felt increasingly that what we are really talking about is not how we can have more civil conversation. What we're talking about in the context of our society, for one thing, is how we can learn how to have a democratic conversation. That is what we need. We are absolutely amateurs at this matter of building a democratic nation made up of many, many peoples, of many kinds, from many connections and convictions and from many experiences. And to know how, after all the pain that we have caused each other, how to carry on democratic conversation that in a sense invites us to hear each other's best arguments and best contributions, so that we can then figure out how do we put these things together to create a more perfect union.

For decades you've been saying that the question of how to be democratic is really taking seriously that question of living into a "more perfect union." I find that helpful as a way to open that word up.

For me, Krista, it also opens up the question of what it means to be truly human. Democracy is simply another way of speaking about that question. Religion is another way of speaking about that question. What is our purpose in this world and is that purpose related to our responsibilities to each other and to the world itself? All of that seems to me to be a variety of languages getting at the same reality.

Let's remember that that community that helped to create King and that he then helped to nurture was a community deeply grounded in the life of religion and spirituality. This was their way of being. For instance, everyone near him knew that he took very seriously this traditional, beautiful terminology when he said that what he was seeking was not simply equality or rights, what he was seeking was the creation of "the beloved community." He saw everything that crushed against our best human development and our best communal development, like segregation, like white supremacy.

When he moved to break down those laws, those practices, he was doing it not simply as an act of civil action, but a deep spiritual responsibility. People like Jimmy Baldwin and others, Malcolm for a certain time, couldn't imagine how Martin could see those possibilities. But I think he was seeing it because he was looking with an eye that was deeply filled by love and compassion and that eye opens us up to see many things that might otherwise be missed.

You've said that most riveting and instructive for young people you meet are stories of how civil rights leaders have worked on society while at the same time constantly working on themselves.

My own sense, Krista, is that there is something deeply built into us that needs story itself. Story is such a source of nurture that we cannot become really true human beings for ourselves and for each other without story—and without finding ways in which to tell it, to share it, to create it, to encourage younger people to create their own story. We also encourage younger people to find the elders, to find the veterans, not the celebrities, not the TV stars, but those folks who nobody else knows have lived such magnificent lives. Find them and then sit with them and learn how to ask the right questions so that the opening can take place. I think that this country cannot become its best self until we find ways more effectively of institutionalizing that process of sharing the stories of the elders.

When you say that we as human beings have a built-in need for stories, what your work shows is that we human beings also know what to do with stories, right? So that, as you say, the young people you work with know how to take those stories as tools and pieces of empowerment in this day, this year.

Yes, as tools for their own best work. Now is a powerful time in this country for young people and others to be asking the question, What are we for? Do we exist for some reason other than competing with China or finding the best possible technological advances? Are there some things that are even deeper that we are meant for, meant to be, meant to do, meant to achieve? Jimmy Baldwin used to like to talk about us "achieving ourselves," finding who we are, what we're for and making that possible for each other.

When the mother with the baby at her bosom starts telling stories, it is clearly not just to pass on information. Most often where I go, where I speak, I start out by asking people to tell a little of their stories. And it is amazing what people discover of themselves, of their connections, of their community. I find this even in some of the strangest situations. It's wonderful.

Walter Brueggemann

Walter Brueggemann's name has been synonymous with the phrase "prophetic imagination" for three decades of Christian preachers and teachers. Sitting with him is to experience something of the fearless truth telling and the fierce hope of this tradition he knows so well. He embodies the idea of "prophetic imagination" in our own complex and chaotic times. And prophets, he insists, have always also been poets.

> Even in the more liberal theological tradition in which I was raised, we only talked about the prophets as moral teachers. There was no attention to the artistic, aesthetic quality of how they did that. But it is the only way in which you can think outside of the box. Otherwise, even liberal passion for justice just becomes another ideology, and it does not have transformative power. That's what's extraordinary about the poetry, that it's so elusive that it refuses to be reduced to a formula. I think a great temptation among liberals who care about justice is to reduce it to a formula and then . . .

. . . to create another ism.

> That's right. And the poetry comes and breaks that open again.

That's that power of language and forms of language. There are words in your writing that come from prophetic texts but are not really part of a modern vocabulary. One of them is lamentation. *Tell me about* lamentation.

> Well, lamentation is a big piece of my research and my passion. The Book of Lamentations is a collection of poems that grieve

the loss of Jerusalem that's been destroyed. But the Book of Psalms, at least one third of the Book of Psalms, are songs or prayers of sadness and loss and grief and upset, so that very much of the Old Testament experience of faith is having stuff taken away from us. What's so interesting is that, in the institutional church with the lectionary and the liturgies, the whole business of lamentations has been screened out.

Because we don't know what to do with those depressing passages.

And we don't want to. The destruction of Jerusalem is the Old Testament equivalent to 9/11. That's their 9/11.

In the days after 9/11, I interviewed a bunch of people, including a rabbi and an Evangelical theologian, who read that first line of Lamentations to me, "How lonely sits the city."

It just fit so well. And because we have neglected the lament pieces, we are ill equipped for the loss that we are facing in our society. So we keep pretending and denying that that's not happening to us.

We think in terms of systems and continuities and predictability and schemes and plans. The Bible is to some great extent focused on God's capacity to break those schemes open and to violate those formulae. When they are positive disruptions, the Bible calls them miracles. We tend not to use that word when they are negative, but what it means is that the reality of our life and the reality of God are not contained in most of our explanatory schemes. And whether one wants to explain that in terms of God or not, it is nonetheless the truth of our life that our lives are arenas for all kinds of disruptions, because it doesn't work out the way we planned.

This larger point that you've been making is about the aesthetic, literary, poetic sensibility of the prophetic tradition—that the very language is different and transformative, and it takes that voice out of political boxes. I'm really aware that a lot of words that religious people treasure and that are core—the word justice, *the word* peace—*these words themselves are tarnished. They have all kinds of political associations and baggage, right? They're liberal or they're conservative or they belong to some agenda.*

I've recently been thinking more and more that it's so astonishing that the Old Testament prophets hardly ever discuss an "issue." What they're doing is they're going underneath the issues that preoccupy people, to the more foundational assumptions that can only be got at in elusive language. Very much the institutional church has been preoccupied with issues. And when we do that, we are robbed of transformative power. Because then it's ideology versus ideology, and that does not produce very good outcomes for anyone.

Can you think of an example where you've seen a religious leader or a community subvert that? I mean, get outside that issues base?

Well, Martin Luther King did sometimes. I think at his best he was a biblical poet. If you just think of the line, "I have a dream"—it soared away. He wasn't really talking about enacting a civil rights bill—except that he was. It happens from time to time like that.

The task is reframing so that we can reexperience the social realities that are right in front of us, from a different angle.

THREE

FLESH

The Body's Grace

We are matter, kindred with ocean and tree and sky. We are flesh and blood and bone. To sink into that is a relief, a homecoming.

Mind and spirit are as physical as they are mental. The line we'd drawn between them was whimsy, borne of the limits of our understanding. Emotions and memories, from despair to gladness, root in our bodies. Bone-deep love, heartbreak, the "hardened heart" of Pharaoh— we've used language like this forever and now we grasp its sense. Our brains lay physical pathways and take bodily direction. Our bodies are longing and joy and fear and a lifelong desire to be safe and loved, incarnate.

Medicine became an art of treating our parts, not our whole. Religion divided us inside with high mystical notions that we are souls trapped in bodies, and theologies that made flesh and sin indistinguishable. Strangely, interestingly, the Enlightenment fed into this too. The philosopher Descartes watched as new science presumed to summarize the whole of reality by way of mathematics. He was preserving a space of dignity for the realm of imagination and spirit when he proclaimed, now so famously, "I think, therefore I am." Later, as a rallying cry—an Enlightenment sound bite—this became a simplification of what makes us human and a demotion of our spiritual and physical selves in that picture.

I taste, touch, smell, see, and hear, and my mind entwines with my senses and experiences. I live and move and have my being, as the Book of Common Prayer more lyrically describes it. Therein, I become.

Philosophers and physicians didn't mean to divide us up. It's what we do instinctively with great truths—we take them to extremes. We try to control this messy reality we are, tugged and torn by desires and needs and holes we fill with excess. Now, we're bringing our sense of ourselves back to earth. We're tethering our yearning for wholeness to the physiology we've known about for a while, the neurons we're just learning to see. Physical, emotional, and spiritual are more entangled than we guessed, more interactive in every direction, and this knowledge is a form of power.

For most of history, religion was a full-body experience, a primary space in common life where we danced and sang and laughed and cried and ritualized the passages of our lives. Rituals are sophisticated ancient intelligence about the body. Kneeling, folding hands in prayer, and breaking bread; liturgies of grieving, gathering, and celebration—such actions create visceral containers of time and posture. They are like physical corollaries to poetry—condensed, economical gestures that carry inordinate meaning and import. Rituals tether emotion in flesh and blood and bone and help release it. They embody memory in communal time.

And all of the traditions that give us meaning and morality have an incarnational, fully human heart. Buddhism carries the enlightened being and the lineages of teachers. Hinduism has its emotive, carnal deities. In Judaism and Islam, there are the prophets and the texts themselves with a kind of embodied presence across time and generations. Christianity, most literal of all, proclaims God entering the fray of physical existence with us, taking on joy and tears and the flu, our flashes of glory, our relentless return to helplessness.

The ancestors of the Protestant world of my childhood had turned worship into a chin-up experience, spine straight on an uncomfortable pew, eyes ahead. And the holy figures who claimed my fascination when I first came back to taking religion seriously in my twenties all seemed, on the surface, to model a sharp boundary between physicality and spirituality. Now I see with different eyes. It's a contained, safe physicality the mystics reject. They plunge into flesh and blood in the raw. There's the Buddha departing his palace to live in the open air and awaken to the range of human suffering. There's the anchorite Julian of Norwich in her cell, surrounded by the ravages of the Black Death, reenacting death, the Passion, as the only way to understand God in its midst. There are the bare, radiant writings of Brother Lawrence, whose *Practice of the Presence of God* was about moving through the most ordinary physical tasks of every day, washing every dish, as a holy act.

Rumi set his dervishes whirling—whirling as a way to stay centered while moving.

I've done walking meditation with Thích Nhất Hạnh and never felt more fully alive in every breath and every cell.

Buddhism in all its variation has cultivated a sophisticated psychology of the heart-mind, never separating the two in its languages of origin. Across thousands of years, it focused on contemplative disciplines to investigate and calm the mind as everyday practice. As modernity and colonialism threatened the existence of the tradition itself, monastics who were its keepers opened these practices wide to everyone. And in the tumult of social upheaval in the 1960s, young westerners began to make their way to India and Burma to learn to meditate. I've interviewed some of those first explorers: Sharon Salzberg, Joseph Goldstein, Sylvia

Boorstein, Mirabai Bush. They came home not so much as evangelists but as importers of spiritual technologies that offer themselves with urgency to the twenty-first century.

Jon Kabat-Zinn was introduced to meditation while he was studying molecular biology at MIT. He says that scientists make the best meditators because they are most comfortable with knowing what they don't know. For him, it felt like a way to tap into different ways of knowing, to reconcile energies that had coexisted uneasily in his childhood with a scientist father and a painter mother. He came to feel that what he was learning should be accessible to everyone and that it held relevance to illness, healing, and stress. In the 1980s, he created something called Mindfulness Based Stress Reduction. He's contributed to a transformation of Western medicine that is still unfolding.

What these technologies or intra-psychic technologies—whatever you want to call them—offer us, is a chance to continually return to what's deepest and best in ourselves. It's not something you have to get by going to Harvard or working in the vineyards for 20 years; you've already got it. And the body is a big part of it. So the practice of mindfulness, whether you're doing it in some formal way, meditating in a sitting posture or lying down doing a body scan or doing mindful hatha yoga—the real practice is living your life as if it really mattered from moment to moment. The real practice is life itself. It is coming to all of those senses in hearing, seeing, smelling, tasting, touching, and also, we could say, minding.

You really put a fine point on what's at stake—that any moment in which we're not aware, any moment in which we're not attentive, is lost. You quote Thoreau in Walden, *"Only that day dawns to which we are awake."*

To which we are awake. Only that day dawns to which we are awake. It's the third to last line in the book of *Walden*. This is a realization that he had in the 1840s in Concord, which we might think of as idyllic. He was describing the residents of Concord, and the farmers, as living lives of quiet desperation. So it's not just e-mail and the Internet carrying us away from ourselves.

It's the human condition.

It's the human condition. We call ourselves *homo sapiens sapiens*. That's the species name we've given ourselves. And that comes from the Latin *sapere*, which means "to taste" or "to know." The species that knows and knows that it knows. And now maybe we need to live ourselves into owning that name by cultivating awareness and awareness of awareness itself and let that be in some sense the guide as to what we're going to invest in, how we're going to make decisions about where we live, where we're going to send our kids to school, how we're going to be at the dinner table. Whether we're going to take our bodies and our children and our parents for granted, or whether we're going to live life as if it really mattered moment by moment.

The more we can sort of learn these lessons, the more we will not be in some sense running towards our death, but opening to our lives. There's a huge distinction between the two. And all the scientific evidence is suggesting that when you choose life in the way I'm talking about, your brain changes in both form and function, your immune system changes, your body changes. I mean, we start to really take care of what's most important. And there are very, very tangible results at the level of the body, the mind, and the heart, and most importantly our relationships with the world and with our loved ones and with our own bodies.

My Southern Baptist preacher grandfather had a love of play, a corny laugh, and a lusty passion for my grandmother. His presence was a counterpoint to his theology, which was underpinned by a joy-killing litany of rules: no drinking or smoking or sex, obviously, but also no dancing or card playing or swimming or wearing shorts. His sermons described the world as a treacherous place, and the body as an entry point of danger. Much later, I grasped that there was an intelligence about the body behind his rules; each one portended a slippery slope that loomed large in his lifetime. My grandfather, like his theology, grew up on the hardscrabble Oklahoma frontier before Twelve Steps made addictions like gambling or alcoholism something less than a death sentence, before sex was unhinged from a high probability of pregnancy, before childbirth out of wedlock upended many lives.

Along with my parents, I looked down on his rules. They no longer made sense in a world of birth control and couples bridge nights and AA. But we had lost a proper humility before nature that my grandfather's generation knew to heed. In large ways and small, we lived a mid-century vision of dominating the world and subduing it. We presumed that the right policies and prescriptions would manage the wildness of our bodies and livelihoods and environment: population control and pollution control and the war on poverty. At home, we tamed the elements of fire and air and water and earth with microwaves and conditioned air, the progress of fast food. My mother studied home economics and discovered, along with her whole generation, the miracle of dinner emerging from boxes and cans. In prosperous postwar America, a newly minted virtue, "convenience," overrode the wisdom of the body.

These days I suspect that, in everything, how we inhabit our senses tests the mettle of our souls. It almost sounds like something my grand-father would have said. But I'm factoring in a love of our bodies he could not imagine, a frankness about them, a fidelity to them. We can trust the wisdom our bodies offer, again and again, and in the most ordinary circumstances. Convenience is an illusion, merely shifting the burden of process and consequences. Labor is real. But so is pleasure real and enduring. In old/new ways, we can factor in pleasure with a heightened awareness. We can insist on delight as a virtue.

Aristotle saw pleasure as a calling, a measure of integrity. So too did the Bible's story of the human condition. The second chapter of Genesis, after order has been crafted out of chaos, is set in Eden, "delight"—a place of righteous desire. The garden is lavish with beauty, the trees as "pleasing to the eyes" as their fruit is good to eat. From the Bible's opening lines, the human everyday is less about sex and sin than it is about eating, as Ellen Davis helps me see—sustenance as a creature among creatures.

> There is tremendous emphasis on the fruitfulness of the earth. "Let the earth grasp forth grass," the Hebrew says. "Let seed-bearing plants, fruit trees of every kind on earth that bear fruit with the seed in it," and it goes on for another verse. Continual emphasis on how the earth is a self-perpetuating system of fertility, of fruitfulness to provide for all. Then there is the creation of the earth creatures, including humankind. And then again at the very end of the chapter, God says to the humans right after they have been given the charge to exercise skilled mastery, God says, "Look, I give you every seed-bearing plant that's upon all the earth and every tree that has seed-bearing fruit that shall be yours for food; and to all the animals and to the birds and to the things that creep on the earth, all green plants for eating." So food has been provided for all.

It seems to me that this is the first and maybe the best clue that we have of what it means for humans to exercise skilled mastery amongst the creatures: that we are the one creature that is conscious that everybody has to eat.

And so it seems fitting to me, just right, that this is one of the elemental places where we are starting, in this century, to become newly attentive to who we are and how we live. Our crises of eating and bodies and food are driving us to revisit the gift of land, the complexity of ecosystems, the structure of economies. At the center of all that analysis, we're relearning that taste can be a measure of moral good—the freshness of the produce, the life and death of the animal, the vitality of the soil. As the era of care-less food comes to a reckoning, we're relearning the astonishingly elemental delight in growing what we eat and preparing it as though it matters. It's a way in to the intriguing connection in that Latin root of the word *sapiens,* between knowledge and wisdom and "taste." Dan Barber is a force of nature—an energetic human being, a fabulous chef and writer. As a passionate voice of the "farm to table" movement, he is reintroducing basic goods of human experience to one another.

> My mother passed away when I was very young and my father tried to cook and was not great. He was a really bad cook. He used to cook scrambled eggs, enough that my memory of my childhood is often having these hard, sort of burnt, really overcooked eggs. What's interesting is that I didn't know they were hard, burnt, overcooked eggs until I was sick with tonsillitis when I think I was 15. And my aunt, who was an expert cook, lovingly prepared food for me. She prepared scrambled eggs whipped over a double boiler with this French butter that she had gotten at the market. This stuff just slid down my throat. I said, God, this is personal. This is food. This is real.

This is real scrambled eggs. This is food. This is love. Now you would say, OK, so I dismissed my father. But actually, it took my father's eggs to make me appreciate my aunt's eggs.

Dan Barber says that when it comes to food, the ethical thing is almost always also the pleasurable thing. I interviewed him in a live event at a synagogue in Indianapolis, as part of a festival on food, spirit, and the arts. One of his restaurants is at the heart of a working farm in upstate New York. There, to Eve's sinful apple, he submits a redemptive carrot.

The most pleasurable thing and the most delicious, they all run along parallel lines. That's the serendipity of what I do. My *shiv* is I want to cook good food in the pursuit of great flavor. It just so happens that they're attached to great ecology by definition. This is one of those things that's so axiomatic that we forgot. We went through this period, especially in the United States, where we forget just the most obvious thing is that a delicious carrot, a delicious slice of lamb, has attached to it these decisions in the pasture and the field that are both thoughtful and intensely ethical as well as ecological. You can't have an unethically raised lamb, an unthoughtfully raised carrot, and have a delicious lamb and carrot dish. It's impossible. Even the greatest chefs couldn't do that.

There's a quick example. We've proved this finally. We grew a variety of carrots called Mokum carrots in the middle of February. We picked them out of the ground and we brought them to the kitchen and we took a Brix test, a sugar test. We squeezed a little bit of carrot juice on a refractometer, which measures part per billion of sugar, and it registered this Mokum carrot 13.8 on the refractometer. Now we, just for curiosity sake, took a Brix measuring of a carrot that we used for stocks in the restaurant. It's the kind of carrot you'd find in a Whole Foods, a high-quality organic carrot. What did it measure on the Brix? 0.0. Undetectable with sugar. This just absolutely wigged me out. I mean, I knew there'd be a difference, because I can taste the difference. But did I know that it was going to be so dramatic?

I finally got to a plant physiologist that I sort of fell in love with. He's a part-time poet. And what he said to me was very poetic and I think right to the point. He said, "The carrot is converting its starches to sugars because, in those hard freezes, it doesn't want ice crystallization. Because if it gets ice crystallization, it dies." What you're tasting is sweetness. But what the plant—that root vegetable—is telling you is that it doesn't want to die.

By the way, there's increasingly a direct connection between Brix levels and nutrient density, which is really interesting when you think about it and it makes sense to us. Of course, the best-flavored food would also be the healthiest and the most nutrient dense. And if we're hardwired to go for that sugar and that flavor, we're also going for the best nutrient density and, as it turns out, the best ecological decisions for a farm.

You say you're not an ethicist, but you're talking about something that's life-giving, that has ethical value.

If I become a rabbi, this will become about ethics.

But those things have ethical value in Jewish tradition.

Indeed true. Look, I feel very fortunate that I believe in something that, from A to Z, is rooted in hedonism. It's really a nice thing to be an advocate of, you know? When you are greedy for the best food, you are by definition being greedy for the kind of world that you want used in the proper way. That's the true definition of sustainability.

My grandfather bought a farm when he retired from preaching, and raised cattle, and picked pecans off trees, and planted a vegetable garden. I can still taste the unbelievable sweetness of his onions, a surprise every time. Of all the memories I love him for in hindsight, this is one of the best and one of the most spiritual, the way I define that now.

I'm drawn to the Jewish notion of the soul, *nephesh*, which is not something preexistent but emergent—forming in and through physicality and relational experience. This suggests that we need our bodies to claim our souls. The body is where every virtue lives or dies, but more: our bodies are access points to mystery. And in some way that barely makes sense to me, I'm sure that we have to have feet planted on the ground, literally and metaphysically, to reach towards what is beyond and above us.

Our bodies tell us the truth of life that our minds can deny: that we are in any moment as much about softness as fortitude. Always in need of care and tenderness. Life is fluid, evanescent, evolving in every cell, in every breath. Never perfect. To be alive is by definition messy, always leaning towards disorder and surprise. How we open or close to the reality that we never arrive at safe enduring stasis is the matter, the raw material, of wisdom.

So many of the wise teachers among us apprehend truths of life from an edge of illness or crisis, where the view is suddenly so stark and so clear. They come back wounded and more whole than before, all at the same time—not cured, but healing, and embodying mystical ideas that seemed strange as abstractions and turn out to be common sense. The core of life is about losses and deaths both subtle and catastrophic, over and over again, and also about loving and rising again. The cancer, the car accident—these are extreme experiences of other trajectories we're on—aging, the loss of love, the death of dreams, the child leaving home. Grief and gladness, sickness and health, are not separate passages. They're entwined and grow from and through each other, planting us, if we'll let them, more profoundly in our bodies in all their flaws and their grace.

My wisest teacher about this, Matthew Sanford, has one of the most vibrant, connected bodies I've ever experienced. He's a brilliant yoga teacher. And he's been in a wheelchair for thirty years, since he was paralyzed from the waist down at fourteen, in a car accident on a foggy Missouri road that killed his father and sister. For twenty years, he took the advice of therapists and physicians to create body-builder arms and forget his legs. Yoga helped him claim the whole of his body, and insist that he could be healed even if his legs couldn't be cured. He's become an innovator of adaptive yoga for people with disabilities, veterans, young women with anorexia. He says that he's never known someone to become more at home in his or her own body, in all its flaws and its grace, without becoming more compassionate towards all of life. This is a wondrous statement, which somehow makes perfect sense.

> There's a reason why, when my son who's six is crying, he needs a hug. It's not just that he needs my love. He needs a boundary around his experience. He needs to know that the pain is contained and can be housed and it won't be limiting his whole being. He gets a hug and he drops into his body.

When it comes to healing, when it comes to aging, we admire that eighty-year-old guy who runs a marathon. We want to see that proof that mind can overcome matter because the body is going to be what ends up shutting down. And believe me, I didn't get this right away. But you need all kinds of strength. You need to be able to also—and it's an overused word—"surrender." Being more present, surrendering into the world, feeling more. I don't mean intellectually. I mean literally having your body as if you're getting hugged like my son. But your heart feels vulnerable when you let yourself be in the world like that. That's why we avoid it. Dominance over bodies is what human beings have done for thousands of years, whether over nature or over each other. That's one thing we want in our tool belt—to use will when you need to have it. But we are just on the beginning of realizing that there are many other ways to integrate with body. And, in fact, I believe our human survival over time is going to depend on getting much more subtly aware of bodies.

When Matthew started to do yoga, he realized that though he had no active memory of the accident, his body did. He uses the term "body memory" to describe his experience. This is consonant with an emerging frontier in the biology of stress and trauma—the realization we're making that experiences lodge in the body and can be addressed there. He says he is on a trajectory we all are on; he simply hit his body's limits and its arc of decline sooner than most and by force.

So you describe how at different times in your life, and through all the operations, and your initial injury and other injuries, you then, at some point, started to realize that healing could look like something different than being able to walk again. You say that you completely disagree when people say, "My body is failing me." I've started to say that now—everyone I know, in our forties, has done it. It's our eyes or our knees or our backs.

And I say that and it's full of grief for me because I took advantage of my body as a 13-year-old by leaving my body to absorb all the trauma that it did. One of the lessons that I've learned is, it was my body that kept me living. Your body, for as long as it possibly can, will be faithful to living. That's what it does.

My body didn't ask to get hammered and break, and to have its spine shredded, and many bones broken. But it went, "OK, let's regroup. Let's go." Only a little part of my body didn't heal—an inch or two of my spinal cord was not able to regenerate. It went to work, right, and that's what it'll do. It might get confused. It might not know how to grow the right cells. But I'm telling you, it's moving towards living for as long as it possibly can.

There's a thing in yoga called *pranayama*. It's yogic breathing. You breathe in a yoga pose for the spaces—I believe this—for the spaces that you can't feel. You don't just breathe for the bicep that you can really flex. And your balance increases, your strength increases, your flexibility increases. Talk about it in terms of honoring your body, but don't make that a moral insight, you know? "Responsibility" to my body—that, boy, doesn't inspire me at all. I like "grace."

Know your body's grace?

Or know that the places you don't feel in you are graceful. They're not lost. They're not absent. They're part of your strength, of your fiber. In a piece of wood, it's not just the grains of wood, it's the empty space and spaces between the grains of wood that make it strong. It's both. And so the world gets lighter and easier when you include more of yourself here.

This is hard. This takes patience. I'd like to tell you there's one magic insight and suddenly it's all easy. No, it's work, like everything else. I think more—not maybe more deeply, but differently—than most people, about how much my body has absorbed and moved towards living still. I look at places—skin on my body, old pressure sores and old stuff that happened—where you can see the skin is struggling to stay and hold. I don't think, "It's not holding, dang it." I feel like, "Man, it's working as hard as it can." My body does not heal as well as it used to when I was 13. That's true. My physical body doesn't do it. But because of the compassion I can feel for my body, for others, something else is healing.

This is the piece of the picture Teilhard de Chardin didn't see—that spiritual evolution would not make biology less important but more so. It would necessitate that we inhabit our bodies with a wiser fullness and reverence. Some of us are claiming this by running or walking or martial arts, or gardening or cooking—manifold ways. I was a swimmer for many years and then, after meeting Matthew Sanford, I began to do yoga. As much as anything I've done as an adult, yoga has saved my life. The salvation is subtle in the moment and profound over time. It was an instantaneous relief to focus by necessity on the placement of my palms, the arches of my feet. I was a beginner at something in midlife, and for the first time in my life I enjoyed the fact that being great at it was not the point. In yoga, the transitions between postures are a measure of grace as much as the postures themselves. I find myself applying this physical experience in minute ways in the more cerebral course of my working days.

There's lots of bad yoga in the world, to be sure, just as there is lots of bad religion in the world. When twentysomething teachers instruct me to "set an intention" for my practice and so, in some mysterious way, send it as a blessing out into the world, I'm not sure I'm a believer. I don't know what I think, honestly. I do know that taking the care to bring body and breath and intention together shifts my capacity to pay attention in moments, and it changes the way I move through the world.

To inhabit my body in all its grace and its flaws appears as a gift for the new/mundane bodily territory I'm on in midlife. Aging is the ultimate slow motion loss, inevitable for us all, and yet somehow for me and everyone I know, it's come as a surprise. You hit a point where it's no longer so incremental, and no longer amenable to cover up. The original dance between order and chaos takes over our bodies inside and out—even with lots of yoga. As I watched my children move through the primal metamorphosis of adolescence, I made a decision to be fascinated rather than terrified. I'm trying to impose the same discipline on my reaction to myself on this end of aging's metamorphosis.

There is grief to be had, to be sure, and fear, and lots of simple dismay. But settling into this as best I am able, I experience a wholly unexpected gift of contentment. Contentment is not something I've known much in my life and not something I ever really knew I wanted. This, too, is the body's grace—a gift of physiology, right there alongside my fading hair and skin. At younger ages, our brains are tuned to learn by novelty. At this stage in life, they incline to greater satisfaction in what is routine. Slowing down is accompanied by space for noticing. I am embodied with an awareness that eluded me when my skin was so much more glowy. I become attentive to beauty in ordinary, everyday aspects of my life. There is nothing more delicious than my first cup of tea in the morning; no experience more pleasurable than when my son, now much taller than me, wraps me in a hug; no view I find more breathtaking, over and over again, than the white pine that stands day in and day out behind my backyard.

The apprehension of beauty, at the life-giving seam between what is sensory and spiritual, is a virtue that clarifies. It has taken me by surprise as a way into the superstar virtues. I was a late bloomer in my reverence for visual beauty in art or the natural world. I didn't see beauty in the red-clayed semidesert of the Oklahoma landscape, though I do now. No one taught me the names of plants and creatures, except for those that sting and poison; and I didn't ask. I pinned grasshoppers to cigar boxes for science projects, and chloroformed more than a few frogs. This was an age—shocking to remember now—when we tossed litter out the windows of cars all over the place, until Lady Bird Johnson came along and told us to stop.

As a young adult in Berlin, I had my eyes locked firmly on the flora and fauna of my inner life, and of the geopolitical intrigue all around me. If you had asked me then about the place of beauty in a meaningful life, I might have responded that it was good but not for everyone as a passion, not necessarily relevant, not obviously reality based. I have boxes full of the writing I did in cafés and on assignment in those years—reams and reams of essays, stories, half novels on A4-sized paper with dot matrix edges, notebooks cover to cover with intense scribbling. There's very little in them that is sensory—smells, colors, sounds. Just Germany's high gray sky and words and ideas piled on words and ideas.

I first looked up and out—literally, that's how I recall it—in Scotland, which I visited from Berlin at the age of twenty-five. I stepped off an airplane shrouded in layer upon layer of black, pencil thin, out of place. Scotland shocked me to attention with its angular edges, cascading hues of green and heather, and extraordinary light. It stilled me. It softened my confusion and my perpetual restlessness by dwarfing them, putting them in their place. I recognized not merely a grandeur but a solid reality that also put high geopolitical clamor in its place. This was the beginning of spiritual life for me.

In my life of conversation, I hear about beauty all the time, beauty as embodied in so many forms, and as reality based as politics could ever be. It comes up vividly in my conversations with scientists. Physicists, mathematicians—those who work with mathematics—have robust vocabularies of beauty. If an equation is not elegant and beautiful, they will tell you with great solemnity, it is likely not true. Meanwhile, astronomers and astrophysicists with telescopes and holographic imagery of radio waves from the beginning of time are planting beauty in the fabric of the cosmos in all of our imaginations.

My Muslim conversation partners across the years have drawn a passionate link between beauty and spiritual virtue: beauty as a core moral value. I received this as a gift, first, in the immediate post-9/11 years, from the UCLA law professor Khaled Abou el Fadl, whom I met in a public dialogue in Los Angeles together with the wonderful Rabbi Harold Schulweis. Khaled has put his life on the line, as the title of one of his books puts it, "wrestling Islam from the extremists." He was raised in Egypt and Kuwait and barely escaped a fundamentalist path as a very young man. He insists that the key to the future of Islam lies in recovering its core moral value of beauty. God delights in beauty, Islam teaches at its core, and is beauty. Beauty is in creation, not destruction, and in balance. It is in the human intellect and the human heart and in their powers to apply sacred text towards creation and knowledge that edifies and enlivens.

That night in Los Angeles, Rabbi Schulweis responded in kind, recalling the evocative Jewish biblical counterpart: "the beauty of Holiness." This is a beauty of wholeness, he said—not just of forms and shapes but of relationships. It contradicts the fractionalizing force of religion—which after all was invented by human beings, not by God. We talked that evening about some of the bitterest issues in modern life: why religion paradoxically is at the heart of so much violence and war. Our conversation drove to high places but by a surprising, disarming route—to a different kind of critique these religious men, a Jew and a Muslim, could make of actions done in the name of religion. Is it beautiful, or is it ugly? This question was proposed as a theological measuring stick, a credible litmus test. Does this action reveal a delight in this creation and in the image of a creative, merciful God who could have made it? Is it reverent with the mystery of that?

Culturally, *beauty* is one of those muddied words. Our minds have been trained to go to perfect bodies and flawless faces on the covers of magazines. But that, as the late great Irish poet and philosopher of beauty John O'Donohue helpfully distinguished, is *glamour.* I've taken his definition as my own, for naming beauty in all its nuance in the moment-to-moment reality of our days: beauty is that in the presence of which we feel more alive. John O'Donohue's own creativity of philosophy and poetry and being emerged from the dazzling raw land of Connemara in western Ireland.

> It's the Burren region, which is limestone. It's a bare limestone landscape. And I often think that the forms of the limestone are so abstract and aesthetic, it is as if they were all laid down by some wild surrealistic kind of deity. Being a child and coming out into that, it was waiting like a huge wild invitation to extend your imagination. And it's right on the edge of the ocean as well, and so there's an ancient conversation between the ocean and the stone going on. I think that was one of the recognitions of the Celtic imagination: that landscape wasn't

just matter, but that it was actually alive. Landscape recalls you into a mindful mode of stillness, solitude, and silence, where you can truly receive time.

John O'Donohue was poetic about the possibility of creating our own inner landscapes of beauty, to keep us vital in the midst of bleak and dangerous surroundings and experiences. He gave voice to the connection between beauty and those edges of life—*thresholds* was the word he loved—where the fullness of reality becomes more stark and more clear.

If you go back to the etymology of the word "threshold," it comes from "threshing," which is to separate the grain from the husk. So the threshold, in a way, is a place where you move into more critical and challenging and worthy fullness. There are huge thresholds in every life. You know that, for instance, if you are in the middle of your life in a busy evening, fifty things to do and you get a phone call that somebody you love is suddenly dying, it takes ten seconds to communicate that information. But when you put the phone down, you are already standing in a different world. Suddenly everything that seems so important before is all gone and now you are thinking of this. So the given world that we think is there and the solid ground we are on is so tentative. And a threshold is a line which separates two territories of spirit, and very often how we cross is the key thing.

And where is beauty in that?

Where beauty is—beauty isn't all about just niceness, loveliness. Beauty is about more rounded substantial becoming. And when we cross a new threshold worthily, what we do is we heal the patterns of repetition that were in us that had us caught somewhere. So I think beauty in that sense is about an emerging fullness, a greater sense of grace and elegance, a deeper sense of depth, and also a kind of homecoming for the enriched memory of your unfolding life.

You've rightly said that we tend to associate beauty with glamour. I think if you just mention the word, if you just throw it into a commonplace conversation, someone might just think of a beautiful face, of a famous beautiful face, right? When you think of the word "beauty," what pictures come into your mind?

When I think of the word "beauty," some of the faces of those that I love come into my mind. When I think of beauty, I also think of beautiful landscapes that I know. Then I think of acts of such lovely kindness that have been done to me, by people that cared for me, in bleak unsheltered times or when I needed to be loved and minded. I also think of those unknown people who are the real heroes for me, who you never hear about, who hold out on frontiers of awful want and awful situations and manage somehow to go beyond the given impoverishments and offer gifts of possibility and imagination and seeing. I also always when I think of beauty think of music. I love music. I think music is just it. I love poetry as well, of course, and I think of beauty in poetry. But music is what language would love to be if it could.

My conversation with John O'Donohue went on for more than two hours and was exhilarating. Two months later, though strong and vital at the age of fifty-two, he died suddenly in his sleep. He left poetry in the world, and a final book of blessings, and our interview was aired as a remembrance and celebration. Life and loss process together, as do grief and beauty.

I begin to wonder if beauty is somehow as elemental to life as carbon and chlorophyll—a key component that imparts life and hope and even transcendence to the natural world and to the religious and the nonreligious of the human species. Might beauty be a bridge we can walk across occasionally to each other, a bridge that might help humble and save us? To insist on beauty in physical spaces where we go to learn and to play and to work and to heal is, we are now learning, to make all of these pursuits more fulsome and life-giving. To attend to the beauty in the other is to redirect the trap of "charity" and "development" in the century now past—to become unable to define and reduce other human beings as problems to help and to solve. The social venture entrepreneur Jacqueline Novogratz, who works in some of the poorest places in the world, asks a question wherever she goes that she experiences to call forth inner abundance: what are you doing when you feel most beautiful?

More and more these days, I'm interested in acts of kindness and works of goodness—beauty incarnate, engaging its own shadows in flesh and blood, time and space. Beauty is visible, palpable, in moments when human beings reach across the mystery of each other. Before he died in 2013, the great sociologist Robert Bellah said that his view of everything he'd studied across his life was tilted on its axis by this late recognition: when mammals began to bring forth offspring from the center of their bodies, spiritual life became possible. With apes and far more with humans, the period of necessary parental care—care in order for the offspring to survive—became longer and longer. The long helplessness of the child generated a sphere of softening, experimentation, and creativity in self-understanding and shared life. This is the biological groundwork for the axial move—stepping out of fear and into care beyond one's self. The religions apprehended this long ago and wove it into language; *compassion* in both Hebrew and Arabic derives from the word for *womb*.

When I left Berlin those years ago, I was questioning the lives of power, and the definition of success, to which I'd grown up aspiring. I didn't study theology in order to be ordained. I studied it to keep exploring the meaning, the necessary nuance, of notions like power and authority in human life and in the exercise of moral imagination and possibility. I was surprised to find myself taking spiritual life seriously. And I needed to know that it could address the complexity of reality I'd experienced. So alongside my discovery of mystics exploring embodied transcendence, I was also attentive to places where spiritual insights were being tethered to hard embodied contradictions in the thick of the human everyday. I was drawn to the L'Arche movement, which remakes notions of power and normalcy by way of shared life between able-bodied and mentally disabled people. In L'Arche communities, people born as strangers practice care that is as fierce, tender, and sustained as the bond of birth. The more "helpless" disabled among them are called, and treated as, the core members, the able-bodied their assistants.

I first read about L'Arche in the books of Henri Nouwen, a spiritual teacher and writer who was immensely prolific and beloved in his day. At the age of sixty-four in 1986, after teaching at Notre Dame, Yale, and Harvard, Nouwen publicly declared himself burnt out. He moved to spend the last years of his life as a resident assistant at the L'Arche community in Toronto, which is called Daybreak. "I moved, that is," he wrote, "from an institution for the best and brightest to a community where mentally handicapped people and their assistants try to live together in the spirit of the Beatitudes. In my house, 10 of us form a family.

Gradually, I'm forgetting who is handicapped and who is not. We are simply John, Bill, Trevor, Raymond, Rose, Steve, Jane, Naomi, Henri, and Adam."

In the early days of my radio adventure, I made a pilgrimage to L'Arche for myself. I traveled to the sleepy town of Clinton, Iowa, on a gorgeous stretch of the Mississippi. There, a revolutionary community shelters among pastel-painted houses on a residential street. It took my eyes and my introverted spirit a little while to adjust to this unfamiliar cross section of humanity testing the most paradoxical of spiritual teachings—that there is light in darkness, strength in weakness, and beauty in the brokenness of human existence. But their dare does not proceed through theologizing; it proceeds through exuberantly inhabiting the given, imperfect raw materials of the everyday. I've rarely been in a place where there is so much laughter and where the rhythm of life includes a real joy in that deceptive phrase, "the simple things of life": cooking, eating together, washing up; the rituals of leaving for work in the morning and coming home at night; walks around the neighborhood and trips to the library; goofing off and making music and playing. I've rarely been hugged so fervently by strangers and enjoyed it. At the same time and not in contradiction to all of that but making it more real, I've rarely been in a place where the grief and imperfection and struggle of being human were more honestly faced moment to moment. L'Arche is like family at its best. And it's a chosen family that then touches the strangers who cross its path. As I moved through the ordinary encounters of ordinary days with L'Arche's core members, I watched how they unsettled everyone they met, at least a little, and left them more joyful and more graceful: bus drivers, librarians, supervisors at work. And me. It's a joy and grace transmitted by bodies, and it settled in my bones and is still with me these many years later.

Jean Vanier, the philosopher and Catholic humanitarian who founded L'Arche, likes to quote his late friend Mother Teresa: "One of the realities we're all called to go through is to move from repulsion to compassion and from compassion to wonderment." When I finally sit down with him for a conversation after following his work for years, I enjoy the insistence with which he uses that word *reality*, which is so often wielded as something hard and unforgiving. Loving reality, for Jean Vanier, is an antidote to living in the imagination, or operating out of what could have been or should have been. Loving reality in all its imperfection is the necessary prelude to discovering God present and alive.

Wonderment in the face of the other is also so beautifully exacting a progression from mere tolerance.

I learn that Jean Vanier's early life did not foreshadow this progression in his own vocation. He grew up in a prominent French-Canadian family, entered the British Royal Naval College as a teenager, and commanded an aircraft carrier in his twenties. But he was consumed with questions of meaning and power. He spent a year in a contemplative community devoted to working with the poor, praying—and studying metaphysics. He wrote about Aristotle's notion of an "ethics of desire," and became a professor of philosophy at St. Michael's College in Toronto. Then at Christmastime in 1963, Jean Vanier went to visit a friend in France who was working as a chaplain for men with mental handicaps. He was especially moved by a vast asylum south of Paris in which all day, eighty adult men did nothing but walk around in circles and take a two-hour compulsory nap. He eventually bought a small house nearby and invited two men from that asylum to share life with him. This way of living became magnetic, and there are now 147 L'Arche communities in thirty-five countries. They are places of pilgrimage for all kinds of people, offering hospitality as a core virtue alongside compassion. I interviewed Jean Vanier in Maryland, where he was leading a retreat for college students from around the United States. I met a few of them, and they glowed, as I know I had in Clinton and now revisited in the presence of this lovely man with immense warmth and the elegant stature of the naval commander he once was. In a very different context to Dan Barber, he, too, draws a connection between the pleasurable thing and the ethical thing.

You say that Aristotle's "ethics of desire" is resonant with who we are today. That people want to have meaning in their lives, which Aristotle identified, and they want to be thrilled by it. You wrote, "An ethics of desire is good news for us at a time when we have become allergic to an ethics of law." People might look at the life you've led and the work that you do and contrast that with what they might call our pleasure-seeking, entertainment-oriented society. But what I hear when you talk about Aristotle is that you're not condemning that basic impulse that we have to seek pleasure. You're just saying that we can take that to a much deeper and more profound level.

It's just finding where, what activity, will give you the greatest, the deepest pleasure. I mean, for some people it might be drinking whiskey. But for me it was to find a meaning through philosophy, through my relationship with Jesus, through justice, through a struggle. And it's true that I sense deeply that I've always been really a happy person. That doesn't mean to say I haven't had difficulties, that doesn't mean to say I didn't go through difficult conflicts. But fundamentally, I've had a pleasurable life, a joyful life.

Talk to me, though, about how you connect a word like pleasure *with the place where I really sense you found your calling, where you understood what was meaningful for you. You went back to France and you encountered men in an asylum. Somehow you were seized by that and that has kind of mapped out the direction of your life.*

Yes, I come back to the reality of pleasure and to the reality of what is my deepest desire and what is your deepest desire. Somewhere, the deepest desire for us all is to be appreciated, to be loved, to be seen as somebody of value. But not just seen . . . Aristotle makes a distinction between being admired and being loved. When you admire people, you put them on pedestals. When you love people, you want to be together. So really, the first meeting I had with people with disabilities, what touched me was their cry for relationship. Some of them had been in a psychiatric hospital. All of them had lived pain and the pain of rejection. One of the words of Jesus to Peter, Do you love me?; so the cry of God saying, Do you love me? And the cry of people who have been wounded, put aside, who have lost trust in themselves: Do you love me? It's these two cries that come together.

Not just in the context of disabilities, you've said the whole question is, how do we stand before pain? All kinds of pain and weakness are difficult for us as human beings. Why is that so excruciating? Why do we do such a bad job with it?

I think there are so many elements. First of all, we don't know what to do with our own pain, so what to do with the pain of others? We don't know what to do with our own weakness except hide it or pretend it doesn't exist. So how can we welcome fully the weakness of another, if we haven't welcomed our own weakness? There are very strong words of Martin Luther King. His question was always, how is it that one group—the white group—can despise another group, which is the black group. And will it always be like this? Will we always be having an elite condemning or pushing down others that they consider not worthy? And he says something I find extremely beautiful and strong, that we will continue to despise people until we have recognized, loved, and accepted what is despicable in ourselves. There are some elements despicable in ourselves, which we don't want to look at, but which are part of our natures. We are mortal.

And as you've also pointed out many times, we all have our weaknesses, our limitations, our disfigurements. They don't all show on our bodily surface, right? We recoil when, on a person with disabilities, it shows. You've written that from the point of view of faith, those who are marginalized and considered failures can restore balance to our world. Talk to me about that.

The balance of our world frequently is seen as a question of power. If I have more power and more knowledge, more capacity, then I can do more. And when we have power, we can very quickly push people down. I'm the one that knows and you don't know, and I'm strong and I'm powerful, I have the knowledge. This is the history of humanity. And it is in the whole educational system, that we must educate people to become capable and to take their place in society. That has value, obviously. But it's not quite the same thing as to educate people to relate, to listen, to help people to become themselves. The equilibrium that people with disabilities bring is precisely this equilibrium of the heart. Think about what happens in families, with children. Maybe a father is very strong. But when he comes home, he gets down on his hands and knees and plays with the children. It's the child teaching the father something about tenderness, about love, about the father looking at the needs of the child, the face of the child, the hands of the child, relating to the child. The incredible thing about children is they're unified in their body, whereas we can be very disunified. We can say one thing and feel another.

And so as a child can teach us about unity and about fidelity and about love, so it is people with disabilities. It's the same sort of beauty and purity in some of these people—it is extraordinary. Our world is not just a world of competition, the weakest and the strongest. Everybody can have their place.

I ask Jean Vanier how he thinks about success. L'Arche is not a solution, he says, but a sign. It's the transmission of a vision and a culture. We don't know how to measure such transmission, moment to moment and life to life. But its reality—to claim that word as Jean Vanier does—is undeniable.

People ask me about the common denominators of the wisest people I've encountered. Alongside all the virtues that accompany and anchor wisdom, there is a characteristic physical presence that Jean Vanier epitomizes with others I've met like Desmond Tutu, Wangari Maathai, Thích Nhất Hạnh. Here's what it feels like, what I can report: an embodied capacity to hold power and tenderness in a surprising, creative interplay. This way of being is palpable, and refreshing, and in its way jarring, hard to figure out. Among other things, it transmutes my sense of what power feels like and is there for. This is the closest I can come to describing the sense I have, at this point, of wisdom incarnate, and it is an experience of physical presence as much as consciousness and spirit.

END NOTES

Bessel van der Kolk

The psychiatrist Bessel van der Kolk is an innovator in treating the effects of overwhelming experiences on people and society. We call this *trauma* when we encounter it in life and news. And we tend to leap to address it by talking. But he knows how some experiences imprint themselves in the body, beyond where language can reach, and how our brains take care of our bodies.

> Way back already in 1872, Charles Darwin wrote a book about emotions in which he talks about how emotions are expressed in things like heartbreak and gut-wrenching experience. So you feel things in your body. And then it became obvious that, if people are in a constant state of heartbreak and gut-wrench, they do everything to shut down those feelings to their body.
>
> One way of doing it is taking drugs and alcohol, and the other thing is that you can just shut down your emotional awareness of your body. And so a very large number of traumatized people who we see, I'd say the majority of the people we treat at the trauma center and in my practice, have cut off relationships to their bodies. They may not feel what's happening in their bodies. They may not register what goes on with them. And so it became very clear that we needed to help people to feel safe feeling the sensations in their bodies, to start having a relationship with the life of their organism, as I like to call it.

I wonder if you have ever heard of somebody named Matthew San-ford. He's a renowned yoga teacher. He's been paraplegic since he was thirteen, and he had no memory of the accident in which he was disabled. But his body remembered it. He talks about "body memory." It's the same thing you say, this imprint that trauma leaves, not just on your mind. The other thing that he's doing recently is working with veterans and also with young women suffering from anorexia, understanding that although that seems to be so much an obsession with the body, they are really in a traumatized relationship with their own bodies.

Really feeling your body move and the life inside of yourself is critical. Western culture is astoundingly disembodied and uniquely so. The way I like to say it is that we basically come from a post-alcoholic culture. People whose origins are in Northern Europe had only one way of treating distress: with a bottle of alcohol.

North American culture continues with that notion. If you feel bad, take a swig or take a pill. The notion that you can do things to change the harmony inside yourself is just not something that we teach in schools and in our culture, in our churches, in our religious practices. But if you look at religions around the world, they always start with dancing, moving, singing, physical experiences. The more "respectable" people become, the more stiff they become somehow.

You said somewhere that PTSD has opened the door to scientific investigation of the nature of human suffering. That's a profound step, right? To me, that's a spiritual way to talk about this field, with a profound understanding of what the word spiritual *means.*

This field has opened up in two areas. One is the area of trauma and survival and suffering, but the other one is that people are studying the nature of human connections and the connection between us, also from a scientific point of view.

As much as trauma has opened up things, I think the other

very important arm of scientific discovery is how the human connection is being looked at scientifically now and what really happens when two people see each other, when two people respond to each other, when people mirror each other, when two bodies move together in dancing and smiling and talking. There's a whole new field of interpersonal neurobiology that is studying how we are connected with each other and how a lack of connection, particularly early in life, has devastating consequences on the development of mind and brain.

And it's true, isn't it, from your study, that if people learn to inhabit their bodies, to be more self-aware, that these qualities and habits can serve, can create resilience, when trauma hits.

Absolutely. There are two factors here. One is that despite your reptilian brain, if you breathe quietly in your body and you feel your bodily experience, even when stressful things happen, you can notice that something is happening out there and you say, oh, this really sucks. This is really unpleasant. But you realize that that something is not you, so you don't necessarily get hijacked by unpleasant experiences. The big issue for traumatized people is that they don't own themselves anymore. Any loud sound, anybody insulting them, hurting them, saying bad things, can hijack them away from themselves. And so what we have learned is that what makes you resilient to trauma is to own yourself fully. So if somebody says hurtful or insulting things, you can say, "interesting, that person is saying hurtful and insulting things." But you can separate your sense of yourself from them. We are really beginning to seriously understand how human beings can learn how to do that, to observe and not react.

I just want to come back to this idea that somehow the point of all of this, the take home for you is that we have to feel safe, and that feeling safe has to be a bodily perception, not just a cognitive perception. Somehow everything comes back to that.

That is the foundation. You need to actually feel that feeling. You need to know what is happening in your body. You need to know where your right toe is or your pinkie is. It's very, very basic, you know, but sorely lacking in our diagnostic system—simple things like eating and peeing and pooping are the foundation of everything. And breathing. These are foundational things, all of which go wrong when you get traumatized. The most elementary body functions go awry when you are terrified. So trauma treatment starts at the foundation of a body that can sleep, a body that can rest, a body that feels safe, a body that can move.

Ann Hamilton

I was very close with my grandmother. And you know, I have really distinct bodily memories of sitting next to her on the couch. You know, when you're little and you kind of get in that space under her arm and her arms were full. We would knit, or needlepoint, and she would read to me. And I think there's something about the rhythm of the hands being busy and then your body falls open to absorb and concentrate on what you're listening to, but not completely, because you have two concentrations. The unfolding of the voice in space, and then the material accreting under your hand, they have really different satisfactions. You know, you can see the material, and . . .

And she was making sweaters . . .

Sweaters. Or we were needlepointing—all those lap things, making by hand, and that was tremendously comforting.

You've also said this lovely thing that textiles are the first house of the body, "the body's first architecture."

Yes. How do we know things? We grow up or we're educated in a world that ascribes a lot of value to those things that we can say or name. And, but, there are all these hundreds of ways that we know things through our skin, which is the largest organ of our body. So my first hand is that textile hand, and text and textiles are woven, always, experientially for me. And when I first started making things out of cloth, it was like it was another skin. I was thinking about it as an animate surface, and thinking about it as something that both covers and reveals.

You also draw this notion of threads, that there are threads of sewing, and threads of ideas, lines of speech—the weaving that happens with both words and substances.

That's ancient and it crosses space and time. You know, when you're reading a book, you're immersed, and you're both inside that book, and you're far away in the world that it might take you to.

The image of your grandmother with her needlepoint, and the knitting sweaters, it's an old art. It feels like a lost art. But it's humanizing when we rediscover these things.

It's interesting, because I teach in a university, and I think about where's the place in that kind of educational institution for embodied knowledge? And how do we cultivate that? And how do we trust it?

But science is now showing us that all these things that we've tried to talk about come in through our bodies first. Trauma, but also our whole experience, our whole experience of the world is never just mental or verbal. And there's also this social aspect in the threads of a garment, or in the words that make a story, or a book. It's also our connection to everyone else.

Right. Well, and to go back to the knitting, in the knitted structure, you can take a sweater, or a sock, and you can see each loop up and around and slip through, and up and around and over. And, so, in that whole that has become, it never loses all the parts that constitute it. Even as you can see the whole, you can see all the parts and you go back and forth between those.

Parker Palmer

Parker Palmer works with people from all walks of life at the intersection of spirituality, professional life, and social change. In his tiny book that I love, *Let Your Life Speak*, he also writes with great heart about two crippling bouts of depression in his forties. His wisdom on this has been lifesaving for me and many others, and carries wisdom for life far beyond the darkness of depression.

There's a sentence from your book in which you talk about your experience of clinical depression, "I had embraced a form of Christian faith devoted less to the experience of God than to abstractions about God, a fact that now baffles me: how did so many disembodied concepts emerge from a tradition whose central commitment is to 'the Word become flesh'?"

That's a baffling question to me to this day. But I take embodiment very seriously, and, of course, depression is a full-body experience and a full-body immersion in the darkness. And it is an invitation—at least my kind of depression is an invitation—to take our embodied selves a lot more seriously than we tend to do when we're in the up-up-and-away mode.

Let's dwell with that for a moment, because there's a critique that Christian tradition does not help people who are suffering sometimes from something like depression, because suffering itself can be said to be glorified. But you're turning that image around in terms of the way you've come to apply it.

I am. I think there's a lot, unfortunately, about suffering in Christian tradition that's hogwash, if I can use a technical theological term. It's awfully important to distinguish in life, I think, between true crosses and false crosses. And I know in my growing up as a Christian, I didn't get much help with that. A cross was a cross was a cross, and if you were suffering, it was supposed to be somehow good.

I do not believe that the God who gave me life wants me to live a living death. I believe that the God who gave me life wants me to live life fully and well. Now, is that going to take me to places where I suffer, because I am standing for something or I am committed to something or I am passionate about something that gets resisted and rejected by the society? Absolutely. But anyone who's ever suffered that way knows that it's a life-giving way to suffer. If it's your truth, you can't not do it, and that knowledge carries you through. But there's another kind of suffering that is simply and purely death. It's death in life, and that is a darkness to be worked through to find the life on the other side.

In Quaker tradition, people know how to be silent. This recalls for me the story you've written about the friend who helped you the most during the worst of your depression, who would just come to be with you physically.

It's such a great image for me. I had folks coming to me, of course, who wanted to be helpful, and sadly, many of them weren't. These were the people who would say, "Gosh, Parker, why are you sitting in here being depressed? It's a beautiful day outside. Go, you know, feel the sunshine and smell the flowers." And that, of course, leaves a depressed person even more depressed, because while you know intellectually that it's sunny out and that the flowers are lovely and fragrant, you can't really feel any of that in your body, which is dead in a sensory way. And so you're left more depressed by this "good advice" to get out and enjoy the day. And then other people would come and say something along the lines of, "Gosh, Parker, why are you depressed? You're such a good person. You've helped so many people, you've written . . ."

"You're so successful."

"You're so successful, and you've written so well." And that would leave me feeling more depressed, because I would feel, "I've just defrauded another person who, if they really knew what a schmuck I was, would cast me into the darkness where I already am."

There was this one friend who came to me, after asking permission to do so, every afternoon about four o'clock, sat me down in a chair in the living room, took off my shoes and socks and massaged my feet. He hardly ever said anything. He was a Quaker elder. And yet out of his intuitive sense, he from time to time would say a very brief word like, "I can feel your struggle today," or farther down the road, "I feel that you're a little stronger at this moment, and I'm glad for that." But beyond that, he would say hardly anything. He would give no advice. Somehow he found the one place in my body, namely the soles of my feet, where I could experience some sort of connection to another human being. And the act of massaging just, you know, in a way that I really don't have words for, kept me connected with the human race.

What he mainly did for me, of course, was to be willing to be present to me in my suffering. He just hung in with me in this very quiet, very simple, very tactile way. And I've never really been able to find the words to fully express my gratitude for that, but I know it made a huge difference. It became for me a metaphor of the kind of community we need to extend to people who are suffering in this way, which is a community that is neither invasive of the mystery nor evasive of the suffering, but is willing to hold people in a space—a sacred space of relationship—where somehow this person who is on the dark side of the moon can get a little confidence that they can come around to the other side.

Eve Ensler

Eve Ensler is best known for her play *The Vagina Monologues*, which has become a global force in the face of violence against women and girls. But she herself also had a violent childhood. And her lifelong work with the difficult, redemptive matter of female physicality came into relief in a new way when she was diagnosed with cancer in her fifties.

So in 2010, you are helping create something called the City of Joy in the Congo. And you discover that you have a huge malignant tumor. In your uterus. You write that cancer landed in your body just as Congo had landed you "in the body of the world." There's something in your story, and I know you know this, that is iconic for this great contradiction of modern women, of most Western women maybe. On the one hand, we are attentive to our bodies and obsessed by our bodies, and yet it's possible to not inhabit them and not even know that we're not inhabiting them.

Exactly.

And for you, this crusader for women's bodies around the world to make that discovery is just, you know, it's remarkable.

Well, I think everything's in stages and is incremental. My whole life, if I look at the body of literature and theater pieces I've written, has been this huge journey and attempt to get back into my body. Every play on some level. But you think you're in your body and then you get cancer. You wake up after nine hours of surgery with tubes and catheters and all kinds of things coming out of it, and you realize that it's the first time in your life you've ever been in your body. You are a body. You are pure body and that experience—it was just so incredible. It was so incredible to be in my body, to not have this be an abstraction.

I'm also thinking a lot lately that Descartes has so much to answer for—his idea, "I think therefore I am." Western culture is so built around this overly cerebral disembodied way we've created all of our institutions, and we're impoverished by it. We're so much smaller for it.

So much smaller. It's so funny that you're saying that, because during my cancer, I used to just chant all the time, "I feel therefore I am." I'm in my body, therefore I can feel my existence. I feel the breath. I feel the living, breathing fiber that is humanness. This notion of objectivity—as if that were ever possible, as if the brain could somehow separate you from your subjective self—has created a level of dissociation on the planet. You can get yourself into a mind-set which keeps you from opening your heart.

I was at a gathering a couple of weeks ago and there were neuroscientists there and artists and poets, a poet from Sierra Leone, a poet from Northern Uganda. There were also contemplatives. And we talked about the Buddhist word for "heart-mind"—that heart and mind are the same thing. And when Western neuroscientists first started studying the brains of meditating Tibetan Buddhist monks, the monks thought this was so hilarious that they were putting the electrodes on the head . . .

As opposed to the heart.

Yes, yes. But actually, the science is also helping us understand that our brain is an organ, right? And that what we experience as feelings lodge in our bodies as well.

And nothing's separate. Again, everything got separated. But there's a direct line that goes from and to, and that is to me the most exciting thing about being alive right now—rewiring ourselves and reconstituting ourselves to understand that this is all connected not only here, but outside of us. You can't dominate people without separating them from each other and from themselves. The more people get plugged back into their bodies, into each other, the more impossible it will be for us to be dominated and occupied. I think that's really the work right now, and I don't mean that in a narcissistic way. I mean, how in our daily lives are we connecting in every single respect with ourselves and everything around us? Because that's where transcendence comes from. That's where real energetic transformation comes from.

This notion that we are "people of the second wind" is how you end your book about your cancer, and it's kind of what you're pointing at now.

I love the idea of the second wind. I've always loved it when you're running and running and running, and suddenly you get that next wind and you can keep going. I've always been very curious what lives in that space of second wind. What's in there—what part of us spiritually, physically? What is it, or what are the ingredients of it? You don't do a lot of thinking about it, it comes upon us.

Again, it's a full-body experience, not so much a cerebral experience.

It's total body. And I feel to some degree that we're kind of in our second wind as humanity. Or, this could be our second wind, but it requires a radical re-conjuring and re-conceiving of the story. What are we doing here? I absolutely believe it's possible, but enough people have to believe it's possible and be willing to move with this wind that is trying to come in, trying to pass through us right now.

Joanna Macy

Joanna Macy is best known as a Buddhist teacher and scholar, but I first discovered her as an exquisite translator of the poetry of Rainer Maria Rilke. Rilke sought the shape of meaning in a now-vanished central Europe at the turn of the last century. Joanna Macy's vision took shape in crucibles of the twentieth century he could not foresee. She became an environmental activist—long before that term entered the global lexicon.

Something that's very present for me as I'm reading about you, and the passion you've had as an environmentalist for a long time, is that you also were always very aware that there is a sense of grief in how we take in news. And you really work with people to hold on to that, to take their grief seriously.

Or not to hold on to it so much as to not be afraid of it. Because that grief, if you are afraid of it and pave it over, clamp it down, it shuts you down. And the kind of apathy and closed-down denial, our difficulty in looking at what we're doing to our world, stems not from callous indifference or ignorance so much as it stems from fear of pain. That was a big lesson for me as I was organizing around nuclear power and around the time of the Three Mile Island catastrophe and around Chernobyl.

That became actually perhaps the most pivotal point in, I don't know, the landscape of my life—that dance with despair, to see how we are called to not run from the discomfort and not run from the grief or the feelings of outrage or even fear. If we can be fearless, and be with our pain, it turns. It doesn't stay static. It only doesn't change if we refuse to look at it. When we look at it, when we take it in our hands, when we can just be with it and keep breathing, then it turns. It turns to reveal its other face. And the other face of our pain for the world is our love for the world, our absolutely inseparable connectedness with all life.

In even thinking that way, a poetic mind-set is more useful than the kind of fact-based or argument-based way we tend to approach problems culturally, even precisely the same ecological problem.

Oh, yeah. That keeps people from even mentioning how distressed they are, because they think that they need to have all the facts and figures and statistics to show that they intellectually can master the problem.

But we get overwhelmed by the facts and the figures and the pictures. They are debilitating, they're paralyzing. As you're saying it's in part because we don't really know how to dwell with grief and turn it into something else. But I think about this a lot as a journalist, as somebody who works in media.

It's a double-edged sword, isn't it? You're taking care of your mother and she's dying of cancer and you can't—you won't—say, I can't go in her house or in her room because I don't want to look at her. If you love her, you want to be with her. If we love our world, we're able to see the scum of oil spreading across the Gulf. We're able to see what it's doing to the wetlands and the marshes, what it's doing to the dolphins and the gulls. When you love something, your love doesn't say, "Well, too bad my kid has leukemia, so I won't go near her." It's just the opposite.

I just want to underline the connection that you repeatedly make, which might be counterintuitive. You talk about spirituality and you are also always equally talking about—these are some phrases from your writing that echo things you said—your "wild love for the world" or even "an erotic connection with the world." Those two things go together for you.

That's right. World as lover, world as self. And it's OK for our hearts to be broken over the world. What else is a heart for? There's a great intelligence there. We've been treating the earth as if it were a supply house and a sewer. We've been grabbing, extracting resources from it for our cars and our hair dryers and our bombs, and we've been pouring the waste into it until it's overflowing, but our earth is not a supply house and a sewer. It is our larger body. We breathe it. We taste it. We are it, and it is time now that we venerate that incredible flowering of life that takes every aspect of our physicality.

So I'm looking at my hand right now as we talk. It's got a lot of wrinkles because I'm 81 years old, but it's linked to hands like this back through the ages. This hand is directly linked to hands that learned to reach and grasp and climb and push up on dry land and weave reeds into baskets. It has a fantastic history. Every particle and every atom in this hand goes back to the beginning of space-time. We're part of that story.

You're always asked to sort of stretch a little bit more. And actually we're made for that. But in any case, there's absolutely no excuse for making our passionate love for our world dependent on what we think of its degree of health, whether we think it's going to go on forever. This moment, you're alive.

FOUR

LOVE

A Few Things I've Learned

If we are stretching to live wiser and not just smarter, we will aspire to learn what love means, how it arises and deepens, how it withers and revives, what it looks like as a private good but also a common good. I long to make this word echo differently in hearts and ears—not less complicated, but differently so. Love as muscular, resilient. Love as social—not just about how we are intimately, but how we are together, in public. I want to aspire to a carnal practical love—eros become civic, not sexual and yet passionate, full-bodied. Because it is the best of which we are capable, loving is also supremely exacting, not always but again and again. Love is something we only master in moments. It crosses the chasms between us, and likewise brings them into relief. It is as captive to the human condition as anything we attempt. "Most people have (with the help of conventions) turned their solutions toward what is easy and toward the easiest side of the easy; but it is clear that we must trust in what is difficult," Rilke said to his young poet:

Everything in Nature grows and defends itself any way it can and is spontaneously itself, tries to be itself at all costs and against all opposition. We know little, but that we must trust in what is difficult is a certainty that will never abandon us; it is good to be solitary, for solitude is difficult; that something is difficult must be one more reason for us to do it. It is also good to love—love being difficult. Love is perhaps the most difficult task given us, the most extreme, the final proof and text, for which all other work is only preparation.

Love is the superstar virtue of virtues, and the most watered down word in the English language. I love this weather. I love your dress. And what we've done with the word, we've done with this thing—this possibility, this essential bond, this act. We've made it private, contained it in family, when its audacity is in its potential to cross tribal lines. We've fetishized it as romance, when its true measure is a quality of sustained, practical care. We've lived it as a feeling, when it is a way of being. It is the elemental experience we all desire and seek, most of our days, to give and receive.

The sliver of love's potential that the Greeks separated out as *eros* is where we load so much of our desire, center so much of our imagination about delight and despair, define so much of our sense of completion. There is the love the Greeks called *filia*—the love of friendship. There is the love they called *agape*—love as embodied compassion, expressions of kindness that might be given to a neighbor or a stranger. The *Metta* of the root Buddhist Pali tongue, "lovingkindness," carries the nuance of benevolent, active interest in others known and unknown, and its cultivation begins with compassion towards oneself.

That religious metaphor of "compassion" as "womb" is beautiful and challenging in equal measure. Consider its implicit complexity in light of the bloody, miraculous, real-world experience of birth, and it tells a

frank story of love in its fullness. A merger of pleasure and risk and sacrifice. A dance of alternating vulnerabilities. A wellspring of joy. A
challenge to endless learning by mistake. The moment to moment evolution of care.

What is love? Answer the question through the story of your life.

I grew up not telling the truth about love. I will try to tell the truth
now. I heard about loving your neighbor in Sunday School, but just like
love of enemy, this was scarcely unfolded with practical application to
daily life. And my parent's church was not my grandfather's church.
"Love Divine, All Loves Excelling," as the soaring hymn goes, was
about God, not about us. Loving the world so much that you would give
up your only son, as the Gospel story had it, was not even humanly
desirable—but it was full-blooded, Technicolor, amazing. The more
domesticated mid-twentieth-century Protestantism in which I spent
Sundays and Wednesday nights read the same Bible with a grain of
modern salt. This was a place for the self-made man and his family to be
thankful for what they had, to be reminded of what was right. It was
nourishing, and well-meaning, in a largely inward way.

My parents, like so many parents of that era, lived married love as
role play. They didn't know themselves, and so they couldn't know each
other. My mother had been raised to find her life in her husband. But her
husband, my father, was too busy fighting his own inner demons to
make an inner life for her.

My father cared as best he could, loved in the only way he'd been
taught to muster—by working hard, providing for his family. He did
this exceedingly well. He supported my education and my early adventures, and for this I am forever grateful.

But I also always perceived fear right up next to love in my father,
fear squeezing the life out of love. He was grandiose with the intention

to love. But he was so alone inside, and so terrified of the countenance of love, even his own. The animal place in him that had been wounded was always vigilant—the body memory I know about now, decades too late. I stayed ahead of his disfavor, which could lapse into cruelty, by impressing with my wits and my ambition. He was fascinated by my forays into journalism and diplomacy. They extended his sense of himself in satisfying ways. When I turned my back on all of that, when I married someone who did not impress in political ways and pursued questions of meaning and theology, he never understood and never forgave me.

Yet for years, I held on tight for dear life to the mantra we'd repeated so often we'd etched it as memory: our happy home; two loving parents; their perfect marriage. This was the pinnacle to which I, too, could aspire. It was a hollow memory, a false memory, but it was a memory that enabled me to move forward with a confidence that was actually beyond my means. Matthew Sanford would call it a "healing story," the kind of story we tell ourselves to survive. Our healing stories are not always true and not always good for us, or not good for us forever. When I was strong enough to bear the truth and live with it, I fell into the full-blown depression of my midthirties. With a gentle and wise therapist, I began the long work of excavating and cleaving to the reality that is truer, and harder, and it gave me new life.

I've known wild in-love-ness and wedded bliss and the fiercest love of all, the one I carry for my children. I've thrived and fallen short at each of these loves and learned to forgive myself some of the time, just as I've had to forgive myself for failing as a loving/beloved daughter.

I met Michael, the father of my children, under deliriously romantic circumstances in Scotland, in the thrall of that mesmerizing, unexpected beauty. I'd traveled the world, accomplished something at a young age, and had interesting, complex relationships. In this pivotal life decision, I gave myself over to every movie with a happy ending I'd ever seen, every love song I'd ever wallowed in. I clung tight to the myth of my parents' marriage, not the reality of it. Michael and I adored each other. Friends came from all over the world to our wedding in Scotland, and it was a fantastic party, the grandest I have ever thrown in my life. But we had practically nothing in common in our backgrounds and lives. And we were held by nothing greater than ourselves when we could no longer be there for each other.

Like so many of our kindred spirits in modern marriage, we were alone in our marriage in the end. We'd moved a few times and taken ourselves far away from people who loved and knew us well, like all of those friends who traveled to witness our vows. The nuclear family is a recent invention and a death blow to love—an unprecedented demand on a couple to be everything to each other, the family a tiny echo chamber: history one layer deep. None of the great virtues—even this—is meant to be carried in isolation.

When my marriage ended, I walked into a parallel universe that had been there all along; I became one of the modern multitudes of walking wounded in the wreckage of long-term love. Strangest of all, on this planet, is the way we continue to idealize romantic love and crave it for completion—to follow those love songs and those movies. After my divorce, I created a welcoming home and took great delight in my children. I cooked dinner for gatherings of friends old and new, invested in beautiful far-flung friendships, and drew vast sustenance from webs of care through the work I do. Yet I told myself, for years, that I had a hole in my life where "love" should be.

This is the opposite of a healing story—it's a story that perceives scarcity in the midst of abundance. I have love in my life, many forms of loving. As I settled into singleness, I grew saner, kinder, more generous, more loving in untheatrical everyday ways. I can't name the day when I suddenly realized that the lack of love in my life was not a reality but a poverty of imagination and a carelessly narrow use of an essential word.

And here is another, deeper carelessness, which I am absolving in a spirit of adventure: I come to understand that for most of my life, when I was looking for love, I was looking to be loved. In this, I am a prism of my world. I am a novice at love in all its fullness, a beginner.

The intention to walk through the world practicing love across relationships and encounters feels like a great frontier.

On the future of my ability to make this move, our ability to make this move together, I have more questions than answers. But good questions, generously posed, seriously held, are powerful things. We've begun to hold the question of hate in public life, creating a new legal category of crimes to name the breakdown where tolerance gives out and the human condition at its worst rushes in. All I know is that, at every turn, I hear the word *love* surfacing as a longing for common life, quietly but persistently and in unexpected places.

We are at such an interesting, unnerving moment. As we take up the task of inventing common life for this century, we are struggling, collectively, with divisions of race and income and class that are not new but are freshly anguishing. Here's what is new: a surfacing of grief. It's not a universal reckoning, but it's a widespread awareness that the healing stories we've told ourselves collectively are far less than complete. There's a bewilderment in the American air—both frustrating and refreshing for its lack of answers. We don't know where to begin to change our relationship with the strangers who are our neighbors—to address the ways in which our well-being may be oblivious to theirs or harming theirs. We don't know how to reach out or what to say if we did. But we don't want to live this way. I don't want to live this way.

The virtue of tolerance told us to keep observations of moral or spiritual imagination to ourselves, to check them at the doors of our places of vocation and learning. We held them close and starved them of the oxygen of living questions as well as answers, communally, in a corrective interplay with each other. Meanwhile, we developed too ready and fluent a vocabulary in the blunt metrics of the market, the numbers. I'm stretching my point only a bit when I say that in American life, every vision must begin and end in an economic argument in order to be heard, on urgent matters of human life: labor, education, immigration, refugees, prisons, poverty, health care.

Rename these "issues" in light of what is at stake in human terms, and consider the complex mix of questioning, applied virtue, and, yes, political and economic wisdom we need to muster for robust, sustained, generative grappling: the future of human vocation, of how we punish wrongdoing and create space for redemption, how we treat outcasts and strangers and the hungry, how we reimagine health in a world of ever longer lives, how we nurture our children's minds and equip them for the world they will navigate and make. We know in our hearts and minds that we are bigger and wilder and more precious than numbers, more complex than any economic outcome or political prescription can describe.

So what if love, as Elizabeth Alexander asked on the Washington Mall on inauguration day in 2009, is the mightiest word? How would this word, openly injected into our grappling, reframe and challenge it, informing all the other necessary computations and strategies? A poet can't carry this question alone, nor can a politician. The question in and of itself invites each of us out of aloneness. The exacting, enlivening aspiration of love does send us inside to know and honor the particularities of our identities and our struggles. But it coaxes us out again to an encounter with the vastness of human identity. Spiritual geniuses and saints have always called humanity to love, as have social reformers who shifted the lived world on its axis. When the civil rights leaders began to force a reckoning with otherness in the 1960s, they did so in the name of love. The political, economic aspirations of this monumental work of social change in living memory grew from an aspiration to create the "beloved community."

I did not grow up understanding this movement and its vision in this fullness, though it unfolded during my lifetime. It was brought home to me tangibly by the intensely dignified, pragmatically loving presence of John Lewis, now a congressman from Georgia, who was beaten senseless on what became known as Bloody Sunday. I was privileged to attend an annual civil rights pilgrimage with him, to holy ground in Tuscaloosa, Birmingham, Selma, Montgomery. I've "remembered" so much in conversation with John Lewis and other veterans and leading lights still among us. The movement they brought into being was a spiritual confrontation in the most expansive sense of that word, first and foremost within oneself and then with the world outside. For weeks, months, before any sit-in or march or ride, they studied the Bible and Gandhi, Aristotle and Thoreau. They internalized practical, physical disciplines of courtesy and conduct—kindness, eye contact, coat and tie, dresses, no unnecessary words. Neuroscientists now would recognize the innate intelligence about the human brain in these rules of engagement. They engaged in intense role-playing—"social drama"—whites putting themselves in the role of blacks being harassed, black activists putting themselves in the shoes of policemen feeling threatened and under orders to gain control.

This was love as a way of being, not a feeling, which transcended grievance and painstakingly transformed violence. Einstein asked a "what if" question, about pursuing a beam of light at the speed of light, on his way to comprehending the nature of light and gravity. John Lewis asked a "what if" question as a tool for social alchemy: what if the beloved community were already a reality, the true reality, and he simply had to embody it until everyone else could see?

When I was 11 years old, I traveled one summer with an uncle and aunt and some of my first cousins from rural Alabama to Buffalo for a visit, for a trip. I had never been outside of the South. And being there gave me hope. I wanted to believe, and I did believe, that things would get better. Later I discovered that you have to have this sense of faith that what you're moving toward is already done. It's already happened.

And live as if?

And you live as if you're already there, that you're already in that community, part of that sense of one family, one house. If you visualize it, if you can even have faith that it's there, for you it is already there. And during the early days of the movement, I believed that the only true and real integration for that sense of the beloved community existed within the movement itself. Because in the final analysis, we did become a circle of trust, a band of brothers and sisters. It didn't matter whether you were black or white. It didn't matter whether you came from the North to the South, or whether you're a Northerner or Southerner. We were one.

You had made that vision real.

For the struggle, for those of us in the struggle. But we studied. We prepared ourselves. It's just not something that is natural. You have to be taught the way of peace, the way of love, the way of nonviolence. In the religious sense, in the moral sense, you can say that in the bosom of every human being, there is a spark of the divine. So you don't have a right as a human to abuse that spark of the divine in your fellow human being. From time to time, we would discuss that, if you have someone attacking you, beating you, spitting on you, you have to think of that person. Years ago that person was an innocent child, an innocent little baby. What happened? Did something go wrong? Did someone teach that person to hate, to abuse others? You try to appeal to the goodness of every human being and you don't give up. You never give up on anyone.

So here's a line from your book Across That Bridge: *"The Civil Rights Movement, above all, was a work of love. Yet even 50 years later, it is rare to find anyone who would use the word* love *to describe what we did." What you just said to me illuminates that. I think part of the explanation of that is the way you are using the word* love *is very rich and multilayered and also challenging—challenging for the person who loves.*

The love is there. How do you make it real? How do you paint the picture? It's like an artist using a canvas. How do you get people to move from maybe A to B and you get C? Or from one to two and get three? You're on a path and you have to be consistent and you have to be persistent.

Again and again, as John Lewis puts so fine a point on it, this work of love exposed the absurdity of de-humanization in the name of race and broke its back. It's hard to imagine such a strategy in our age. And maybe, just maybe, the time for such strategies has passed.

But I question my own wariness in Birmingham, where John Lewis muses aloud half whimsically, half seriously, that he would like to bring nonviolent role-playing to Congress—the personal training he learned half a century ago in putting oneself in the other's shoes.

In that city, after four little girls were killed in a firebombing of the 16th Street Baptist Church, Martin Luther King made one of the most radical statements I've ever encountered: "At times life is hard, as hard as crucible steel. In spite of the darkness of this hour, we must not lose faith in our white brothers."

To insist on faith in the common humanity even of our enemies and live accordingly; to begin with the assumption that love is there and it is up to us to make it real. Could we imagine that now?

A half century after John Lewis went from fighting for his life on the bridge in Selma to attending the signing of the Voting Rights Act in the White House, we are still, and again, face to face with the unfinished work of love. It's a key without which all the laws that were passed remain inadequate and precarious. We elected a black president, a multiracial president in fact, but we mostly talk about race when we acknowledge that we still don't know how to talk about it. To be racist is not condoned, unthinkable for almost all of us within ourselves. Yet too many of our children of color are unable to reach their human potential. Too many of them are literally in danger. The primal bond of birth, the original source and apex of love, does nothing more fiercely, in the first instance, than protect. We are not close to being the Beloved Community. What is new, perhaps, is that we have come to acknowledge this in places, to repent of it even, though we scarcely know how to move forward.

I use the "we" I so freely wield on other subjects more self-consciously here. In the awakening by force of racial tumult of the early twenty-first century, I realize that I've reflexively pondered race as something that is about skin color, a matter primarily about people of color. We've expected people of color to be the visionaries among us, to shoulder the complex constellation of conditions that is racism, and have expected them to show us the way forward to healing.

They often do. In 2015, the Confederate flag was finally lowered and transferred from state houses to museums in several southern states, but not before a horrific shooting of nine African Americans inside their church in the center of Charleston, South Carolina, by a young white supremacist. That very day and in the days that followed, the loved ones of those murdered spoke publicly to forgive and express their concern for this young man in the same breath with their grief and remembrance of their mothers, fathers, sisters, brothers, children. In the ensuing weeks, an image went viral of a black South Carolina state trooper, Leroy Smith, gently guiding a white supremacist to a seat after he was overcome by heat at a rally protesting the move of the Confederate flag. What he saw, he told a *New York Times* reporter, was a fellow human being, an older man, in trouble: "Mr. Smith said he was taken aback by the worldwide attention but hoped the image would help society move past the recent spasms of hate and violence. Asked why he thinks the photo has had such resonance, he gave a simple answer: love. 'I think that's the greatest thing in the world—love,' said the burly, soft-spoken trooper, who is just shy of fifty. 'And that's why so many people were moved by it.'"

"Love" is not always or often the first response to violence and violation, one human being to another, nor can we expect it to be. Anger is also a moral response. On the front lines of the worst that has happened to bring the unfinished work of racial reconciliation to the fore in the American twenty-first century, the nonviolence of the civil rights elders feels inadequate to many. Love, muscular and resilient, does not always seem reasonable, much less doable, in our most damaged and charged civic spaces.

But it seems to me worth insisting that those spaces where the worst has happened do not utterly define us as individuals or a people. Together, and politically, we have to reckon with excruciating questions of how we reform the culture of policing, the well-being and flourishing of people of color, and the innate injustice of so many of our civic structures. Alongside that reckoning, there remain the quiet spaces of the everyday in which we live and move and have our being. In these spaces, there is abundant and immediate possibility for the power of conduct, of unromantic practical love, towards creating new realities that might just, over time, accompany and shape those larger challenges.

With my faith in the power of words, I appreciate how the esteemed legal and racial scholar john powell opens up the question of race into the question of belonging. His counsel and wisdom are being sought on the front lines of renewed racial anguish and longings. He's a generation younger than John Lewis and the civil rights leaders, though he's known and learned from many of them. His ancestors were slaves and sharecroppers; he attended Stanford and started the Black Student Union there. He's lived long enough, he says to me, to have been Negro, then black, then African American. He has a long sense of how change happens quickly and too slowly, all at the same time; and we must always, he says, keep both paces of change in mind and in intention.

Race, john powell says, is like gravity, experienced by all, understood by few. But it's never been a quality some possess and others don't—it's as much about "whiteness" as about color. It's relational. I find that labels like privilege and disenfranchisement can function like containers—ways to categorize each other that can actually make it harder to imagine and step onto kindred human ground. But john powell speaks of "whiteness" as a cultural way of being that infuses imaginations across the color spectrum. Whiteness is the narrative voice of Western culture, even where we perceive a third-person account. It's part of the ethos of dominating the world and subduing it, the root idea behind the self-made men and women I grew up with in the middle of the middle of America—alone, and ultimately lonely.

W.E.B. DuBois called "the color line" the problem of the twentieth century. The conundrum of the twenty-first is that with the best intentions of color blindness, and laws passed in this spirit, we still carry instincts and reactions inherited from our environments and embedded in our being below the level of conscious decision. There is a color line in our heads, and while we could see its effects we couldn't name it until now. But john powell is also steeped in a new science of "implicit bias," which gives us a way, finally, even to address this head on. It reveals a challenge that is human in nature, though it can be supported and hastened by policies to create new experiences, which over time create new instincts and lay chemical and physical pathways. This is a helpfully unromantic way to think about what we mean when we aspire, longingly, to a lasting change of heart. And john powell and others are bringing training methodologies based on the new science to city governments and police forces and schools.

> What we're finding now in the last 30 years is that much of the work, in terms of our cognitive and emotional response to the world, happens at the unconscious level. We moved from the discussion of race partially because we were trying to move from the Jim Crow era and the white supremacy era. We said, to notice race is bad so let's not notice it anymore. But it was still deeply embedded in our biology, in our structures, in our arrangements. And the unconscious was saying to the conscious, "You can do whatever you want to. We're going to keep noticing race." It responds to race in some pretty powerful ways.

You make this really fascinating point that there are two "parents" to the way we are now, the way we grapple with race. One is slavery—I get that. The other is the Enlightenment—that, in fact, it's from the

Enlightenment that we inherited this idea that the conscious mind could know everything, and that we could be reasonable.

Yes, and the United States became extremely, extremely attached to the notion of individuality and independence. Though think about the groups who were not independent. They were the Africans, they were the Indians, they were women, they were anyone who was not a white male. The Enlightenment Project had this hubris that we could control everything, including the world, when we can't even really control ourselves.

And if we were having this discussion in 1980, we'd say, "OK. Let's not do race. Let's look at everyone as an individual. Why do we have all these categories?" Well, now if you ask the question of why we have all those categories, science will tell us that's the way the mind works. The mind actually works with categories. We simply cannot process the world, we simply would not exist as a species, without categories.

And yet this condition of each of us in isolation, which you associate with whiteness, which is this culture of domination, is not sustainable. And it's not desirable. And I feel like we've run into the limits of our ability to convince ourselves that it is desirable.

There are so many expressions that help us see this. Sometimes people talk about how we need to do things to connect. And on one hand that's right, but on the other hand, it understates what is. We *are* connected. What we need to do is become aware of it, to live it, to express it. Think about segregation. Segregation is a formal way of saying, "How do I deny my connection with you in the physical space?" Think about the notion of whiteness. Whiteness in the United States, as it took form, believed that one drop of black blood—whatever that is—would destroy whiteness. It turns out that most white Americans actually do have black blood. White blood and black blood have been mixing up for a long time. And so as we deny the other, we deny ourselves. Because there is no other. We are connected. How do we actually acknowledge that? How do we actually celebrate that?

There's language that you've been using that I really appreciate, of belonging. As we try to move beyond the language that's divided us and the behavior that's divided us, tell me what that means for you and how you think that might be powerful.

The human condition is one of belonging. We simply cannot thrive unless we are in relationship. I just gave a lecture on health. If you're isolated, the negative health consequence is worse than smoking, obesity, high blood pressure—just being isolated. We need to be in relationship with each other. And so, when you look at what groups are doing, whether they are disability groups or whether they're groups organized around race, they are really trying to make the claim, "I belong. I'm a member." If you think about Black Lives Matter, it's really just saying, "We belong." How we define the other affects how we define ourselves.

Right.

And so when we define the other at an extreme distance from ourselves, it means we have to cut off large parts of our self. In the early debates around integrating schools, the white segregationists said, "We can't have integrated schools because black and white children might get to know each other and might marry each other and have babies." The Civil Rights Movement said, "This is not about marriage." But the white segregationists were right. You bring people together, they will actually learn to love each other. Some of them will marry and have children. It will actually change the fabric of society. When people worry that having gays in our community will change what marriage really means, actually, they're right. When people worry that having a lot of Latinos in the United States will change the United States, they are right. We're constantly making each other. Part of it is our fear that we are holding on to something and the other is going to change it. And the other *is* going to change it—but we're going to change the other. If we do it right, we're going to create a bigger "we," a different "we."

And there's no way we can approach that challenge, as you just described it, which is a human challenge, with laws or policies or school reform alone. Let's just say it this way—it's a way of taking up the language of the "beloved community," which was the language and goal of Dr. King and John Lewis and all those people, and you use that language too.

That's right. I mean, we've learned some things since then. At one time, we talked about integration, and we equated integration with assimilation. Arthur Schlesinger talked about that in some of his work. That was clearly wrong. We're not going to all melt into each other. And yet, we do have to have a beloved community, not in a small sense, but in the large sense. And I would even extend it beyond people, to a beloved relationship with the planet. And to live that, and to have structures that reflect that, is a very different way of ordering society.

Then I think we can also learn to relax. Then we don't have to be afraid of the force. Yes, it will take us beyond what we're comfortable with, who we are right now. But I think we need help in getting there. And right now, we don't have the language for that because we still have the language of the Enlightenment Project. We still have the language of, "You can be anything you want to be, you can control, you're in charge of your own destiny." Even the notion of sovereignty is very problematic. Whether it's a community or a nation, there's no such thing as sovereignty. We are in relationship with each other. It can be a bad relationship or a good relationship, but we are in relationship with each other.

OK. So what's also relaxing about what you just said about belonging and reframing our relationship with the other is that we tend to talk about clusters of issues—race, income inequality, schools, crime, incarceration, segregated neighborhoods. On a global scale, this gets into issues of scarcity, including scarcity of natural resources. And all of those things are problems, they are big issues. But when you start lumping them all together as what we have to tackle, it's completely overwhelming and paralyzing. It's not that the project of belonging is simple . . .

No, it's not.

But somehow I feel that it might open our imaginations in a new way, which also might open possibilities for action.

I think that's right. One reason the problems seem overwhelming is because we're using the wrong tools to understand them and fix them. We're actually talking about a profound change in paradigm. It's like trying to think about computers as fancy typewriters. So if you're using the framework of typewriters to try to make sense of computers, it's very clumsy. It doesn't work. You have to really shift it altogether. Or think about automobiles. Automobiles were initially thought of as a horseless carriage, right? The metaphors break down, and they don't work. And so, right now, we're trying to use, I would say, the language of individuality, the language of the Enlightenment—to understand something that heads into a different area. It makes it incredibly complicated. Actually, I think that because everything is connected—I say this to my students sometimes: if you want to infect all of the people in San Francisco with the measles, you don't have to go around to each person one at a time. Just go to BART, which is our subway, on a crowded day. Expose it, it's done. Because people are in relationships, they will do the rest of the work for you. If we can figure out where the inflection point is in a system, it populates the whole system.

So the question is, how can we make belonging infectious?

How do we make it infectious? I think actually people are longing for this. People are looking for community, right now, though we don't have confidence in love. We have much more confidence in anger and hate. We believe anger is powerful. We believe hate is powerful. And we believe love is wimpy. And so if we're engaged in the world, we believe it's much better to sort of organize around anger and hate. And yet, we see two of the most powerful expressions, certainly Gandhi, certainly the Reverend Dr. King. And, even though he came out of a violent revolution—Nelson Mandela—when I met him, he just exuded love. And as you know, he had a chance to leave prison early. He refused to unless it included structuring the country. He actually tried to lean into a notion of beloved community. He didn't want the blacks to control or dominate the whites. Even today, he's loved in South Africa, and he's loved around the world.

So I think part of it is that we don't have to imagine doing things one at a time. We claim life, our own and others. We celebrate and engage in life. To me the question is not "how do we get there?" It's "how do we live?" In a healthy family or society, we do not just have the words that we're related, we actually learn to care for each other, and we celebrate that. Policy can help, like Good Samaritan laws. There are a lot of things we can do. But it needs to be animated by a sense that we are connected, that we share each other, and yes, that we in fact love each other.

I circle back again and again to the gap between who we are and who we want to be—and how to open wisely, fruitfully, to it. I'm helped by a gentle notion from Buddhist psychology, that there are "near enemies" to every great virtue—reactions that come from a place of care in us, and which feel right and good, but which subtly take us down an ineffectual path. Sorrow is a near enemy to compassion and to love. It is borne of sensitivity and feels like empathy. But it can paralyze and turn us back inside with a sense that we can't possibly make a difference. The wise Buddhist anthropologist and teacher Roshi Joan Halifax calls this a "pathological empathy" of our age. In the face of magnitudes of pain in the world that come to us in pictures immediate and raw, many of us care too much and see no evident place for our care to go. But compassion goes about finding the work that can be done. Love can't help but stay present.

There are windows in public life, every now and again, when we wake up to the reality of our bond to each other, even to hurting strangers far away, and keep attending through our sorrow. September 11, 2001, was such a moment. I believe that Hurricane Katrina was also such a moment, though we rarely commemorate it as such. Racial isolation, entrenched poverty, and environmental fragility converged in catastrophe. We watched for days as thousands of fellow human beings in New Orleans sheltered in sub-human conditions in their flooded city. I couldn't turn my eyes away from the TV screen. A FEMA official said, with spiritual acuity beyond his intention in that moment, "We're seeing people we didn't know existed."

For a few days, that is, we were shocked into seeing and to attending. How could this be happening? What would it possibly mean to be a neighbor? A major poll in those days, john powell tells me, showed that 70 percent of Americans were willing to have their taxes raised if that would help relieve the human crisis in New Orleans. In American political life, where money is how we nod to what matters, this would be as close to a revolutionary, federal declaration of love as it gets.

Then the pictures stopped. The story moved on to the ineptitude of FEMA. The revolutionary poll wasn't pondered or followed up. We turned away from the question of love because we couldn't begin to live into it. But it remains urgent in New Orleans and every American community. The reality of poverty in our midst is interwoven with the reality of race, and if anything, it is more paralyzing and conflicted. As a land of self-made men and women, we have scarcely begun to notice the poverty line in our heads. And yet, and still, there is an unease growing, a sense of dis-ease, at the widening specter of "income inequality."

This is antiseptic language, which puts our human dramas in political and economic boxes and holds us at arm's length from the heart of the matter. Still, I feel more and more of us willingly seeing, choosing to care about the heart of the matter, holding the question of love, if you will, across all kinds of ingrained ideological, political, economic difference. Opinion polls, our way of taking the civic temperature, are telling this truth too in undeniable numbers: income inequality is a concern that crosses partisan boundaries. Counterintuitive impulses to care are forming left to right, religious to secular, across class and income boundaries, as though many of us are recalling that we do in fact belong to each other and are ready to make that real.

Sister Simone Campbell is one of the people who is giving this form and voice. She became known as a face of "the Nuns on the Bus," a "road trip" in 2012 that brought all kinds of people onto the streets to welcome these sisters and listen to them and be listened to by them. If she must be categorized, she is definitively on the progressive side of the American political border. But she's an outside-the-box political and spiritual animal—more like the rest of us, as I want to continue to insist, than the neatly categorized, all-answers, no-questions remaining voices who steal the air from our civic room. She's a Catholic sister, and a lawyer and lobbyist, with a serious Zen practice. Her political passion started with the civil rights movement. She took vows in 1967 with the Sisters of Social Service, one of the many lesser-known offspring of the Benedictine family tree. The order's foundress became the first woman in parliament in Hungary when she was the head of her community. She wondered, if God would bless the people who wiped away the tears of people who suffered, wouldn't God also bless the people who made it so that tears were not shed?

Sister Simone is executive director of NETWORK, a small lobbying organization founded in 1972 in Washington, D.C., by forty-seven Catholic sisters with an initial collection of $187. In 2012, they used the publicity they'd received from a censure by the Vatican of Pope Benedict to publicize their opposition to what was known as the Ryan budget, which included sweeping budget cuts on programs that served "the most vulnerable among us," in Sister Simone's parlance. I admire the winsome words her nonprofit uses to describe its twenty-first-century policy vision: "enacting a living wage," "crafting a faithful budget that benefits the 100 percent," and "mending the wealth gap"—as though we are working with a fabric that is torn, in want of repair, as opposed to an "income inequality" that reduces fragile livelihoods to a matter of math.

I also like the way Sister Simone speaks of Republican leaders who are her political opponents in the early-twenty-first-century political climate. In the course of our conversation, she speaks with a genuine respect and affection for Paul Ryan, the Republican congressman and House Budget Committee chairman turned Speaker of the House, telling stories about how her interactions with him have been good for him and good for her—"loving" in the polarized political context in which they operate together:

> In many ways, Paul Ryan is doing his part. And I'm doing my part. And we spend our lives annoying each other kind of. I mean, he enjoys sparring with me and I enjoy sparring with him. So even though we've been working on opposite sides in a way, my intersection has affected him and he's affected me. And I think we're better for it. One thing that happened was, I got to testify in front of the House Budget Committee when he was chairing it. One of the Republicans went out after me, saying how I shouldn't be believed because I was censured by the Vatican and so nothing I said was trustworthy. And Paul Ryan defended me. He said, "Well, Sister Simone is well within the teaching of the Church, though we may not agree on these things."

I am amazed at the cross section of people who come to my Monday night conversation with Sister Simone in our studio in Minneapolis, the delight they take in her—and the way they experience the choices she's made with her life to be informative, useful, for their own. She models a commitment to both contemplation and action and so brings the synergy between inner life and outer life into intriguing relief.

You've said somewhere that over the years, your spirituality and prayer life have deepened to become what you called a contemplative life of "walking willing" that defines who you are and how you do this work—and, I think, how this work continues to evolve both in vision and action. So, what do you mean by that?

Well, the heart of who I am is the contemplative. Gerald May, in this amazing book *Will and Spirit,* says that the only thing that we bring to the contemplative life is a willing heart. And that the two things that shut down the contemplative life are fear and holding on, grasping. So what I've come to realize is that, for me, this journey is about continuing to walk willing towards the hope, the vision, the perspective, the opportunities that are given. But it's all about where people are hungry. I get invited to where people are hungry. And I'm willing to try to be food for them, just be available, just be present, and listen to their stories or tell mine. But it's all about keeping my heart open to what's around, and not closing up.

I know that you also have a serious Zen practice. And that, as busy as you are, and as big a job as you have, you cultivate that. You take time to immerse in meditation and contemplation.

I meditate every morning. I mean, it's essential. It's essential. The first time I did a Zen retreat, it was at the retreat house my community runs in Encino. It was like, I don't know—it was like diving into this pool, this refreshing pool. It was so exciting, I didn't want to go to bed at night. I was really a little nuts. I had been dabbling in centering prayer and trying to find a way. But this was like a doorway to a form that could be used with any content because Zen is the discipline of the meditation. My experience was of having in my imagination the sense of a sage inviting me to go deeper. And being willing to do that was the biggest gift of my life ever. And being willing to know that—how can I say this? Well, to know that we're one body. All of creation is one body. I'm only just a little piece of it. But the freedom of knowing that means I just have to do my part. I don't know how to communicate how freeing that is.

And I think what you're describing is really being immersed in that knowledge, then . . .

It's visceral.

So being able to then walk out of meditation and live out of that place? You write, "Staying open-handed, treasuring but not grasping, is critical to the contemplative stance. I also believe that's how we have to think of our economic life together." That's a really intriguing statement.

Well, if we're open-handed, then I know a few things. One is, no guarantees. All is fragile. It's all gift. And being willing to share what I have or what I have been given then becomes the way that we can really engage each other. One of the pieces that gets lost is that it's as much about our stories as it is monetary. How could I leave you out if I've heard your story? I can't.

You tell a lot of stories of people you met on the road. And they're the kind of stories that we're becoming familiar with. Stories of good people who are working too many jobs and still not getting by. Stories of college students who are carrying way too much to be able to focus on college. Stories of people who don't have the money to get the care they need and die too young. I am aware in myself and I think all around me, maybe, those of you in this room—there are so many of us anguished about these gulfs that seem to be growing in our society, in our community, and in our nation. And it's not that we don't care. We care deeply. But we don't know how to connect that care in meaningful, practical ways. To do something about it.

There are several levels of that. One is the doing something. I sometimes think we, in the United States, think we ought to do something about everything and that it's my job to fix everything. Well it's not. That's way beyond us. It's more important, I think, that we listen deeply to our stories and then see where it leads. And that's the piece. If we all do our part . . .

Whatever our part is, wherever we are.

Whatever our part is. Just do one thing. That's all we have to do. The guilt—or the curse—of the progressive, the liberal, the whatever, is that we think we have to do it all. And then we get overwhelmed. I get all those solicitations in the mail.

And I can't do everything. And so I don't do anything. But that's the mistake. Community is about just doing my part.

I really like the way you talk about being for "the 100 percent." In some ways, a lot of the issues you take up and the policies you take up are on the surface associated with this language of "the 99 percent," which had its moment and its meaning in Occupy Wall Street.

And that set it up for me to be able to say the 100 percent. We're doing business roundtables, and I got this chance to talk to some entrepreneur, C.E.O. types. I got to ask them finally this question that I've been really wondering about. A report had just come out that the average C.E.O. of a publicly traded company got $10 million in salary a year, and they were going for $11 million. I got to ask them, "Is it that you're not getting by on $10 million that you need $11 million? I don't get it." And this one guy said, just like this—"Oh, no Sister Simone. That's not it. It's not about the money." He said, "It's that we're very competitive. And we want to win. And money just happens to be the current measure of winning."

Then I think, well, could we have a measure that's a little less toxic? Because that's it. It's not that they want to hoard this money, they want to win. And if we can understand for the common good what is underlying their desire, then we could find some other measures that would free up money. Having the curiosity to see their perspective allows for finding new solutions. Because if we just fight and resist—this is the other piece about contemplative life—if we just fight against something, it reinforces it.

Now, the other piece that I haven't really talked about is

joy. I goof off a lot. Joy is at the heart of this journey. Too often, progressives are really grim. It's not a very good advertisement: "Come join us. We're so miserable." The amazing wonder is that we get to live this life in relationship. We live in a hugely complex, multicultural setting, which is not shared in very many places in our world. There are tremendous possibilities. So the giving, the finding your niche, is about life giving, and enjoying the life that is given to you and to others in the process.

This humanizing balance Sister Simone describes and embodies— between contemplation and activity, passion and curiosity, hard work and having fun—adds color and complexity to the notion of *agape*, practical love, public love. "Deep listening" is a virtue that anchors every kind of love relationship and it is the compass Sister Simone cites again and again as a creative, openhearted anchor to her life of strong passions and advocacy. She offers these lines of self-appraisal on whether one is being true to deep listening in any situation: "Am I responding in generosity? Am I responding in selfishness? Am I responding in a way that builds up people around me, that builds me up, that is respectful of who I am?" Such questions are tools to start walking willingly towards the more exacting question of what would it mean, day to day, year to year, to become the beloved community. And how, concretely, to begin.

I can't end this reflection with a single story, or a voice that sounds the right summary note on love. Instead, I offer a handful of memories and metaphors.

An exuberant and lyrical astrophysicist, Natalie Batalha, tells me that her life in science has led her to think about love differently. It's like dark matter, she says, this force that permeates everything and yet remains essentially mysterious, something we have scarcely begun to understand and to mine. As a person who hunts for planets hospitable to life—a search she says is a matter of when not if—she has the grandest of all perspectives on her assertion that love makes a fundamental sense: what is good for me is good for you, and on a planetary scale.

A renowned geophysicist named Xavier Le Pichon has found in his understanding of how the earth works a metaphor for understanding the power of care at the center of human community. He was a pioneer in the field of plate tectonics in the 1960s, pivotal in one of those moments when science not only radically revised its view of the world, but changed the way all of us see it. He's also spent decades living with his family in communities of care—for a time in Jean Vanier's L'Arche community in France—with families facing disabilities and later mental illness. He is a person who has lived a life of love. A capacity to accommodate fragility, he says, is a fundament of vital, evolving systems, whether geological or human. At the right temperatures, geologic faults allow for movement, ductility, flow. Earthquakes happen when weaknesses cannot be expressed. "And communities which are rigid, which do not take into account the weak points of the community—people who are in difficulty—tend to be communities that do not evolve. When they do evolve, it's generally by a very strong commotion, a revolution."

Xavier Le Pichon has taken his perspective into a personal study of the Axial Age, exploring the qualities that gave way to a larger canvas of human potential across the history of our species. He is puzzled when we tell the story of humanity through milestones that only have to do with skills and tools. He is intrigued by fossil evidence that Neanderthal and early humans cared, at great effort and sacrifice, for people who were injured and disabled.

They reorganized themselves around the small ones, the babies, because otherwise no life is possible. That we share with all the mammals. But they also organized around people in great difficulty through suffering or sickness, because of handicap, or because life is coming to an end. And that's really very new and special. It becomes a society which we call *human*, *humane*—in French we use the same word. There is a new touch, a new kindness, a new softness, a new way of living, which is completely introduced by the fact that you put the weakest at the center of the community.

I think a great deal about the journalist and Catholic humanitarian Dorothy Day. She's up for sainthood in the Catholic Church, which is fascinating given the Bohemian nature of most of her life. But I'm intrigued too that I hear her name on many lips these days, including young people looking for role models across space and time. She was eight years old, growing up in Oakland, California, when the 1906 earthquake devastated San Francisco. She stood on the street watching for the next few days as the people of Oakland helped each other and helped the people of San Francisco who were coming across the bay in boats. With the clear eyes of a child, she was captivated. Somehow, though this was not the ordinary pattern of ordinary days, they'd known in their being how to do this all along. Dorothy Day gave voice to a question, which she then lived into across the trajectory of her own very human, messy, adventurous life: why can't we live this way all the time?

I'm drawn to her, surely, because she was in equal measure a person passionate about words, about talking about what matters, but also about doing what needed to be done. In her memoir, *The Long Loneliness*, she wrote in a stream of consciousness way about the *Catholic Worker*, the journalistic project and social movement she helped to found and which continues to feed and clothe needy people across American cities to this day:

"We were just sitting there talking when lines of people began to form saying, 'We need bread.' We could not say, 'Go, be thou filled.' If there were six small loaves and a few fishes, we had to divide them. There was always bread. We were just sitting there talking, and people moved in on us. Let those who can take it, take it. Some moved out and that made room for more. And somehow the walls expanded. It is not easy always to be joyful, to keep in mind the duty of delight . . . The most significant thing about the Catholic Worker is poverty, some say. The most significant thing is community, others say. We are not alone anymore. But the final word is love. We have all known the long loneliness and we have learned that the only solution is love and that love comes with community. It all happened while we sat there talking and it is still going on."

Love is hard to talk about in public, but intriguingly, when a person of integrity—like the patrolman Leroy Smith, like a Dorothy Day—speaks plain truths they live by, it adds up. We recognize what they are describing. Now, you can dismiss their magnanimity too. You can say that extreme moments of crisis bring out heroic impulses that otherwise lie dormant and return to being dormant. You can certainly argue that moments of public love don't define humanity. You can point out that Dorothy Day went on to create a life of self-sacrifice, including eventually a vow of celibacy—and that most of us, within the confines of our vocations and families and livelihoods, aren't capable of this and can't reasonably be called to it.

I often ask people I'm interviewing, who themselves are wise and loving, about this argument I sometimes have with myself. The writer Paul Elie studied Dorothy Day when he wrote a lyrical biography of the intersecting lives of Thomas Merton, Walker Percy, and Flannery O'Connor, and Day. She lived by a conviction, he says, that it's not merely great crisis moments that call forth that lovingness in us. She lived also by a recognition that at any given moment, someone somewhere is having a crisis of that magnitude.

> And that you have to be there when the person is having his or her crisis, and not wait for the city to burn down. She thought it possible for society to be different than it is because she thought that we're naturally oriented toward love. We're made to love one another. Strife and war are a deformity of that. But what we're created for is to love one another and to love one another in community. She was a radical and a formidable organizer, but she was always clear that it was not a programmatic effort that got the Catholic Worker going. It was people doing what came naturally, which was loving one another in community—and talking about it.

I'm comforted and buoyed by insights of the philosopher Anthony Appiah, who has studied how moral evolution happens across history and the world—how deeply rooted practices deemed not merely right but honorable can shift relatively quickly. His parents' interracial marriage in the 1950s was one of the stories that gave rise to the movie *Guess Who's Coming to Dinner*. In his family as in his scholarship, he's experienced one of these recurring places in human life where within one generation, we look back at something that seemed normal forever and ask, "What were we thinking? How could we have lived that way?" Appiah studied how foot binding ended in China; how dueling ceased to be a way for honorable gentlemen to settle disputes; how slavery was abolished as a fundament of the British Empire. As he tells it, change begins to happen in the human heart slowly, over time. Only then do the movements and leaders come along and topple the structures.

This is a way to tell the story of what is happening in the realm of marriage and love and gender in the early twenty-first century. It is a way to tell the story of how we are finally, fitfully, reckoning with bullying. It is a way, I would contend, to talk about the reasonableness of holding the question of love, whoever we are, however we can, in the places and circumstances each of us inhabits.

For all his erudition, Anthony Appiah's prescriptions for the everyday are refreshingly simple. He talks about "sidling up" to difference, not attacking it with a solutions-based approach as Americans are wont to attack what they see as problems. The way to set moral change in motion, he says, is not to go for the jugular, or even for dialogue—straight to the things that divide you. Talk about sports. Talk about the weather. Talk about your children. Make a human connection. Change comes about in part, as he describes it, by way of "conversation in the old-fashioned sense"—simple association, habits of coexistence, seeking familiarity around mundane human qualities of who we are.

I've been deeply formed, finally, by a kindred insight of John Paul Lederach, the haiku-writing, globally esteemed conflict resolution and transformation practitioner. He says that imaginations are too narrowly oriented to "critical mass" when we imagine how social change happens. Critical mass—rallies, galvanizing leaders, large numbers of bodies on the street—plays a cathartic role in toppling old realities and making way for the new. But in his experience with people who have transformed conflicted realities across time and continents, new realities are envisioned and brought into being before and beyond those cathartic points—patiently, doggedly, over years and decades—by a new quality of relationship in small, unlikely groups of people. They are not obvious compatriots, at least at first; they represent different places on the societal spectrum and embody divergent passions and perspectives. But they see the dead end of the polar opposite conflict in which their lives have become enmeshed, and they step out of fear and into care. John Paul Lederach calls what they create "critical yeast."

Here are specific qualities in the lives of yeasty groups he's seen transform realities in places from Northern Ireland to Colombia to Nepal: they refuse to accept a dualist approach—us against you. They are armed with love and courage, and these things in action are closely connected with creativity: "Reaching out to enemies, embracing complexity, creativity, and risk add up to moral imagination in action. . . . They are artists."

Lovers are artists.

I write that sentence with such pleasure, and now rush to qualify it with caution and confession. It is a biological truth that safety is almost always a prerequisite for the best in us to emerge. I have been estranged from my father for several years. I am frightened to write the truth about the failure of this central love of my life in these pages. But it's a failure that I must forgive, in myself and in him. Love doesn't always work as we want it to, or look like something intimate and beautiful. There are times and places in human existence when love means life on the line, but most of us need not live that way most of the time. Love as a public good needs yeasty groups of social artists, and it also requires bridge people to stand with, speak for, and protect those whose very identities are threatened by conflict. Sometimes love, in public as in private, means stepping back.

We all live lives that are complicated and that at times, with infinite variation, feel overwhelming. But we know people in our immediate world who step beyond themselves, into care. If you know them up close, you know they are not saints or heroes—take note of that, and take comfort. Feel how when you extend a kindness, however simple, you are energized and not depleted. Scientists, again, are proving that acts of kindness and generosity are literally infectious, passing from stranger to stranger to stranger. Kindness is an everyday byproduct of all the great virtues, love most especially. It's appeared on too many bumper stickers for my taste. But it is a form of instant gratification.

Some of us have literal work to do in knowing our neighbors, being present as neighbors. I do want to glorify this with the word *love*—such relationships are the basic connective tissue of common life. It's worth repeating that as love crosses the chasms between us, it likewise brings them into relief. The challenge of standing before open ruptures in civic life is matched, and complicated, by the challenge of standing hospitably before those who offend and harm and drive us crazy in an everyday way. So is standing hospitably with our own, perhaps justified, righteous indignation.

I use the word *hospitably* with intention. *Hospitality* is a word that shimmers, softly. It offers itself as an accessible entry point to love in action. As creatures, we imagine a homogeneity in other groups that we know not to be there in our own. Yet in our own groups of family and colleagues and circles of friends, there are people we admire and people we dislike, people we adore and people who drive us crazy. We find ways, if we can, to stay in relationship—to find out what love can mean with this person at this moment, and a year later, and ten years later. With people we love most, we often know what subjects not to broach or not to broach now. With people we love most, we are often not talking, just staying in the room companionably. This is a piece of intelligence for the world around us.

What is love? Answer the question through a story about the last time you saw it.

Then go and be critical yeast.

END NOTES

Elizabeth Alexander

"Praise Song for the Day," final stanzas

at the inauguration of Barack Obama on January 20, 2009

Some live by *love thy neighbor as thyself,*
others by *first do no harm* or *take no more*
than you need. What if the mightiest word is love?

Love beyond marital, filial, national,
love that casts a widening pool of light,
love with no need to pre-empt grievance.

In today's sharp sparkle, this winter air,
anything can be made, any sentence begun.
On the brink, on the brim, on the cusp,

praise song for walking forward in that light.

So one thing you did in that inaugural poem, "Praise Song for the Day," having said in "Ars Poetica" that "poetry is not about love, love, love . . ."

This poem is.

You invoked love in a political moment, into a public space. It's hard for me to imagine that could have been done politically and have any integrity. But it had incredible weight and also I think strangeness. It was so out of place and yet so powerful, and it worked. These have been

hard years, these years since the inauguration, with all kinds of press-
ing problems on which to talk about love would seem even more super-
fluous than it might have on that day.

Well, when I say "poetry is not all love, love, love," I mean romantic love is where we go first with the word. But really there is so much more to the word. The word is sober. The word is grave. The word is not just about something light and happy and pleasurable. The word calls up deep, deep responsibilities.

The question you posed is, what if the mightiest word is love?

And that's a real question in a lot of my poems. I was thinking about this as I was coming towards this interview. I was think-ing about the act of asking real questions in poems as a kind of spiritual practice. I ask questions relatively often in poems and I ask them because I don't know the answer. And I ask them because I think that poems are fantastic spaces with which to arrive at real conundrum-y kinds of questions, to go as far down the road as you can of understanding something and then sometimes that road ends with a real question.

So "what if the mightiest word is love?" is a question that asks in these times, as an incredibly heterogeneous collective, as an incredibly diverse country, is there such a thing as a love that can supersede or guide or take us through disagreement? What would that mean? What would that love look like? *Mighty,* that's a very, very particular kind of word. Is there a kind of enduring power of love, as I so fervently want to be-lieve? But, once again, love with no need to preempt griev-ance, love that is not about marital love, not just about familial love. It's not even about national love. In fact, love cannot just be for the people in our nation, even in an incredible national moment of the inaugural.

I think you're injecting the word love *into our encounter with otherness, which is more and more just a defining fact even of our national life, right? Even of our family life. Something I think about a lot is how the word that we took after the 1960s to live together with otherness was* tolerance, *and it's not nearly a large and mighty enough word. Love demands much more.*

Well, yes, and especially if it's a love with no need to preempt grievance. You know, love that can even do more than tolerate dissent in difference. That can sit with it, can take it in, can listen to it, can let it stand whole and not necessarily feel the need to engage it argumentatively.

There are a lot of ways, I think, that people who are aggrieved can be addressed. We all have our grievances. And this we understand on the intimate level—when grievance is really heard on the intimate level, that does a great deal of the work of moving people forward.

To living together even if the problem isn't solved, right?

That's right.

So something that I'm really interested in is the connection between what is universal and what is particular and how what is particular illuminates the universal. Recently I had a conversation with the Chief Rabbi of Great Britain, who said this striking thing—that he thinks moral imagination begins with universality and ends with particularity. Which is kind of the reverse of how we've come to think superficially of diversity in Western culture. We have the goal to get to a place where we realize how alike we are—where we can celebrate what we have in common. But you use phrases like "Negro esoteric quirks, oddnesses, particularities," that your poems archive and preserve. How do you think about the force of bringing very particular black experience to our common life? I'm not sure I'm asking the question right, but maybe you understand what I'm getting at.

Well, I have a bunch of responses, though, yeah. I mean, we are always speaking out of our particularities, and that was true in ancient Greece and that's true in England and that's true in all kinds of languages and that's true for white people and that's true for everybody. We speak out of what we know and what we have lived. And then, hopefully from that comes something that we might call the universal. But I also think that because our education is not integrated enough, people don't realize that African American experience is one way of telling the American story and that, in fact, actually it's a profoundly centered way of telling the American story. In fact, if you don't get it and if you move around it, if you don't pass through it, I think people will profoundly misunderstand America. This speaks more in a way to my educator self because my poet self, she's all intuition. There's no program. She's just doing as Adrienne Rich says, "diving into the wreck." The job of the poet in me, again to quote that great poem from Rich, is, "I want the wreck itself, not the story of the wreck, I want the wreck itself." So that's what that part of me is doing, but the educator part of me argues much more forcefully for the necessary centering of African American culture and experience if one is thinking about the United States.

Well, the American story, but also the human story.

Absolutely, absolutely, absolutely.

Xavier Le Pichon

I love the story about Dorothy Day, the Catholic social activist, how she experienced the San Francisco earthquake when she was a child. She saw what happens after a catastrophe. She saw people pouring out to care for each other and to take care of each other. And she asked herself, why can't we live this way all the time? Life has a tendency to go back to normal, at least on the surface. Do you have a sense of what happens when people actually do turn their lives over to this and make this normal? And do you have any sense from the sweep of your lifetime that maybe more people might move in that direction?

That's a very important question you're asking, and this is one I've often asked myself. I've known some people that I've considered very generous, very open, and so on, and I've seen them progressively close themselves, begin to shut the doors, begin to be afraid of being invaded by this problem from the outside. It's as if their hearts were shriveling. And why is that? I don't know. Others, you have the impression that they become more and more open. I've known some extraordinary people. I met Mother Teresa and of course Jean Vanier and so on, people who have this extraordinary capacity to enter into a relationship with others, always open and in a relationship in which they immediately join the part which is most hidden and hurt in them. They have this capacity to enter into new life, and it seems to deepen and deepen with time. It's as if you had two different ways. Now for most of us, it's something in between.

You have these kinds of big awakenings when the catastrophe happens, either a collective one like a war or major accident, but it can be also a tragedy inside the family, not just outside. And people may react in a way that you cannot predict. Sometimes it's very bad. Sometimes it opens them up. But my experience is that once you enter into this way of, I would call it companionship, walking with the suffering person who has come into your life and whom you have not rejected, your heart progressively gets educated by them. They teach you a new way of being.

Your heart gets educated. I like that.

Yes. We have to be educated by the other. My heart cannot be educated by myself. It can only come out of a relationship with others. And if we accept being educated by others, to let them explain to us what happens to them, and to let yourself be immersed in their world so that they can get into our world, then you begin to share something very deep. You will never be the person in front of you, but you will have created what we call communion. I feel that that is the essence of life and that's what Jesus came to teach us. Learn how to enter into communion with your neighbors—that's what he called it, neighbors. And then you will discover something completely new.

Eve Ensler

One of the big realizations that you came to, during your experience of cancer, was about the nature of love. I really took that in; it's something I've also been thinking about a lot. You wrote how, in that extreme moment, the loves that we tend to focus on—love with a capital L, the romantic love, the marriages, the lovers—didn't really come through for you, didn't feel very substantial. And yet you realized that did not amount to the equation we would often make—that you don't have love in your life. You realized you were surrounded by love, that you were held by love, and that you'd had too small an imagination about that word, that thing.

Romantic love, absolutely. Our notion of love—it just seems a very unevolved and very unenlightened notion. That it's this one person who you will meet.

The One.

The One. And, by the way, I've yet to meet anybody who has that experience in that way. Yes, there are people who have good marriages that have lasted long. But I don't think you will talk to anybody who will tell you this is the panacea and this is the only person whom I've ever loved who fulfilled me. Of course not. And I feel so excited now in my life, now that my notion of love has been dispelled, that old notion. Though it still haunts you and lingers. How do we get rid of so much of that stuff? It's in your cells. You just gotta keep purging. But since I recovered from cancer, I feel so joyful. To be sitting here occupying this space with you. This summer, I had my friends and we were in Italy and we were dancing and we were swimming and we were talking and we were having amazing evenings. And every moment of that was so dear to me and precious. We find our fulfillment where we choose to find our fulfillment. And if you're told you can only find it here and you don't look at where it is, which is your life, you keep thinking it's coming. Oh, it'll be here one day. I'll get the big love. Well, you have the big love. It's already here.

You talk about "the daily, subtle simple gathering of kindnesses." It was that love you felt. It was also the love you felt from women in the Democratic Republic of the Congo who were praying for you.

Absolutely. I had one of those bad nights where I was thinking about all my past lovers and husbands and the failure of love in my life, with a capital L. I just didn't get it, and my own intimacy issues, and blah, blah, blah, blah. And then I suddenly realized, okay, how many beautiful people had shown up for me? Marie Cecil, who was cooking me eggs at five in the morning to settle my stomach when I was in chemo. Or my granddaughter, who packed my bags when I went to see my mother for the last time. Or my sister who was there every minute on the couch with me, putting washcloths on my forehead. And it was just this moment of, "Oh, my God, my life is so rich." There is the love. The paradise is here. Paradise is right in front of us. In capitalism what is engineered is longing, engineered longing and desire in us for what can be in the future. It's always about the next product, the next big thing.

You look at clothes and you always see some hot, sexy, fabulous couple wearing those jeans—the jeans, i.e., the love. Everything's all hooked into the seduction. And when you wake up you don't actually look like that, but the reality is delicious in its own messy, human way. I think we're always comparing the messy, human to that, and to celebrity culture, so whatever this is doesn't come up right. Come on. What if we actually were content with our lives? What if we actually knew this was paradise? It would be very hard to control us.

Marie Howe

So your poetry about your brother John's death from AIDS has been really very important for many people. But what intrigued me as I started really steeping in your work is how you've always written a lot about family and families. You've put poetry to family, or you've put family to poetry.

Family is the stage where so much happens in our lives—the family of origin and our family of friends or children or whatever. It's where everything happens. You know, there were 11 people in my family and a lot happened in a given day. There was a great deal going on; the boys downstairs playing pool, the kids in the backyard. Sometimes there would be 40, 50 people over, no big deal. My life now is so different from that life. I'm raising my daughter by myself in a tiny rent-stabilized apartment.

And there's only one of her.

One of her and one of me, and we're in a tiny rent-stabilized apartment in Greenwich Village, which would not even be considered a room in my family of origin's house. No one ever got enough attention through all those people, you know. And people in my family were afflicted by the disease of alcoholism, which brings a terrible chaos into a home as well. Things get violent or things become very dramatic. But that happens in so many places, so many families. Ours was no different.

I want to ask you about a line that was in a poem called "Letter to My Sister."

Oh, dear.

"This no one told us / There is no such thing as family." Somehow that rings true to me, despite what we've just said.

Well, in a big house, different people experienced different things, depending on where you are and the age. One thing I grew up understanding was that multiplicity of viewpoints and truths. But that particular poem was to my sister, a sister who I love very much, who was experiencing trauma. I was trying to speak to how, in our case, alcoholism shatters a unity. It can fragment a community, so that you are now in separate shards. As much as you want to be all in the same room, the nature of that illness fragments any unifying understanding or even experience. That's what those lines were trying to say. One sister is trying to speak to another from that fragmentation, shard to shard.

This is something you wrote or said maybe in another interview, that art helps us to let our heart break open. We've talked about your childhood, and family, and families of origin, and then going through life and becoming a poet, and becoming a mother rather late in life. How do you think about art helping us let our heart break open—how the form and the stakes of that are different at different points in your life and maybe in all of our lives?

Well, that's one of the only choices that we have, right? Things are going to happen. The unendurable happens. People we love and we can't live without are going to die. We're going to die—one day are going to have to leave our children and die, leave the plants, and the bunnies, and the sunlight, and the rain and all that. Art holds that knowledge. All art holds the knowledge that we're both living and dying at the same time. It can hold it. And thank God it can, because nothing out in the corporate world is going to shine that back to us, but art holds it.

People are suffering now an endurable suffering, way beyond what I did. Right this minute, someone is in a prison being tortured for no reason. I don't know how I would live through that without going psychotic. But I did know that when John died, I could either just let this crack my heart open or closed.

And the good news about open is, I turned around and there were of course the billion other people who live on this earth who have lost a person they love so much. There they all were. It was so great to be in their company.

Alternatively, the day I said to my daughter for the first and maybe only time, when she was four years old—I was standing in Austin, Texas, making her bed—and she said, Why do I have to do it? And I said, Because I said so. And I turned around, and there they all were again. There were millions of people clapping—yeah, we said it too! And I'm like, Hi, everybody, I just joined you! I was so glad to be with them. We join each other, you know. It's easier. We're not alone. And I feel that's the only answer. Otherwise, we'd just think it's only happening to us. That's a terrible and untrue way to live our lives. I think art constantly mirrors that to us, whether you're reading Thomas Hardy, or Doris Lessing, or Virginia Woolf, or Emily Dickinson, you know, it's just holding human stories up to us and we don't feel alone. It's so miraculous.

Kate Braestrup

Kate Braestrup is a Unitarian Universalist chaplain to game wardens in the parks and forests of Maine. These are law enforcement officials in the wild, called in on search and rescue missions to respond to danger and disaster. Her work with them takes her, as she describes it, to hinges of human experience, moments where some lives are altered or ended and others swung in wholly unpredicted directions.

You've said that the Tibetan notion rings true for you, that whether we know it or not, we're spending our whole lives preparing for our death. But a lot of the cases you deal with are people who are experiencing the death of people they love. And I don't think any of us feel like we can prepare for that. Or that the universe even makes sense if we're supposed to.

Right. And that's why it's a good thing we don't have to consciously prepare.

And then there's the story you tell of Christina, and Anna Love.

That was one name I did not change in my book.

She has an improbable name, this policewoman Anna Love, and you met her in a context in which you ponder the idea of a miracle in all its complexity.

Well, Christina was a young woman who was abducted and raped and murdered and left in the woods. And so the warden service was involved, along with many, many other agencies, in both recovering her body, and gathering and evaluating the evidence. It was a very painful experience for everybody involved. Obviously, for her family it was excruciating. It was one of those events that test our sense of what it means to live in Maine, of whether our children are safe or whether we are safe. What do you do about evil that swoops down completely at random? I suppose that's where the issue of miracles comes in, that so many things had to happen in the right way, or the wrong way, depending on how you put it, for this particular young woman to meet this particular guy in the parking lot at 7:00 in the morning. That is as improbable as any miracle.

And because of that, a miracle to me can't just be something that was providential, that everything had to line up just right in order for it to happen. Bad things happen that way too. Really bad things happen that way too.

If I look at it from another perspective, and this is really the perspective I maintain, I don't look for God or God's work in magic or in tricks or in, you know, "this is what I want" and then I get it. I look for God's work always in how people love each other, in just the acts of love that I see around me. This event tested that for me because, in general, I don't get involved with a lot of sexual predators and murderers. I'm much more likely to be dealing with accidents or people who've done something stupid or they got drunk and did something stupid, but they weren't actively malicious.

So to look for where love was in this situation, the very obvious place to look would be in the hearts and the hands of the guys who did their best to find her and to make things right for her and for her family. And with all the limitation in that.

That they couldn't, in fact, turn back time or make her be alive. Make that not have happened.

They couldn't fix it. And the fact, actually, that they are willing to go and respond to these things when they can't fix it is actually, in some ways, the most beautiful thing I see. It's one thing to get to be Superman. You swoop in and save the day, and it's very satisfying when that happens. I love it, you know, when they find the kid in the woods before the last breath has left his body. That's wonderful. They bring him out alive; I love it. But what's amazing to me is that these police officers and the game wardens have actually deliberately set up their lives so that they're going to have to go and do these things that are excruciatingly painful and that don't fix or undo the harm and the evil that they see.

And in this particular case it was a woman, a police officer named Anna Love.

Anna was the primary detective on the case. She's this very serious young woman. I've known her actually for quite a long time now. And she's very easy to picture as a detective. She's very smart, you know, very serious, kind of a little pale heart-shaped face. And as a result of her investigating this, which meant combing through all of this information and trying to come up with plausible places to look for a suspect, they found the suspect. Then she had to interview him repeatedly and interview all the witnesses and interview him again and then go with him to the scene.

And this is all within just three days, right? She really closed this case.

She did. In between all of this, she would duck into the lieutenant's office with a breast pump, because she had a newborn baby at home and she was sending bottles of milk home to her husband, who's also a police officer, so that he could give them to the baby. I thought, There's something just gorgeous about that.

You wrote, "If ours were a sensible culture, little girls would play with Anna Love action figures, badge in one hand, breast pump in the other."

And kind of the perfect detective for this case somehow. There are these paradoxes that you can't fix or make fit together. You can't shave away the edges so that they match. You just have to let them sit there as separate things. On one hand you had this terrible event that was not right and not just and was cruel and on every level harmful and hurtful and terrible. On the other hand, you have all of these guys responding. All of these guys motivated by love. And one of them is Anna Love, who is a breast-feeding mother. And she's the one who nails this guy.

It's not as if all of that fixes Christina's death; it doesn't. It's just that they both exist in the same time and the same space, which, I guess, isn't enough and is enough.

You point out something that's very simple, but really striking and unsettling in good ways and bad. That even when the miracle is of a life restored, that is always a temporary restoration. And you say that most of the time, perhaps, "a miracle can only be the resurrection of love beside the unchanged fact of death."

This is a continual argument I have with Christianity. I always felt that it was answering a question I wasn't asking. If you decide that the most important thing, the highest possible value, is life—breath in the body and walking around and eating sandwiches and whatever—then you're lost. Then you've lost. Because we're all going to die. So then you have to posit this whole other set of things that you can't see and you can't connect with. As I said, I'm a practical person. I want to be able to see it and I want to be able to do it.

So if I posit instead that the most important thing is love, then what I have is, yes, I have a world that's full of suffering and evil and pain. And I have something to do. I have something to look for, and I have something to do. For me that works better.

john powell

There was a period of time when I was feeling really overwhelmed with a lot of this stuff. And I was talking to my dad, and I said, "Dad, this is just too much. I can't do it all. I'm trying to do all of this stuff by myself." And he looked at me and said, "John, you know you're not alone." I said, "What do you mean?" He said, "Well, you've got God with you." And I realized, although I don't organize around God the way he does, my mistake was I thought I had to do it, that I was defining it in terms of "I" instead of "we." So . . .

. . . you were in that white mode.

Exactly, exactly. So I think we should both get out of the white mode and do it together.

So here's something you said in another interview: "If you look at 1950s attitudes toward integration versus today, the majority of whites today say they'd prefer to live in an integrated neighborhood and send their kids to integrated schools. What they mean by that is a different question. But the world and the demographics of the country are changing. And to live in a white enclave is not to live in the world. It has a certain deadness to it. It has a certain spiritual corruption to it." And you said, "I think most people, white, black, Latino, and otherwise, would like to see something different. We just don't know how to do it. And we've been so entrenched in the way things are. It's hard to imagine the world being different."

You speak for me, you speak for so many people. This is what we're up against. I feel like this is what we have to attack first, this inability to see differently. You've told one story about Oak Park near Chicago. It was just really helpful to me. This is a story we've all heard—you integrate neighborhoods, and housing values go down. And the way we always tell the story is that people of color moved in. And the way we could tell the story is whites moved out. But you talked about how just this very practical measure was taken so that the housing values didn't change. I feel like these little stories are really crucial as well.

And there are really a lot of them. They're little, and they're big. So Oak Park is in Chicago. Chicago's one of the most segregated areas in the country. Cook County has the largest black population of any county in the United States, and a lot of study of segregation takes place in Chicago. So here you have Oak Park, this precious little community. They were liberal whites there, and blacks started moving in. And they were saying, "Look, we actually don't mind blacks moving in, but we're concerned that we're going to lose the value of our home. That's the only wealth we have. If we don't sell now, we're going to lose." And the local government basically said, "If that's the real concern, not that blacks are moving in, what if we were to ensure that you would not lose the value of your home? We'll literally create an insurance policy that will compensate you if the value of your home goes down." And they put that in place.

They haven't had to pay one policy. Whites didn't run further out to the suburbs. And that's a stable community. It's been that way for 50 years. This is interesting on a number of levels, because you could say those white people were just being racist. They were just using the insurance policy as an excuse. Maybe, maybe not. Are you willing to actually take them at their word? Are you willing to embrace them and engage them where they are? Because people do have anxieties, and they're multiple.

I want to give two other examples very quickly. Think about Katrina. These examples are all around us, and yet we don't tell stories about them. The face of Katrina, when you remember it, was blacks stuck on roofs as the water was rising. What's not told is that Americans, all Americans, gave to those people. It was the largest civilian giving of one population to another in the history of the United States. So here you had white Americans, Latino Americans, Asian Americans trying to reach out to what they saw as black Americans. They were actually claiming that we have a shared humanity. And the fastest growing demographic in the United States is not Latinos. It's actually interracial couples and interethnic couples. That's people who are themselves right now, not tomorrow, trying to imagine a different America, trying to say, "I can love anyone. I can be with anyone." So if we start looking for it, we see expressions of it all around. Oftentimes, they're not celebrated. They're not talked about. There are no structures for them. We have to embrace them and lift them up.

Vincent Harding

I was listening to the BBC in recent weeks, as they watch us from afar. A comparison was made with the 1960s, another moment of social turmoil, including many assassinations. A journalist said that he thought the difference between the 1960s and now was that even though there was incredible tumult and violence, it was at the very same time a period of intense hope. People could see that they were moving toward goals, and that's missing now. What do you think about this analysis?

I think that is such a complicated issue that I can only pick at it and tease it out and play with it, in the best sense of play. I think that what I see now is the fact that all over this country wherever I go—and, of course, where I go tends to be sort of self-selective, because I am most often going into situations where people are operating out of a sense of hope and possibility, where in their local situations—whether it be Detroit or Atlanta or a campus someplace or a church community in Philadelphia—there are women and men and young people who are operating out of hope.

My sense is that, in the '60s, there was probably a larger canopy of hope that we could see and we could identify and that people could name and focus on. I have a feeling that one of the deeper transformations that's going on now is that for the white community of America, there is this uncertainty growing about its own role, its own control, its own capacity to name the realities. It has moved into a realm of uncertainty that it did not allow itself to face before.

And I think that that's the place that we are in, and that's even more the reason why we've got to figure out what King was talking about when he was seeing the possibility of a beloved community and recognized that that cannot come until some of us realize we must give up what we thought was only ours. Can there be a beloved nation? Why don't we try and see?

There's a question that you pose in your writing—that you've posed in recent years: "Is America possible?" When you answer that question, is America possible?, what people come to mind? What answers come to mind in the form of the hope that you see embodied?

One of the great benefits of living past my 80th birthday is the great privilege of being able to meet and be with all kinds of marvelous people. I spend a lot of my time in places like Philadelphia, where, on the northwest side, I've been deeply involved with a church community there, a Methodist church led by a magnificent woman pastor who has embraced the young people of the community in ways that churches often do not. Young people who were considered marginalized have become the heart of her work and they have seen their own possibilities.

I remember when a group of them came out to visit us at our project in Denver. They were true Philadelphians. They were dressed from the Philadelphia streets, they moved like Philadelphians and they ran into some very interesting encounters in Denver. But at one point, two of them—one young man, one young woman—took me aside and said, "Could we talk to you for just a minute?" They had started to call me Uncle Vincent, and they said to me, "Uncle Vincent, why do you love us so?" And what I saw was that they had this great capacity to know that they were being loved, to feel it in their being, and that they had power and responsibility to do something for their community that had not been done for them.

I see young people like that all over this country, and I know that they exist. I know some of the adults who work with them in places like Greensboro, North Carolina, in Detroit, Michigan, on the reservations in New Mexico, out in the LA area. We've got working connections with young people and their adult nurturers in all of those kinds of situations. Because I see that, feel that, receive their returning love, I know they are capable of building the beloved community.

And so it is that kind of constant engagement with people who have been considered hopeless, useless, purposeless, just like I saw them in the Deep South in the 1960s. People who were considered backward, unable to do anything, became the creators of a new possibility for the whole nation. And when I think about Tiananmen Square and Prague, I realize that those folks in Mississippi and Alabama who were considered useless were able to speak to the world. I see that again and again and again right in this country, see it with young people, see it with those who are loving them into new possibilities. And so that's why for me the only answer that I can give to the question that I raise is, yes, as we make it possible, yes. Yes.

FIVE

···|————————|···

FAITH

The Evolution

When I summon up the memory of faith of my earliest life, I find it acquainted with fear, but not fear alone. Longing lived there too, and moments of transport, and of comfort, and of a bracing vastness of possibility. That was all there for me sometimes when I plunged my mind into the Bible's puzzles; and it was always there in the music of church. I wouldn't have said it this way then. But I would feel all the cells in my body as I sang hymns that connected my little life with the grandeur of the cosmos, the Christian drama across space and time. This was my earliest experience of breath and body, mind and spirit soaring together, alive to both mystery and reality, in kinship with others both familiar and unknown. That's one way I'd define the feeling of faith now.

Who am I to speak for God? But this I believe:

If God is God—and that in itself is a crazy shorthand, begging volumes of unfolding of the question—he/she does not need us craven.

He/she desires us, needs us, grateful and attentive and courageous in the everyday.

To invoke some of my favorite classic approaches to a definition, if God is the "mind behind the universe," God honors our minds. If God is the "ground of being," God blesses our wholeness.

That fear of the religion of my childhood was about measuring up—about moral perfection, and the eternal cost of falling short. For me now, faith is in interplay with moral imagination, something distinct from moral perfection. I am still figuring out what that means, how to nurture it in myself and in others. I am playing and wrestling with how this language—and the character it implies—might find expression in common life. What I am coming up with takes me by surprise. It is all so removed from the public face of religion in living memory, and far from where I began. But in taking in this vocabulary, the great traditions in all their fraught, lumbering majesty become comprehensible for me again.

Faith is evolutionary, in every culture, and in any life. Even a person who could proclaim, all of their days, "I believe in God" or "I trust in prayer" would fill those words with endlessly transforming memories, experiences, connotations. The same enduring fundamental belief will hold a transfigured substance in the beginning, the middle, and the end of one lifetime. Wisdom, of the everyday sort, is about how we reckon with the surprises and mysteries that make life *life* as opposed to stasis. Mystery lands in us as a humbling fullness of reality we cannot sum up or pin down. Such moments change us from the inside, if we let them.

Western Christianity lost some of the cleansing power of mystery when it became a bedfellow with empire and later, again, in its headlock with science. I sensed a discomfort in my grandfather at his own large and active mind, a nervous reluctance to acknowledge things the Bible did not or could not explain. For they might be delivered over to science's godless certainties, and then they were lost to the faithful forever.

He could not foresee that twentieth-century science would come to the edge of what it thought to be final frontiers and remember its own core virtue of humility, be delighted by surprise. We learned, among other premise-toppling things, that the expansion of the universe is not slowing down but speeding up; and by way of explanation, that the vast majority of the cosmos is brim full of forces we had never before imagined and cannot yet fathom—the intriguingly named "dark matter" as well as "dark energy."

As this century opened, physicists, cosmologists, and astronomers were no longer pushing mystery out, but welcoming it back in. Scenarios of string theory and parallel realities, the multiverse, still sound like science fiction. They are attempts to achieve the "theory of everything" that eluded Einstein—to reconcile the great puzzle that how the world works at the cosmic level does not cohere with how we understand its workings at the micro level, the quantum realm. But quantum physics, whose tenets Einstein compared to voodoo, has given us cell phones and personal computers, technologies of the everyday by which we populate online versions of outer space.

In turn, these immersive science-driven experiences are renewing ancient human intuitions that linear, immediate reality is not all there is. There's reality and there's virtual reality, space and cyberspace. Use whatever analogy you will. Our online lives take us down the rabbit hole like Alice. We wake up in the morning and walk through the back of the closet into Narnia. The farther we delve into artificial intelligence and the mapping of our own brains, the more fabulous our own consciousness appears.

The late wise physician Sherwin Nuland, an agnostic born a Hasidic Jew, liked to quote Saint Augustine's observation that

> Men go forth to wonder at the heights of mountains,
> the huge waves of the sea,

the broad flow of the rivers,

the vast compass of the ocean,

the courses of the stars,

and they pass by themselves without wondering.

We have come, in our time, to wonder at the mystery we are with a newly adventurous vigor. Einstein saw a reverence for wonder at the heart of the best of science and religion and the arts. Wondering is a useful way to begin to speak of a shared vocabulary of mystery we might embrace across our disciplines, our contrasting certainties, and our doubts. It is an animating impulse the psychiatrist Robert Coles discerned in the origins of a human lifetime—in childhood—and the origins too of faith. I interviewed him in his book-lined home outside Boston in the early days of my radio adventure, and it grounded all that came later.

> We come out of nowhere, don't we, in the sense that we're a total accident. Our parents met. Obviously, we come from someplace physiologically. And then comes the emergence of our being. That takes time, experience, education of a certain kind with parents and neighbors and teachers and relatives and from one another humanly. And this slow emergence of our psychological being and our spiritual being is itself a great mystery . . . I think there is no doubt that a lot of the religious side of childhood is a merger of the natural curiosity and interest the children have in the world with the natural interest and curiosity that religion has about the world.

Robert Coles came to this kind of language accidentally himself. He began his career in the crucible of social change of the 1960s. As a young psychiatrist in New Orleans, he happened to drive by crowds of adults heckling nine-year-old Ruby Bridges as she became the first black child to desegregate an elementary school in the south. He was mesmerized by her dignity, got to know her and her family, and went on to write award-winning books about the psychological, political, and moral lives of children. Then one day relatively late in his career, his friend Anna Freud suggested that he might look back at all his research and see if there was anything he'd missed. And he found, to his surprise, that his notes were full of religious and spiritual observations from children, insights he'd largely ignored for the sake of academic respectability. These were the seeds for the book for which he is now best known: *The Spiritual Life of Children.*

When Robert Coles describes the spiritual lives of children, he's not describing a childish exuberance we outgrow. It's a delving and wondering he went on to trace in adult lives of greatness, creativity, and resilience—the Dorothy Days and William Carlos Williamses and Dietrich Bonhoeffers of this world. Robert Coles has a growly voice wonderful for radio and in his eighties he remains one of those luminously wise, ever-delving people too.

It's interesting to me that a "questioning spirit" is a quality you found in children from religious and nonreligious backgrounds—and even in children who came from homes in which the tradition was much more conservative and the answers set. And what you discovered in speaking with children and listening to them is not only revealing about childhood. It's revealing of an aspect of religion which we probably don't pay as much attention to as we should.

That's the great tragedy, isn't it? Because after all, if you stop and think about Judaism, the great figures in Judaism are those prophets of Israel, Jeremiah and Isaiah and Amos. They were prophetic figures who asked the deepest kinds of questions and were willing to stand outside the gates of power and privilege in order to keep asking those questions. And then came Jesus of Nazareth, who was a *teacher*. You might call him a migrant teacher, who walked about ancient Israel—now called Israel, Palestine, the Middle East—seeking and asking and wondering and reaching out to people and daring to ask questions that others had been taught not to ask or even forbidden to ask. This inquiring Jesus, this soulful Jesus, searching for comrades—let's call them, in our vernacular, buddies. They were his buddies, and they were willing to link arms with him in this kind of spiritual quest that he found himself impelled toward or driven toward.

Now, both in Judaism and Christianity, of course, there are rule setters, and at times they can be all too insistent, some would say even a bit tyrannical. But the spirit of religion, I think, is what children connect with—the questions, the inquiry, the enormous curiosity about this universe, and the hope that somehow those answers will come about.

Also what I think you're getting at, and what is also in this compatibility between children and religion, has something to do with the mystery of those questions themselves.

Mystery is such an important part of it. And mystery invites curiosity and inquiry. You know, Flannery O'Connor—talk about a religious person, she was Catholic in background but she was beyond Catholicism; she was a deeply spiritual person. And she once was talking about the kind of person who becomes a good novelist, hoping that she would be included in that company but not daring to assume that that had happened.

She said, beautifully, "The task of the novelist is to deepen mystery." And then she pauses and says, "But mystery is a great embarrassment to the modern mind." And there's our tragedy, that we have to resolve all mystery. We can't let it be. We can't rejoice in it. We can't celebrate it. We can't affirm it as an aspect of our lives. Because, after all, mystery is an aspect of our lives. And mystery, you bet—mystery is a great challenge. It's an invitation, and it's a wonderful companion, actually.

Once upon a time I took in mystery as a sensation best left unexamined. Now I experience it as a welcome. I'm strangely comforted when I hear from scientists that human beings are the most complex creatures we know of in the universe, still, by far. Black holes are in their way explicable; the simplest living being is not. I lean a bit more confidently into the experience that life is so endlessly perplexing. I love that word. Spiritual life is a way of dwelling with perplexity—taking it seriously, searching for its purpose as well as its perils, its beauty as well as its ravages.

In this sense, spiritual life is a reasonable, reality-based pursuit. It can have mystical entry points and destinations, to be sure. But it is in the end about befriending reality, the common human experience of mystery included. It acknowledges the full drama of the human condition. It attends to beauty and pleasure; it attends to grief and pain and the enigma of our capacity to resist the very things we long for and need.

I admire the perfect, succinct opening line of Reinhold Niebuhr's twentieth-century classic *The Nature and Destiny of Man*: "Man is his own most vexing problem." This is the basic conundrum behind the notion of "original sin," which was drilled into me by my preacher grandfather like the Church drilled it into Western civilizations for centuries, to the point of trivialization. The world beyond Oklahoma proved itself full of life-giving pleasure, even in what I previously perceived to be the throes of sin. Yet at this point in my life, I find "sin" a useful inheritance from my religious mother tongue, not merely a condemnation of this act or that act, this transgression or that wrong, but a piece of psychological clarity.

I was living in England when I circled back to religion in my late twenties, and the Anglican Book of Common Prayer drew me with its poetry and its vigorous description of the vexing human condition. "We have done those things we ought not to have done," Thomas Cranmer penned for King Henry VIII, who was as vivid an embodiment of the vexed human condition as ever walked the earth. "And we have left undone those things which we ought to have done"—naming the ordinary, everyday failure to join inner aspiration with outer reality. A failure to take in beauty and let it put things in their place. A failure to be grateful, as a habit. A failure to take the time to attend to the hurting stranger. A failure to be my best self with those I share life and work with. A failure to forgive others for not being their best selves with me.

So much of what we orient towards in culture numbs a little going in and helps us avoid the reckoning we actually long for—the push to self-knowledge and deeper lived integrity. Poetry, says Marie Howe, hurts a little going in. It soothes and deepens us and hurts a little all at the same time. So do many of the elements that give voice to the soul—silence and song, community and ritual, listening and compassionate presence. They wake us up—the apt Buddhist language for spiritual illumination. But there is that window of choice, moment by moment, to go for distraction instead, to settle into numb.

Maybe this is another way to think about original sin—the ingrained lure of the possibility of going numb, a habit of acquiescence to it. It takes forms profound and banal. It is there in the way I am itching, with each sentence on this page, to heed the background call of technology and head down a rabbit hole of distraction that will scatter my ability to follow this line of reflection to the end. In that western half capital of Berlin in the cold war days, I found myself in a place and time where every distraction held geopolitical import. It was thrilling. But up close, I experienced diplomats, journalists, and policy makers who spent all of their personal energy on cultivating powerful, reactive, external lives. I wouldn't have used this language then, for I, too, was a mostly political animal—but they were underdeveloped spiritually, beginners when it came to inner landscapes of beauty that would anchor and nourish them on the inside, beyond work, in the intimate spaces that in the end define us all. The ambassador with whom I worked was a nuclear arms expert of some renown, who captivated audiences with brilliant speeches and faced off with the Soviets. At home, he sent terse, adolescent messages through his staff to his wife, who was upstairs.

This was a pattern of unintentional self-destruction glorified in the twentieth century—to enrich on the outside, and impoverish within. Our kids want us to finally get this right. They have injected the language of *transparency* and *authenticity* and *integrity* into our civic vocabulary. These are fragile words, like all words meant to convey deep truth, at risk of overuse and simplification. Behind them I hear a wise refusal to disconnect what we know from who we are, what we believe from how we live and who we are to each other. Such words carry heart-breaking, holy longings for us to see ourselves in our wholeness—to make the move from intelligence to wisdom, from the inside.

Spirituality is a word I've used sparingly in my life, wary of its vagueness and promiscuity of attention, of the teachings of the ages individualized and customized and rendered superficial. But I've watched our cultural encounter with spirituality—and the relationship between spirituality and religion and culture—come of age in important ways.

Here's what I know: the whole picture confounds any neat analysis, any sure prognosis. The phrase "spiritual but not religious," now common social parlance, is just the tip of an iceberg that has already moved on. We are among the first peoples in human history who do not broadly inherit religious identity as a given, a matter of kin and tribe, like hair color and hometown. But the very fluidity of this—the possibility of choice that arises, the ability to craft and discern one's own spiritual bearings—is not leading to the decline of spiritual life but its revival. It is changing us, collectively. It is even renewing religion, and our cultural encounter with religion, in counterintuitive ways. I meet scientists who speak of a religiosity without spirituality—a reverence for the place of ritual in human life, and the value of human community, without a need for something supernaturally transcendent. There is something called the New Humanism, which is in dialogue about moral imagination and ethical passions across boundaries of belief and nonbelief.

Then there are the "Nones," the awkwardly named, most rapidly growing segment of spiritual identification, as calculated by opinion polls. Beginning in the first decade of this century, pollsters began to register that 15 percent of the U.S. population, and a full third of people under thirty, answered "none" when asked to fill in a multiple-choice question about their religious affiliation. Masses of air and print time have been given over to punditry on this shift that defies America's age-old self-understanding as a Christian nation.

I don't find it surprising that young people born in the 1980s and 1990s have distanced themselves from the notion of religious declaration, growing up as they did in an era in which strident religious voices became toxic forces in American cultural life. Figures like Jerry Falwell and Pat Robertson were granted inordinate air and print time as the voice of "religion" in all kinds of media, long after they ceased to represent most Evangelicals and Fundamentalists, much less all Christians or people of faith.

More to the point: the growing universe of the Nones—the new nonreligious—is one of the most spiritually vibrant and provocative spaces in modern life. It is not a world in which spiritual life is absent. It is a world that resists religious excesses and shallows. Large swaths of this universe are wild with ethical passion and delving, openly theological curiosity, and they are expressing this in unexpected places and unexpected ways. I think of Nathan Schneider as a millennial public intellectual, straddling journalism, the academy, social activism, and religion. He wrote an unorthodox and captivating journalistic account of the Occupy Wall Street movement, which arose in the wake of the economic crisis of 2008, from the inside. He observed a spiritual dynamic missed by other commentators.

> When young people in the secular social political movement that was Occupy Wall Street started turning their attention to churches—sometimes actually protesting in front of churches—it wasn't that they were protesting the things that a church would claim to believe. What they were actually saying was, "Church, act like a church!" These were people who, many of whom, had never really been part of a church community or another kind of religious community. Or if they had, they'd had some experience of alienation. The general identity was that of the Nones.

Nathan Schneider has a distinctly twenty-first-century category-defying life. He was raised by parents who exposed him to every spiritual tradition and invited him to create his own. He explored intellectually and experientially throughout adolescence—and when he was eighteen, he was baptized into the Catholic Church. After millennia in which human beings inherited their denominations like DNA, we are free even to choose orthodoxy. Nathan has written another book about the search for proof of God "from the ancients to the Internet." This vision backward and forward in time is a hallmark of wise seekers I experience in emerging generations. Among things that need correction, Nathan suggests, speaking my language, is that we are asking the wrong questions when we analyze the validity of religion in our time, the place of religion, and the changes religion is undergoing.

> One thing I noticed as I got older, especially as I started studying religion in a more formal context, was that the kinds of struggles that we're going through were known by many of the great thinkers and experimenters of our religious traditions, who we kind of ossify and contain, and put into boxes and try to own and control. This was a time just after 9/11, when the new atheists were just getting going. Is religion real? What is its relationship to violence? The stakes of these questions were very, very high. They were swirling around me. And they were framed in terms of the question, Does God exist? Is there anything there? As I started diving into the tradition of what I thought would be people trying to answer that question, I actually realized that that was not so much what was on the minds of people who've sought proof for God across the ages. The real power of a lot of these arguments is in the kind of relationship that they're forging—the way in which they express God in and through an account of relationship between people.

So your generation—this age right now—has given rise to this phenomenon that's been defined as "the Nones." It seems to me that what you're describing, in yourself and for them, is not so much trying to figure out who God is but trying to figure out what these traditions are about at their heart, across time and space, and in their best expression.

On the one hand, when I became a Roman Catholic, I was drawn in by this medieval contemplative tradition as well as this tradition of courageous social witness—exemplified by something like Dorothy Day's *Catholic Worker*, and many other examples throughout history and around the world. I came into Catholic churches and realized that many of the people who were going to those churches didn't really know about that stuff. They didn't know their own tradition. They were kind of keeping on, in many cases though certainly not all, with a kind of inertia.

On the other hand, people I've found outside of these spaces, outside of these churches, were intensely interested in these questions and had very good questions they were trying to think through and work through. They didn't feel like they could really commit themselves to these institutions, but they were curious, and they were looking for something. It was so striking to me, that cry of Occupy: "Act like a church." I still keep on the background screen on my cell phone, while I'm pulling up my Facebook and Twitter and all that stuff, a picture of what happened after Hurricane Sandy, when those Occupiers filled churches with rescue supplies.

And that was what became Occupy Sandy. I don't think that was quite as much in the headlines or covered as much. I'm not sure people necessarily know that Occupy Sandy grew out of Occupy Wall Street. Tell some of that story.

So when Hurricane Sandy hit New York City and surrounding regions, immediately a small group of people who had been involved in Occupy Wall Street decided that they were going to organize some kind of relief effort. They had to do something. And they did. They had the first website up, the first place on the ground where people could deliver supplies—in churches. And they ended up becoming a major part of the early phases of the relief effort.

But it was really interesting to see, in the course of that process, this group of people—many of whom did not have comfortable relationships with traditional religious institutions—work with religious folks, work with these religious communities. On the one hand, they would see the power of those communities, see the resilience of those communities in a way that their movement had not been able to build for itself. And they would see what they could draw from the ideas of those traditions. They started talking about "jubilee." They started recognizing that there was something real in this religious language that connected with the frustrations that they were feeling with the society around them.

I was just at a place in Southern Italy where activists—hackers mainly, from around Europe, technology activists—have been gathering and actually adopting and playing with hacking, so to speak, the rule of St. Benedict. They're looking at this rule that's the basis of Western Christian Monasticism as a kind of basis for building sustainable, sustaining communities. They look at the way in which monasteries carried civilization through the Dark Ages, you know, preserving the art of writing. They're looking to this religious legacy as a means for starting from scratch. And they're thinking about what kinds of reorientations they could make in their relationships with the technology that they're using, and how they could build livelihoods for themselves in a way analogous to monks.

Again, these are not people who affiliate themselves with

any religious communities in particular. Yet they're drawn to something that is in these traditions. They recognize that something is there, and they don't feel that they can go to the existing institutions to explore them. So they're playing around on their own.

The connection points I hear to monasticism, nearly everywhere in the emerging spiritual landscape, are beyond intriguing. The wandering ascetic, eccentric sages known as the Desert Fathers and Mothers, the visionaries like Benedict or Francis or Ignatius of Loyola across the many centuries in which Catholicism was the only way to be Christian—they all emerged at a distance from a Church they experienced to have grown imperial, externally domesticated, and inwardly cold—out of touch with its own spiritual core.

And there is a kindred shift in the Nones' generation of young Christians, including Evangelicals and others—people who have not rejected the faith of their childhood, but grew up allergic to stridency and determined to reform it. One pivotal, loosely federated movement is called the New Monasticism. Shane Claiborne is now one of its guiding lights and, at forty, one of its elders. He was born in Tennessee in 1973, in the heyday of the Moral Majority, and spent part of his teenage years canvasing for a Republican vice-presidential candidate, Dan Quayle. He is a lanky, charismatic, dreadlocked figure, who looks like he might have been at home with the Desert Fathers and Mothers. While at Eastern University outside Philadelphia, an Evangelical college with a long history of social action, he and some friends became involved in championing and caring for a large number of homeless people who had moved into an abandoned church in North Philadelphia and were facing forced removal. The irony was not lost on them. They began to wonder if Jesus would recognize what went on in the churches they grew up in. He tells me this story of what happened next, in his long Tennessee drawl:

You know, I start reading this stuff that Jesus said. And I'm just, like, "Man, does anyone really believe this anymore?" Mother Teresa was one of those people that I felt just lived so magnetically and authentically the simple words and teaching of Jesus. So we wrote her a letter, you know? We said, Hey, we don't know if you give internships out there in Calcutta, but we'd love to come work. And we didn't hear back. I guess she got a lot of mail. So we called Calcutta. I'm expecting a polite, "Missionaries of Charity, how can we help you?" And I hear this raspy, old voice go, "Hello?" And I'm thinking I've got the wrong number and it's $4 a minute. So I started talking really fast. I'm like, "We're trying to get hold of the Missionaries of Charity or Mother Teresa's order out there, the Sisters." And she said, "Well, this is the Missionaries of Charity. This is Mother Teresa." And she says, "Yeah, come on out."

I learned so much. We had been sucked up into this real movement of social justice, going out and getting arrested and protesting everything that was wrong. We knew what we were against. We just didn't know what we were for. And in a leper colony in Calcutta, I learned from a group of people who had been, basically, forced by their society to create a new society in the shell of the old one. It's really there that I kind of caught that vision of, let's build something new together. As one of my heroes, Dorothy Day, said, "Let's build a society where it's easier for people to be good to each other."

When Shane and his friends came back from Calcutta, they founded a community called The Simple Way. This is not a monastic order in the traditional sense, but an "intentional community" that does draw on some monastic wisdom about structuring a rhythm of life together. Single people and couples and families share life with each other and the city around them. Over time it's grown from one house to six and a multitude of projects and ministries. It's a place of pilgrimage for young people, from many backgrounds. It's a beacon for a larger web of community, a constellation of other groups in other places, and for church and spiritual life reimagined.

> There was a group of us that ended up going, "Let's try to do church like the old days." We would read in the Book of Acts that all of the believers were together and shared everything in common. No one claimed any of their possessions were their own, but they shared everything. And there were no needy persons among them. We had all kinds of baggage from the church, you know, recovering Evangelicals and disenchanted Catholics. But we decided that we were going to stop complaining about the church that we'd experienced and try to become the church that we dreamed of.
>
> We had no huge visions for transforming our neighborhood or something. We were coming very much as learners. We opened our door up to people. Our mission was just to love God, love people, and follow Jesus. And we said, "If we can figure that out, then we'll be doing well," you know? And so we had a lot of homeless folks that came by the house; we had a lot of kids that needed help with homework. And everything that we do just sort of bubbled up out of that. In North Philly, there's a lot of struggle, but there's also a lot of hope. We tried to feed each other hope and to reclaim abandoned spaces. I'm missing out on all the gardening today. We're reclaiming two lots on our block where they were formerly just filled with trash and needles. We're reclaiming that space and doing gardens with our neighborhood. We have a little thrift store. As soon as I leave here, we'll be giving out about 50 bags of food

to folks who need food. But initially, when we started the community, we were just responding to crisis, you know. And then there comes a point, as Dr. Martin Luther King said so well, where we're called to be the Good Samaritan and lift our neighbor out of the ditch. But after you lift so many people out of the ditch, you start to say, Maybe the whole road to Jericho needs to be transformed.

There's something in the way—not just the way you see your Christianity, but the way you look at the world. It's a very holistic vision. So, for example, you've taken the old adage that if you give someone a fish, they'll eat for a day, but if you teach them how to fish, they can eat for a lifetime. And you say, "We also need to ask who owns the pond and who polluted it." I'm not sure human beings have previously lived in a world where they could think that way, or see all the connections. Have you thought about this—about your generation and this time?

Everywhere I go, I am so encouraged by the questions that people are asking, especially even within the Evangelical church that's been so scared of a lot of those questions. Most people my age that I see, even within the Evangelical church, transcend categories of left and right, and really are wanting to know how to create a better world. And they know that the world that we've been handed is very fragile. They say, we need to figure out how to live differently ourselves and how to live with some imagination and some creativity, and give ourselves to something bigger than just our own little circle of friends.

To me, that's so encouraging. And I'm convinced that if the Christian church loses this generation, it will be not because we didn't entertain them, but because we didn't dare them with the truth of the world. It won't be because we'd made the Gospel too hard, but because we made it too easy, and we just played games with kids and didn't actually challenge them to think about how they live. And what I really love about much of what's happening in the younger generation is that there's a sense that, man, we all have a lot of contradictions and we don't need to feel like we have it all figured out. There's something just as magnetic as a church that seems to pretend that we've all got it together, which is definitely the church that I grew up in. There's something magnetic about a group of people that say, "Hey, we don't have it all figured out, and we need each other."

The Nones of this age are ecumenical, humanist, transreligious. But in their midst are analogs to the original monastics: spiritual rebels and seekers on the margins of established religion, pointing tradition back to its own untamable, countercultural, service-oriented heart.

This life-giving heart of religion, of course, is not the whole story. Religion, in the sweep of the drama of human history and the contemporary globe, has a power to magnify the worst of what humanity is capable of as well as the best. Human fear and rage—almost always a pair, two sides of an emotional coin—are combustive when mixed with a cosmic worldview and a vocabulary that equates wrong with evil and damned. Violent catharsis in the name of the second largest religion in the world, Islam, is the framing crisis of this century, which no one foretold the day Berlin's Wall fell so peacefully. We might have seen that the cold war's unraveling took the lid off ethnic and religious tensions that had been suppressed by the superpower division of the world. We might have known that peoples who had been on the captive side of history so long—their very borders and livelihoods the stuff of geopolitical whimsy and barter—could not make a joyful transition to a world without fear alongside us. Fear comes out in public looking like anger, when it comes to nations as well as individuals.

The raw human condition, the interwovenness of Islam with cultures and of those cultures with globalization, the Nones' generation of young people unmoored from tradition and confounded by the world in which they're growing up—this brew of social complexity has created the crisis of terrorism that primarily lays waste to the lives of other Muslims but which, in a globalized world, touches us all. Islam is six hundred years younger than Christianity, and six hundred years ago Christians were waging holy wars, defiling ancient sacred spaces, and burning heretics at the stake. But Islamist militants and crusaders function with high visibility in the Internet age while jarringly out of sync with the secular modern West's self-understanding. In a strange, illuminating way, they revive the usefulness of religious imagery. After visiting a refugee camp in Syria created by a group calling itself the Islamic State, the Harvard-educated, South Korean–born, Buddhist-raised UN secretary-general called it "the deepest circle of Hell."

The longer I live, the less comprehensible I find the notion of a God who listens, yields, takes account of our struggles. Yet at the very same time, I see that an undeniable aspect of the science of our age, mirrored in the disarray of journalism as I first learned to practice it, is the acknowledgment that the very notion of objectivity is an illusion. Simply put, the human participant is always a participant, never merely an observer. Somehow our subjectivity, our presence, our wills matter cosmically, whether we want them to or not. A new puzzle takes shape in my spiritual imagination: if on our end there is no such thing as disinterested detachment, true dispassion, can that be a defining state behind the universe from which we come and to which we return?

And as uncertain as I grow about some of the fundaments of faith, in a way that would have alarmed my grandfather, I grow if anything more richly rooted in one of the most inexplicable things he taught me: God is love. I understand the contradiction here. I am unable to state, with conviction, that God exists in any way that sentence would have made sense to me in childhood or makes sense to me now intellectually. I have my eyes wide open to horrors that unfold in my city, and halfway across the world, in any given moment. But I apprehend—with a knowledge that is as much visceral as cognitive—that God *is* love. That somehow the possibility of care that can transform us—love muscular and resilient— is an echo of a reality behind reality, embedded in the creative force that gives us life.

One of the great ongoing debates in the history of mathematics is whether mathematics is invented or discovered. Did Einstein invent $e = mc^2$, or did he discover it embedded in the fabric of reality, waiting to be seen? In human life and in the history of faith, I think, love has a quality of a bedrock reality we discover—adventurers, travelers, each of us, only fitfully apprehending its potential. I take some solace in the fact that I'm not alone in this intuition that the reality of evil, of injustice, of suffering notwithstanding, "at the center of this existence is a heart beating with love." That's how Desmond Tutu put it to me, with greater authority than mine from a life that has known extremes of human cruelty one to another.

I'm also inspired, and persuaded, by the Maine game warden chaplain Kate Braestrup. She became Unitarian Universalist in adulthood and says that she, like some scientists I know, is "religious but not spiritual." For her, this means that the idea that God is love has nothing to do with beliefs or transcendence and everything to do with actions and people.

> I mean it pretty literally that God is, if nothing else—and
> that's a big if—but if nothing else, God is that force that drives

us to really see each other and to really behold each other and care for each other and respond to each other. And for me, that is actually enough. That cultivating it, that thinking about it, worshipping it, working towards it, taking care of it, nurturing it in myself, nurturing it in other people, that really is a life's work right there, and it doesn't have to be any bigger than that. God doesn't have to be out in the next solar system over bashing asteroids together. It's plenty, just the God that I work with.

And then the question is, and this is something I know you grapple with all the time, how do you draw that line to this God of love from the child who's gone missing, the beloved husband who just skated on lake ice that was too thin, the young woman who was raped and whose body is left in the woods?

Well, the first two are easier than the last one. The child is loved. The people who show up have no trouble at all loving that child enough to risk themselves to try to find her or him. And if you accept, as I do, that death is a given for all of us, then that becomes the thing to look for and to mark.

The love and the care that surrounds.

Yes. If someone asks, "Where was God in this?" I'll say, "God was in all the people that came to try to help, to try to find your child." This helps people, it really does.

You know, the question isn't whether we're going to have to do hard, awful things, because we are. We all are. The question is whether we have to do them alone.

Natalie Batalha, the astrophysicist who compares love to dark matter, tells me that the great physicist Carl Sagan said that "for small creatures such as we, the vastness of the cosmos is bearable only through love." But Carl Sagan was definitively atheist, and would not connect that thing called love to anything called God.

I cherish my conversations with cosmologists and physicists. They are standing on ground where religious thinkers reigned until very recently in human history, the sphere in which we imagine the nature of the cosmos and our place in it. Only a modest proportion of them are religious in a traditional sense of that word. In fact, they are clear with me, their current math shows no real room for human will and choice, much less for love to have any ultimate reality, our intuition of these things notwithstanding. We may be living, breathing illusions of freedom, determined by complex natural laws and forces that merely elude our minds and senses for now.

As the brilliant physicist Brian Greene explained to me, at once playfully and provocatively pushing back on the question of the reality of love, I'm composed of particles just like the table I'm writing on now. My perception that this table is solid and red, or that the sky is blue, is not a matter of reality; it is a projection in my mind based on the sensory input of my hands and my eyes. Likewise, we intuit that time is universal, ticking off at the same rate for everyone, and this, too, is an illusion. The fundamental nature of reality, as far as we can grasp it now, he says, is fundamentally hidden from us at this stage in our development as a species. It's not just that I can't comprehend the true nature of the forces that compose and determine my presence and action in the world; rather, what I feel and experience and believe is leading me astray.

One of the scenarios suggested by string theory is that reality as we observe it is akin to a holographic projection of a real base of information. Our civilization and selves, in this theory, are like a skyscraper to an architect's blueprint. But that blueprint/base of information is some-where else, something else more real than us and beyond our imagining. And this idea returns me to the excruciatingly imponderable question of my otherwise certainty-soaked childhood: If God made the universe, who made God? Likewise, one might reasonably ask, who or what was the architect of the blueprint?

This is not a question physicists might pose, but it is a question they plant in me: might our evolving insights into the laws of physics eventu-ally fill in for what our imagination and our words have always called God? Or to turn that question at an angle, might science, as it evolves, actually point at "God" in a way the classic scientists like Copernicus, Galileo, and Newton—who believed their inquiry into the natural world would reveal the personality of its maker—could not have dreamed? My exchange with Brian Greene ends like this—tying things up for him, opening them wide for me:

This hiddenness of reality is perplexing to me. It doesn't seem elegant—a word you use to describe truths you discern in science. You said once that assessing life through the lens of everyday is like gazing at a Van Gogh through the lens of an empty Coke bottle.

We can do a calculation using quantum mechanics to 10 deci-mal places, to point whatever, 13596, you know. That's the re-sult of a mathematical calculation. We then go out and measure magnetic properties and we find that, digit by digit by digit, 10 decimal places long, the observation agrees with our scribbles on a piece of paper. How can you not be in awe of that? And how can you not be convinced that this is revealing some deep truth about reality that you simply are not privy to with your eyes or your hands or your ears? There's no sense that allows us to directly experience the quantum world, but the mathematics allows us to understand it and make predictions that agree with observation. That's a very powerful story.

An image Einstein used was of a "mind" or an "intelligence" behind the universe, by which he did not necessarily mean a creator God. If you think about mind or an intelligence or even order behind the universe, how do you imagine that? It has to be something that incorporates hiddenness as a way of making its point.

So the important thing to bear in mind is that many physicists have this perspective. We don't envision that there's some mind behind it all, but I would say that we do envision that there are these powerful laws that can do things that you wouldn't expect them to be able to do. I mean, how could it be that general relativity, the simple equation in quantum mechanics, and the standard model of particle physics, over the course of billions of years, can somehow conspire to yield you and me, this complex cognizant being? How could we really just emerge from the laws of physics acting through evolutionary change? But that's the power of the math. So if you want, there is the hidden hand. Call it the hidden hand of God, if you want. I would simply call it the hidden hand of the equations. And that gets us from the beginning to here.

An idea handed to me in the earliest years of my life of conversation comes back with new resonance—the idea of a kinship between the spirituality of the scientist and the spirituality of the mystic: a constant endeavor to discern truth while staying open to everything you do not yet, cannot yet, know. A geneticist shared this with me, a lovely man named Lindon Eaves, who created groundbreaking long-term studies of twins and is also an Anglican priest. He told me how he often has to keep the scientist and the theologian in himself at bay. He compares the great creeds of the Church to the operational hypotheses in his laboratory— the best we've been able to articulate up to now, but also not the last word. Both the scientist and the mystic live boldly with the discoveries they have made, all the while anticipating better discoveries to come.

Several years ago, while I was writing my first book, I retreated to the lush, craggy edges of the west coast of Ireland, reminiscent of the west coast of Scotland that first awakened me to beauty. It's one of those landscapes the ancient Celts called "thin places," where the veil between the temporal and the eternal seems to wear thin. From this respectable writer's retreat, a number of people had made pilgrimages to a woman named Mary Madison, a gorgeous, ageless, wizardlike presence who "read stones." To be clear, despite my commitment to drawing out the meaning of spiritual life, I have always been wary of things that smack of "new age," and I did not think reading stones would be my thing. But person after person came back amazed, with stories of this woman who somehow saw into their souls, into their families of origin, into their life and loves beyond time.

And so I found myself, on a July afternoon, sitting with my bare feet in a bowl of smooth, cool stones of every hue, gathered from the seashore beyond her window. The stones were not really the point, I quickly realized. This woman had a gift that is impossible to explain, and difficult to write about comfortably even now. Knowing nothing except my first name, she proceeded to tell me about the essential qualities of my vocation and the personalities of my children, even to "see" people I had loved and lost—as somehow still present and speaking to my ongoing life. She saw my grandfather. He looks very serious, she said. He was a brainy man. He must have had a long list of dos and don'ts. He was strict with himself too, deprived himself of little things unnecessarily. But he did like his cars. (I had forgotten this funny inconsistency in his outward asceticism—the oversized purple Ford of which he was ridiculously proud.) He's raising a glass to you, she said, of my lifelong teetotaling grandfather. Mary Madison spoke words that went right through me: "He understands now that we become closed-minded when we could be investigating."

The question of where this thought came from—Mary Madison's imagination; or my grandfather from whatever heaven might be; or perhaps through an echo from a parallel universe in which he could evolve to make that observation—this I treat as mystery. The notion itself— the virtue of investigation over against familiar closed categories—is insightful and pleasingly stated. I honor the integrity and necessity of doctrine and theologies that have emerged in conversation across generations and across time. But so many of our categories, defined and wrapped in forms and institutions that no longer quite work, had become too narrow. Certain kinds of religiosity turned themselves into boxes into which too little light and air could enter or escape. So did certain kinds of nonbelief. Dogmatic atheism is no more intellectually credible than dogmatic faith. Both presume a certainty in things unproven that a spirit of inquiry, a virtue of investigation, inclines to nuance. In life, in religion, in science, this I believe: any conviction worth its salt has chosen to cohabit with a piece of mystery, and that mystery is at the essence of the vitality and growth of the thing.

The spirituality of the mystic and the scientist—a reverence for wonder and the possibility of never-ending discovery—also points a way forward for the orthodox of every tradition to live with the mystery of a world of kinship with the religious other and the nonbeliever. At their orthodox cores, all of our traditions insist on a reverence for what we do not know now and cannot tie up with explanation in this lifetime. This is an invitation to bring the particularities and passions of our identities into common life, while honoring the essential mystery and dignity of the other—and to do so not as an adjunct to faithfulness, but as an article of it.

Rabbi Lord Jonathan Sacks, who held the august title of Chief Rabbi of the United Hebrew Congregations of the Commonwealth—otherwise known as chief rabbi of the UK—for over twenty years, until 2013, is one of our most eloquent thinkers on the multitudinous and redemptive both/ands of the religious present. He finds in Jewish tradition, and in the religious enterprise as a whole, a profound well of tools to take on "the dignity of difference" and keep vibrant identities intact, across boundaries of faith, science, and culture.

I remember a statement of a very intelligent, excellent American journalist after September 11, 2001—that what those events demonstrated was that in order for the three monotheistic religions in particular to survive and be constructive members of society in the twenty-first century, they would have to relinquish their exclusive truth claims. That, I think, made a lot of sense to many people. The case you make also aims towards the traditions being constructive parts of the twenty-first century, but you take it in a different direction. So let's talk about how it is possible in your imagination to retain the essence, the truth claims, of Judaism and also, as you say, honor the dignity of difference, understand one's self to be enlarged rather than threatened by religious others.

I use metaphors. Each one may be helpful to some and not to others. One way is just to think, for instance, of biodiversity. The extraordinary thing we now know, thanks to Crick and Watson's discovery of DNA and the decoding of the human and other genomes, is that all life, everything, all the three million species of life and plant life—all have the same source.

We all come from a single source. Everything that lives has its genetic code written in the same alphabet. Unity creates diversity. So don't think of one God, one truth, one way. Think of one God creating this extraordinary number of ways, the 6,800 languages that are actually spoken. Don't think there's only one language within which we can speak to God.

The Bible is saying to us the whole time: Don't think that God is as simple as you are. He's in places you would never expect him to be. And you know, we lose a bit of that in English translation. When Moses at the burning bush says to God, "Who are you?" God says to him three words: *"Hayah asher hayah."* Those words are mistranslated in English as "I am that which I am." But in Hebrew, it means "I will be who or how or where I will be," meaning, Don't think you can predict me. I am a God who is going to surprise you. One of the ways God surprises us is by letting a Jew or a Christian discover the trace of God's presence in a Buddhist monk or a Sikh tradition of hospitality or the graciousness of Hindu life. Don't think we can confine God into our categories. God is bigger than religion.

Although at the same time as you say that God is bigger than religion—and I think this is an "and" for you and not a "but"—there is also a special relationship that is evidenced in those texts and a covenant that is particular to the Jewish people. So even as you honor the dignity of difference in the contemporary world, you are upholding the dignity of particularity.

By being what only I can be, I give humanity what only I can give. It is my uniqueness that allows me to contribute something unique to the universal heritage of humankind. I sum up the Jewish imperative, very simply—and it has been like this since the days of Abraham: to be true to your faith is a blessing to others regardless of their faith. That's the big paradox when you really reach the very depth of particularity.

I don't know why it is. An Isaiah comes along and he delivers his prophecies and they're so particular to that faith, that place, that time. Yet I call Isaiah the poet laureate of hope. At the height of Martin Luther King's "I Have a Dream" speech, at the very height of it, there he is quoting verbatim two lines from Isaiah, Chapter 40. I doubt whether Isaiah, 27 centuries ago in the Middle East, could envisage that one day a black civil rights activist would be moved by his words. But it's the particularity of Isaiah that spoke to a Martin Luther King. That's how we are as a people. I don't know why it is, how it is, but it's the authentic, the unique, the different that makes us feel enriched when we encounter it. And a bland, plastic, synthetic, universal can't-tell-one-brand-of-coffee-from-another-brand-of-coffee by contrast makes life flat, uninteresting, and essentially uncreative.

There's a line of yours—and it might please you, I think, that I first heard it quoted by a young Muslim interfaith leader, Eboo Patel. You said: "Religion is not what the enlightenment thought it would become—mute, marginal, and mild. It is fire and, like fire, it warms, but it also burns and we are the guardians of the flame." What do you see when you look at the world, in terms of seeds of a deeper moral and spiritual imagination emanating from your tradition and other traditions? Where are you finding hope?

I think God is setting us a big challenge, a really big challenge. We are living so close to difference with such powers of destruction that he's really giving us very little choice. To quote that great line from W. H. Auden, "We must love one another or die." That is, I think, where we are at the beginning of the 21st century. And since we really can love one another, I have a great deal of hope.

Our traditions are vast repositories of conversation across generations about the intricacies of really loving one another and of living in hope. They have not always practiced these things robustly in private or in public or across certain boundaries of difference. But they are keepers of intelligence and practices that offer themselves with urgency to the twenty-first century, the virtues to which I return so often in my life of conversation and which flow through this writing—the constellation of habits large and small that add up to compassion and reconciliation, mercy and mindfulness, love of neighbor, love of enemy. Something new, in our time, is an outpouring and transfer of such wisdom—of virtues and teachings as spiritual technologies more freely on offer to read and hear and learn about across traditions, and from traditions to individuals and communities.

What is also new—revolutionary, I feel—is the way social and life sciences have become a companion in illuminating how these virtues and teachings work and why they matter. The physicist's question of whether we have any real capacity for choice, for morality, for love, remains open. But biologists and neuroscientists and psychologists have become partners in unlocking the wisdom of the ages for contemporary people. They are taking the great virtues—forgiveness, compassion, empathy, love—into the laboratory, describing the practical conditions we can create for this way of being to flourish among us. Rabbi Sacks is observing this gleefully, as work of fleshing out and refreshing the "operating instructions" of ancient sacred intelligence:

Here we are reading those instructions afresh through the eyes of quantitative and experimental science and discovering what the great traditions of wisdom were saying three or four thousand years ago. We now know that doing good to others, having a network of strong and supportive relationships, and having a sense that one's life is worthwhile are the three greatest determinants of happiness. Somehow or other, against our will sometimes, we are being thrust back to these ancient and very noble and beautiful truths. And we can now do so in a fellowship, awkward perhaps and embarrassed, between religious leaders and scientists and social scientists as well.

So the clinical psychologist Michael McCullough is investigating the conditions that make forgiveness more likely and more lasting and as biologically natural as revenge. The neuroscientist Richard Davidson contributed to the discovery of neuroplasticity through studies he did, at the invitation of the Dalai Lama, on the brains of meditating Tibetan Buddhist monks. He is now probing his conviction that children are hardwired to learn compassion just as they are hardwired to learn language. There is a vast field of study on the health and societal effects of acts of kindness and gratitude. There are experiments now that actually shrink the amygdala—the part of our brain that carries the fight or flight instinct, which evolved to shield us from mortal danger but also is in charge when we are at our moral worst, individually and globally. The epigeneticist Rachel Yehuda has shown that the physical and psychological effects of trauma cross generations, and she and others are using this knowledge as a form of power to instill resilience and healing across generations. Institutions like Berkeley and Stanford are sourcing Silicon Valley and simultaneously conducting serious ongoing investigation into subjects like awe and empathy and experimenting with teaching compassion through virtual reality.

On the other side of this new equation, religious institutions are struggling to reimagine their institutional health and their contribution to the unfolding world. This struggle itself is leading to invention and renewal of sacred spaces as common spaces where the virtues we're better understanding can be practiced and applied. As pews become less full, food shelves and humanitarian practical care move in, like those churches the Occupy Sandy kids took refuge in even as they railed against their limitations.

Monasteries have a place in this end of the story too. Centering prayer, spiritual direction, retreats, and meditation sat quiet for centuries, largely reserved for "experts," the cloistered, monks or nuns or dedicated oblates and pilgrims deep inside all of our traditions. Now, even as many Western monastic communities in their traditional forms are growing smaller—the Benedictines of Collegeville and Sister Simone's community of sisters among them—their physical spaces for prayer and retreat are bursting to the seams with modern people retreating for rest and silence and centering. They are learning arts of contemplation to take back into their families and workplaces and communities and schools.

The millennial Nathan Schneider began to make his way to faith on retreat at a Trappist community to which his avowedly nonreligious mother had sent him in a period of furious existential searching. And he tells a story that centers on that experience and holds, for me, the pathos and irony of this moment we're in when it comes to faith—of the strange, somehow comforting ways faith itself lives and dies and is born again, evolving all the while in individual lives and in our life together. The story emerged when I asked him about some poetry of William Blake that he quoted in his writing as important: "He who binds to himself to joy doth a winged life destroy / He who kisses the joy as it flies lives in eternity's sunrise." Nathan explained,

> I found those lines pasted to the wall of the monk who was my baptismal sponsor. He was one of the great friends and mentors of my life. And pretty much the whole time I knew him, he was dying. At the time he was getting close, it would be one scare after another, always hooked up to some machine or another. This was a man who lived a rich and complicated life in the world before entering the monastery, and then lived a rich and complicated life there. And at around the time I saw that on his wall, I asked him what role his faith in God had played in the course of his process of dying, what comfort it had given him.
>
> He said something that I had kind of suspected, which was that he no longer really had that belief anymore. The first feeling that I had was, I knew one could feel betrayal, feel sadness, a sense of loss. But his honesty about that made me feel a sense of gratitude, and joy, and also a sense of the mystery of how our lives intertwine, and how they play out: that a person who had been losing his faith was the same person who guided me into mine.

In so many ways I see the new dynamics of spiritual life in our time as gifts to the wisdom of the ages, even as they unsettle the foundations of faith as we've known it for what feels like forever. The transfer of knowledge across boundaries of religion and culture and science is strengthening the efficacy of spiritual technologies. It is making the practice of virtues, indeed the elements of righteousness, more humanly possible. So is the profusion of ways modern people are finding to explore what the wise writer Pico Iyer, one of those people who routinely retreat to a hermitage, calls the "inner world" and the "art of stillness." Our greatest aspirations and virtues have always relied on a measure of inner equanimity. And this is something many of us are learning to tend better, more consciously, precisely as the noisy world feels like it is pulling us apart. We are learning, if fitfully and always imperfectly, to nurture inner wisdom that shapes outer life and accordingly enlivens the part of the world that we can see and touch. This is a dialectic by which faith, in order to survive, lives more profoundly into its own deepest sense than it ever could before.

END NOTES

Pico Iyer

The writer Pico Iyer is not a spiritual teacher or even, he says, a spiritual person per se. But with degrees from Eton, Oxford, and Harvard, and a quintessential lineage in the twenty-first century's global spiritual melting pot, he's lavishly equipped to bridge intellectual and spiritual worlds. In his family life and his full name—Siddharth Pico Raghavan Iyer—there are influences of the Buddha, a Renaissance Catholic heretic, Hindu priestly culture, and theosophy.

> I grew up traveling a lot—first being born to Indian parents in England, and then we moved to California when I was 7. And in those days, it was actually cheaper to continue getting my education in England and flying back to my parents in the holidays than to go to the local private schools. So from the time I was 9, I was living on planes and flying across the North Pole

to school by myself. And then when I was loose upon the world in my 20s, I quickly, literally tried to map the world and to see as many places as possible and try to take in—I always remembered that I felt I was part of the first generation ever to be able to wake up one morning and to be in Tibet or Bolivia or Yemen the next day. My grandparents couldn't have imagined that.

It's one of the things that's worth pausing every once in a while and taking in, isn't it—this dramatic change in our lifetime.

Yes, and also the dramatic change that goes with it, that my grandparents almost had their home in their community and their tribe and their religion handed to them at birth, whereas I felt that I could, in some ways, create my own. Which is a challenge, but it was a beautiful opportunity. And at some point, I thought, well, I've been really lucky to see many, many places. Now, the great adventure is the inner world, now that I've spent a lot of time gathering emotions, impressions, and experiences. Now, I just want to sit still for years on end, really, charting that inner landscape because I think anybody who travels knows that you're not really doing so in order to move around—you're traveling in order to be moved. And really what you're seeing is not just the Grand Canyon or the Great Wall but some moods or intimations or places inside yourself that you never ordinarily see when you're sleepwalking through your daily life. I thought, there's this great undiscovered terrain that Henry David Thoreau and Thomas Merton and Emily Dickinson fearlessly investigated, and I want to follow in their footsteps.

*You've given a name to this life you lead, to what I would call a con-
templative practice, which is "stillness." I think it's such a wonderful
way you've injected that word in your writing and into our cultural discourse. I wonder, can you trace when you started to use that word to
name this impulse in you in this way?*

I think I can, very distinctly. As I said, I've always traveled
a lot, and even in my 30s, I noticed I'd already accumulated
one million miles on a single United States airline. So I realized I have a lot of movement in my life, but not maybe enough
stillness. And around that same time, our family house in
Santa Barbara burned to the ground, and I lost everything I
had in the world. I bought a toothbrush from an all-night su-
permarket that evening, and that was the only thing I had
the next day. So I was unusually footloose. A friend who was
a schoolteacher recommended that I go and spend a few
days in a Catholic hermitage. And although I am not Catholic, and although I am not a hermit, he told me that he always
took his classes there and even the most distracted, restless,
testosterone-addled adolescent boy felt calmer and clearer
when he went there. So I thought anything that works for an
adolescent boy ought to work for me.

And I got in my car, and I drove north along the coast following the sea, and the road got narrower and narrower, and
then I came to an even narrower barely paved road that snaked
up for two miles to the top of a mountain. I got out of my car
at this monastery, and the air was pulsing. It was very silent,
but really the silence wasn't the absence of noise, it was almost
the presence of these transparent walls that I think the monks
had worked very, very hard to make available to us in the

world. And I stepped into the little room where I was going to stay, and it was simple. But there was a bed and a long desk, and above the desk a long picture window, and outside it a walled garden with a chair, and beyond that just this great blue expanse of the Pacific Ocean.

One thing I noticed was when I was driving up, like many of us, I was conducting all kinds of conversations or arguments in my head, and I was feeling guilty about leaving my mother behind, and I was worried that my bosses wouldn't be able to find me for three days. And as soon as I arrived in that place, I realized that none of that mattered and that, really, by being here, I would have so much more to offer my mother and my friends and my bosses. The last thing I'll say about this is that nowadays my mother lives in the hills of California at exactly the same elevation as the monastery—1,200 feet, and she enjoys a beautiful view over the Pacific Ocean. And to anybody looking at her house, they would say it's the last word in tranquility and seclusion. But of course, when I'm at home, if ever I'm tempted to read a book, a part of me is braced for the phone to ring or the chime of "you've got mail" in the next room. So I interrupt myself even if it doesn't interrupt me. And if ever I'm tempted to look at the stars, I think, oh no, there are a thousand things I have to do around the house or around the town. Or if I'm involved in a deep conversation, I think, oh, the Lakers game is on TV. I should do that. And so one way or another, I always cut into my own clarity and concentration when I'm at home. And it reminds me why sometimes people like me have to take conscious measures to step into the stillness and silence and be reminded of how it washes us clean, really.

So I've been going now for 24 years. I've stayed there more

than 70 times. I really think that's my secret home. In a world of change and sometimes impermanence, that, along with my wife and my mother, is really the still point of my world. Wherever I'm traveling in the world, I have the image of that little room with the Pacific below it in my head and the chapel there too. And I feel that really steadies and grounds me in the way I need in a world of tumult.

And I think that's such an important point. Because as you pursued that place of stillness that you found both physically and inside yourself, it seems to me you've held that in a creative tension with moving back out into the world. Here's something beautiful you wrote: "The point of gathering stillness is not to enrich the sanctuary or the mountaintop, but to bring that calm into the motion, the commotion, of the world." You know, a couple of years ago, after you published your book about Graham Greene, I went to a conversation you had with Paul Holden-gräber at the New York Public Library. You said something that night—all these years I've been looking forward to the day when I would be able to discuss it with you. There was a question about the difference between religion and spirituality. You said that spirituality is like water, and religion is like tea. But I wondered—what if spirituality is water, and religion is the cup which carries it forward in time, although it may be flawed, and we may drop it and break it.

I love that notion of the cup. And if you had just asked me that question now, I would say that spirituality is the story of our passionate affair with what is deepest inside us and with the candle that's always flickering inside us and sometimes almost seems to go out and sometimes blazes. And religion is the community, the framework, the tradition, all the other people into which we bring what we find in solitude. So in some ways,

I would say very much exactly the thing that you just said. And I should also say when I talked about water and tea, I was probably stealing from the Dalai Lama. Because what he often says is that the most important thing, without which we can't live, is kindness. We need that to survive. He says kindness is like water, religion is like tea. It's a great luxury. It increases the savor of life. It's wonderful if you have it. But you can survive without tea, and you can't survive without water. And so everyday kindness and responsibility is the starting block for every life. It's a nice reminder to ground ourselves in the people around us before we start thinking about our texts and our notions of the absolute.

Arthur Zajonc

Arthur Zajonc is a physicist and contemplative who believes that the furthest frontiers of science are bringing us back to a radical reorientation towards life, and even back to the foundations for moral life. Integrating sciences and the humanities is simply a way of talking, as Zajonc puts it, about "bringing all of who we are to all that the world is."

It's possible to have a spirituality that is not simply about faith, as interesting and complex as that is on its own, but that actually understands itself as committed to knowing. The practice of meditation and contemplation, which has been an important part of my life since my 20s, has led me to the conviction that there's an experiential domain in contemplative spirituality, which can become clarified, which can become in some sense scientific—in the sense that it's a repeatable basis of human experience, one that's shared over thousands of years and that we can be engaged with today in a way that is congruent with my activity as a scientist.

Here's a definition you penned of morality: "Morality concerns the nature and quality of our relationship with other people and with the world of which we are a part."

For me, I guess morality goes back to my Catholic upbringing. So it was a lot about guilt. You know, sins and venial sins and . . .

Missteps.

Yeah. And you were always worried about being caught out somehow. But at some point, that felt impossible. It couldn't just be about a kind of legislation given by an ecclesiastical hierarchy. There had to be a deeper source. And there also had to be the possibility of ethical conduct. Not necessarily with all of your being, but a foothold. And so science became an interesting place to explore the failure of deterministic thinking. Whether chaos dynamics or quantum mechanics, you begin to feel that, well, maybe it's more porous, and maybe the biological imperatives aren't complete. Maybe there is a space for freedom. And maybe there is a question of right action that's morally grounded and true. But if you take away all of the imperatives of parents, priests, teachers, peer group, biology—all of which have tremendous force on us— and you create a space, well then what is your moral compass? What is the means by which you live a life? Can I explore that directly? Not hypothetically, but can I begin to feel my way or meditate my way into that space of openness? Is there a way in which I can know that feels morally connected to a center that I can place my life inside of? That's become a lived experience for me.

It's a presence that you cultivate moment to moment.

Exactly.

But what you are bringing home is that reality is expansive, that subjectivity is real, it is "our friend," that in fact this new science is "a radical reorientation toward life." And in it, we regain the foundations for our moral life.

Yeah. The argument goes something like this, that since the 17th century, mechanism and matter have dominated. From 1900 to 1925, physics went through a revolution where we began to realize, well, to a certain approximation, we can neglect the observer. But we can't neglect the observer if we look carefully, if we do our science carefully. We are always implicated. We are always implicated in quantum mechanics and relativity. There is a subjective dimension—subjective not in the sense of arbitrary or capricious—but there is an observer or an imagined observer everywhere. And the universe requires this. This is not something where you can say, well, it's a nice way of thinking about things. In order to make sense of the cosmos, in order to have a cosmos at all, you need that element in there. There is no objective view from outside the system, where you're looking at the whole thing play out according to some universal story. So it's always a story to me.

Our experience, our story, is in some way the only real thing?

Exactly that. It's odd, but it throws us back on experience, throws us back on subjectivity, not in the sense of, again, capricious or arbitrary. But in the sense that reality is connected to my person. From that standpoint, subjectivity becomes, rather than the enemy, the friend. Can you feel how then, once you have that, the moral dimensions of life come back in? Because by sanitizing the world of subjectivity, you basically leave out the moral possibilities.

And the moral dimension of life comes back in because what you do matters ultimately?

What you do, what you experience, is reality. It's a strange thing, that what we experience in life as our real world—the world of children and suffering and getting old and getting born and all the rest of it, that sensual lived world of experience—gets explained away, in the old view, in terms of a whole set of other things. Sometimes I think of this as a kind of idolatry. If you're pointing at the gods, but you can't really see the gods, you create a statue. Same sort of things in physics. You can't see that far, so you create a model. That's what we call it, right? And then you fall in love with the model, and it becomes a form of idolatry. You end up worshipping the model as opposed to the thing you were trying to understand, which was the human being or the planet or the whole cosmos. So you need to be an iconoclast in some sense, to take those down and reanimate your direct experience, your direct epiphanies and insights into that world of pattern. Yet taking that turn also connects back into lived experience in a way that, to me, opens up the moral and ethical dimensions of life once again.

Richard Rodriguez

Richard Rodriguez is one of America's great writers on self and society. He sees the racial categories of previous generations transforming in what he calls the "browning" of America. He's also been searching to understand his kinship, as a Roman Catholic, with Muslims in the post-9/11 world. His life and mind straddle discourses of left and right, of immigrant and intellectual, of secular and religious.

I grew up Roman Catholic. Though that doesn't even do it justice. I grew up in Sacramento, California, in a neighborhood that was—I hate to use the term "white," because "white" doesn't tell me anything; "white" doesn't tell me enough; "white" doesn't tell me that your father was a coal miner; "white" doesn't tell me that your son died in a canoe accident. But it was white. I went to a Catholic school where everyone was Catholic, with one exception, Bobby Wright, who was Episcopalian. And he would bow his head when we prayed. I was surrounded by Irish voices. Those were my first English voices. And that's how I learned the English language, through Ireland, oddly enough. All the priests, all the nuns, were Irish. They were truly the first feminists of my life. I was also an altar boy. That is, I was on the altar responding in Latin to the priest. And to this day I remember being at a graveside helping to carry a coffin to the open pit. And then going back to arithmetic class in an hour. You know, the seamlessness of that life. But I remember also, this is the power of memory, the power of poetry to instill itself on a child's imagination, the first lines I would say in response to the priest, in Latin: "I will go to the altar of God, the God who gives joy to my youth." So people ask me now, what was the church to you? It was completely embracing.

There's this line in your memoir, Hunger of Memory, *that I thought was so striking. You said, "Of all the institutions in their lives, only the Catholic Church had seemed aware of the fact that my mother and father are thinkers, persons aware of their experience of their lives."*

Yes. This I think is the power of liturgy and ritual, the seasons of grief and triumph, the seasons of renewal and sorrow. The power of religion to make us reflective of the lives we are lead-ing seems to me to encourage an inwardness, which I would call intellectual. And when I think of what the peasant Church, all over the world, is still able to give people, that same conso-lation of the inner life, that's no small gift. I must tell you, Krista, I live most of my life now among people who are not religious, people who are anti-religious. My brother considers himself not an atheist, but an anti-theist. He says that the word atheism doesn't grasp the fullness of his negativity toward re-ligion. And so when I write about religion as I do, I'm always worried about what the secular reader is going to make of this line. The worry I have is always that my writing will be too pious.

For the secular?

For the stylish, I'd call them. Or too stylish for the pious. You know what I mean. The uses of irony and paradox are not al-ways apparent in religious writing.

And you took yourself on a fascinating journey after September 11, 2001, which was a moment in this culture where we absolutely saw a dangerous "Other." Islam—this religion of over one billion people— had been there all along. But we saw this terrifying face of the "Other." And you made a countercultural move of exploring your kinship with these men who were terrorists. You wrote, "I worship the same God as they, as a monotheist. So I stand in some relation to those men." And you set out to understand what had happened in that sense.

Well, the first thing I understand is mystery. I moved to the desert, to the great desert of the Middle East. And I realized that the God of Abraham, who is the God of the Jew, the Christian, and the Muslim, revealed himself in the desert. This is a holy landscape. It is also a landscape that drives us crazy. Somehow, in this landscape, we got the idea that there is a God who is as lonely for us as we are for Him. And there is in this landscape, also, a necessity for tribe. You do not live as an individual on the desert. You live in tribes. And that tribal allegiance, that tribal impulse, leads on the one hand, to great consolation, but also to the kind of havoc we are seeing now.

You have to acknowledge when you wander the desert, how bright and blinding is light. And how consoling is twilight and darkness. In these religions, oftentimes shade and darkness come as consolations, or gifts, so that Mohammed has his revelation in a cave, in the darkness. In Judaism, God puts Moses in the mouth of a cave so that he will not be blinded by the brightness of God. And also the resurrection happened in a cave. We sometimes forget that we are people of dark. And we should accept that darkness as part of our faith.

Well, I guess that leads into what I want to ask you. How did you come to realize how the desert in this tradition and the cave, how these things had formed you, the Catholic spirituality that you find to be redemptive.

I end my book *Darling* with Mother Teresa, who was hounded by Christopher Hitchens, our great American atheist going from cable channel to cable channel to tell us God was dead. I live part of the year in London. And I assure you, God is not dead in London. Muslims are plentiful, as are Hindus. After Mother Teresa's death, a number of her letters to confessors and bishops were revealed. For 40 years of her life, Mother Teresa describes her life as a darkness.

I wanted to ask you why you ended the book there, with the juxtaposition of Christopher Hitchens, with his exuberant certainty that there is no God to the very end of his life, and Mother Teresa, in her despair.

I once was with her in San Quentin prison. It was the most remarkable afternoon I can remember, religiously. There was a group of thugs, and she was supposed to meet these guys from death row, and they were all like schoolboys. This tiny little woman, you know, four foot tall or something, in her sari. She tells them in that little tiny voice that if you want to see the face of God, look at the prisoner standing next to you. These tattoos coming up over their necks: look at the man next to you. This man who has murdered and raped: that's the face of God. And I think, I didn't know that. I didn't know. I'd been looking at the holy picture all this time when I should look more closely at the face of the sinner to find the face of God.

Father George Coyne and Brother Guy Consolmagno

There are more than thirty objects on the moon named after Jesuits. Jesuits, after all, mapped the moon. A Jesuit was one of the founders of modern astrophysics. And four Jesuits in history, including Ignatius of Loyola, have had asteroids named after them. Vatican astronomers Brother Guy Consolmagno and Father George Coyne are the two living men with this distinction.

I'd like to hear from both of you about how your take on life, which is very much informed by your science, resonates with Catholic theology and tradition in particular. So, Guy, you wrote somewhere that "Catholic intellectual achievement has human fallibility with all the accompanying richness and pathos at its center." And you weren't necessarily talking about theology, but the world of literature and art and poetry and culture that has been defined by Catholicism.

Brother Guy: Right. I remember when I wrote that thinking, Oh that's going to come back and haunt me. But it is that sense of not knowing ahead of time where it's going to go, that it's not all pat. And yet you can approach it intellectually. I think one of the joys of being a Catholic is that we've got this rich intellectual tradition at the same time that we've got the smells and bells, and the hymns and all of the other emotional part, that are all responses to the awareness that there is this God and I want to do something about it.

Father Coyne: I would add just a little note. I think it's exciting to be ignorant and I think our ignorance in pursuing science has something to do with this whole idea of the uncertainties involved in a relationship of love with God that I call faith. I'll give you a story. I gave a paper at a scientific meeting on the uncertainties in our determination of the age of the universe. There are several methods we use for determining the age of the universe and there is a degree of uncertainty involved with each of them. Well, whenever I'm at a scientific conference, I'm usually not dressed as a priest because it just confuses things. But I had just given a talk in a church or something, so I gave this talk and I was wearing my Roman collar. A gentleman stood up in the discussion period, and the first thing he said was, "Father." And I trembled at the thought that he had, first of all, called me "Father," but then he proceeded to build upon that. He said, "Father, it must be wonderful that, with all the uncertainties we have in our scientific pursuits, you have this faith, this rock of faith to stand upon." I took off my Roman collar and faced him down and said, "Who told you that my faith was kind of a rock?" I said, "Every morning I wake up I have my doubts. I have my uncertainties. I have to struggle to help my faith grow." Because faith is love. Love in marriage, love with friends, love of brothers and sisters is not something that's there once and for all and always kind of a rock that gives us support.

What I want to say is, ignorance in doing science creates the excitement of doing science, and anyone who does it knows that discoveries lead to a further ignorance.

Brother Guy: The more you know, the more you know you don't know.

And you feel that's true with faith as well?

Brother Guy: Oh, exactly. I keep going back to this wonderful phrase that Anne Lamott came out with a few years ago: "The opposite of faith is not doubt. The opposite of faith is certainty." If you're sure about something then you don't need faith.

It's when you have the doubts that faith kicks in. And that's true in science as well as anything else.

Didn't she also say faith *is a verb, not a noun?*

Brother Guy: Oh, very good. Yes. But what George is saying about the joy of ignorance, this is, of course, an old tradition that goes back . . . well, Socrates himself says, "I'm wiser than everyone else because I know I don't know." And Nicholas of Cusa, who wrote about extraterrestrial beings in the 14th century, did so in The Book of Ignorance—that's one way of translating the title.

Father Coyne: We have examples of it in science down through history. But to take just the past two decades, we knew the universe was expanding. We marveled at the fact that it was expanding at just such a rate that it was on the borderline of expanding forever or collapsing. Right on the borderline. Now, that itself is a marvel. Of all the possibilities—expanding so fast at the beginning that nothing could come to be, there could be no self-gravities so that galaxies and stars formed; or expanding so slowly that it collapsed in upon itself almost as soon as it began to expand—of all those possibilities, it was right on the edge. So we were delighted with that and marveled at that until within the past 15 years, with very accurate observations of distant quasars, we know now very well that the universe is not only expanding, but it's accelerating in its expansion.

I mean, it challenges gravity, which is very fundamental to all of our understanding, and always has been, since Newton.

But I think you're saying that ignorance in this sense is something to take delight in.

Father Coyne: Educated ignorance.

Brother Guy: The awareness that we don't know. You know, if we had all the answers, boy, we'd have nothing left to do. It'd be a terrible universe.

When I was a little kid, nine years old, I remember a rainy Sunday afternoon when I couldn't go out to play and was stuck in the house. And my mom came out with a deck of cards and dealt them out and we played rummy together. Now, my mom can beat me in cards because I'm nine years old. That wasn't the point of the game. The point of the game was that this was her way of telling me she loved me, in a way that she couldn't by just saying "Son, I love you," because I was nine years old. In a way, being able to do science and come to an intimate knowledge of creation is God's way of playing with us, loving us. It's as invented as the card game. Is it an act of love? It's as much an act of love as the card game.

Father Coyne: I like that. Playing games with God. Or God playing games with us. That's true. Made a universe that has a fascinating attraction about it. Doing science to me is a search for God. And I'll never have the final answers, because the universe participates in the mystery of God. If we knew it all, I'd sit under a palm tree with my gin and tonic and just let the world go by.

Brother Guy: Which is not a bad thing to do every now and then.

Father Coyne: Well, every now and then, but it'd get kind of boring.

Margaret Wertheim

Margaret Wertheim studied physics and became a science writer in order to translate the thrill of scientific questioning across human history and culture and its relevance for all of us. Australian born, she started the Institute for Figuring in Los Angeles together with her identical twin and artist sister.

As a little child, I was obsessed with the question of how mathematical concepts seem to appear in nature. I can remember, when I was maybe 6 or 7, lying on the grass and staring up at the sun. We'd just had a lesson at school about Pi, the number embedded in circles. And I thought, Is Pi real? What does it mean that there is this sort of mystical number at the heart of the sun or in a hubcap or any circular thing that you see? And the more you study physics, the more astounding are the examples of that—that math is everywhere in the world. How do we interpret that? What is the meaning of the fact that there are these incredibly complex equations that describe phenomena like lasers? And that, therefore, the understanding of those equations then leads us to have technologies like microchips? It's the great philosophical question that I want to understand in my life: what does it mean that the math is in the world?

So, I like this fact that in science, light can be a particle or a wave, depending on what question you ask of it. It's kind of a way of demon-

strating something we all experience, that contradictory explanations of reality can simultaneously be true. And I want to read something quite beautiful that you wrote: "Wave particle duality is a core feature of our world. Or rather, we should say, it is a core feature of our mathematical descriptions of our world. But what is critical to note here is that, however ambiguous our images, the universe itself remains whole and is manifestly not fracturing into schizophrenic shards. It is this tantalizing wholeness and the thing itself that drives physicists onward like an eternally beckoning light that seems so teasingly near. It is always out of reach." That's very beautiful. Do you want to say anything about that thought?

Yes. Physics, for the past century, had this dualistic way of describing the world. One in terms of waves, which are usually conceived of as continuous phenomena. And one in terms of particles, which are usually conceived of as discrete or sort of digitized phenomena. And so quantum mechanics gives us the particle, discrete description. General relativity gives us the wavelike, continuous description. General relativity operates at the cosmological scale. Quantum mechanics operates so brilliantly at the subatomic scale. And these two theories don't currently mathematically mesh. So the great hope of physics for the last 80 or so years has been, "Can we find a unifying framework that will combine general relativity and quantum mechanics into one mathematical synthesis?" Some people believe that that's what string theory can be. And when contemporary physicists write about the world, they talk about this as being a fundamental problem for reality. But it's not a fundamental problem for reality. It's a fundamental problem for human beings. The universe is just getting on with it.

Right.

So I think the universe isn't schizophrenic. It's not having a problem. We're having a problem. And I don't think it means that there's anything wrong with what physicists are doing. Quantum mechanics and general relativity have both been demonstrated to be true in their domains of expertise to 20 decimal places of experimentation. That's a degree of success which is mind-blowing and awe-inspiring. But the fact that these two great, fabulously functional descriptions don't fit together means we haven't, by any means, learned all we've got to know about the world.

You've said that you don't think neuroscience is finally going to have a theory of everything that explains us to ourselves—that explains happiness and love and pain and why we do what we do or whether we have a choice to do it. You think there is something more that will remain. You've spoken a lot and very movingly about your legacy of Catholicism, but you also are atheist, is that correct? I've heard you say that.

I—no, I'm not an atheist. I'd like to put it this way. I don't know that I believe in the existence of God in the Catholic sense. But my favorite book is the *Divine Comedy*. And at the end of the *Divine Comedy*, Dante pierces the skin of the universe and comes face to face with the love that moves the sun and the other stars. I believe that there is a love that moves the sun and the other stars. I believe in Dante's vision. And so, in some sense, perhaps, I could be said to believe in God. And I think part of the problem with the concept of "Are you an atheist or not?" is that our conception of what divinity means has become so trivialized and banal that I think it's almost impossible to answer the question without dogma. I'm very, very saddened by the fact that militant atheism has come so to the fore of our society. It's destructive and unhelpful. And I don't think it does science any service.

And I hear you saying, also, that the language of God itself gets ruined. We turn it into cliché or we fight about it. So whether you use that language or not, I almost feel that with your history and the history you have delved into, our human history of science, you don't speak about the God of religion, but you do speak about a "beyond" that is somehow kind of a third way behind the God who is discredited in some ways by us or the cold, hard materialism of the scientific worldview.

Well, one way I think we can understand the God question in relation to science is this: that prior to the coming into being of modern science, the Christian conception of God had two functions. God was the creator of the universe. But he was first and foremost the redeemer of mankind. And with the coming into being of modern science, God's position as redeemer got shoved into the background and all of the questions and the public discussion became about God the creator. And that was why Darwin was so critical. He appeared to challenge the idea of God as the creator of man. And we, I think, in the modern West, we focus so much on the debate about the creative function of God that, outside of theological circles, we don't seem to be able to discuss, as it were, the concept of redemption. I think we need to be able to discuss that. You don't have to believe in an idea of original sin to speak of redemption. I don't think that humans are innately sinful, but I think we all make mistakes. Every single one of us. And collectively, we're making massive mistakes. And the question is, How can we redeem ourselves, in the sense of making amends?

Reza Aslan

Reza Aslan has a challenging and ultimately refreshing perspective on religion in the world—a long view of history and humanity that news cycles obscure. He was born in Tehran and grew up in the San Francisco Bay Area. He is a scholar of religions who has written bestselling books about Islam and Jesus, and is a curator of independent media and information from the Middle East.

I like to sometimes joke that I come from a long line of lukewarm Muslims and exuberant atheists. My mother was the lukewarm Muslim, my father the exuberant atheist. The kind of atheist who always had a pocketful of Prophet Muhammad jokes that he would pull out at inappropriate times. In a sense my father's atheism actually ended up serving us well, because if you recall, in the Revolution of 1979, when the Ayatollah Khomeini returned to Iran, he made a great show of pretending that he had no interest in any political or government position. He said that he wanted to just simply go back to his home and his mosque and his family, and be left alone. My father, who's never trusted anyone wearing a turban, didn't believe him for a minute, and thought that it would be a good idea for us to leave Iran until things settled down. That, of course, was three decades ago, and things did not settle down.

You've said, "Religion, it must be understood, is not faith, it is the story of faith."

Well, it's certainly true that all great religions deal with the same conflicts of politics and violence, and the struggle to reconcile with the realities of a changing, evolving and modern world. I think there's this misunderstanding, amongst most people of faith, that prophets sort of grow up in some kind of cultural or religious vacuum. That a prophet is somebody that just plopped down to earth from heaven, and with a ready-made message, in which they found a brand-new religion. But prophets don't invent religions. Prophets are reformers of the religions that they themselves grow up in. Jesus did not invent Christianity. Jesus was a Jew. He was reforming Judaism. The Buddha did not invent Buddhism. The Buddha was a Hindu. He was reforming Hinduism.

We have to understand that our prophets are intimately connected to the worlds out of which they arise. And so, for me, when I write about the origins of particular religions, it's very important to recognize how seamless that transition from the era before and during and after the prophet actually is. And that's certainly the case with the prophet Muhammad.

I've experienced, in these years speaking with Muslims, that the notion of Islam needing a reformation, the language of reformation, doesn't work for a lot of people. Certainly what doesn't work is Christians saying, well, what Islam needs, what Muslims need, is a reformation like ours.

But I notice that you do use that language. And you make this interesting suggestion that a reformation within Islam has been taking place already for nearly a century. That the Islamic reformation is already here and we are living in it. So tell me what you see, what you're describing, when you make that statement.

When we use the term "reformation," what we mean is the fundamental conflict that is inherent in all religious traditions, as I say, between who gets to define the faith. Is it the institution? Or is it the individuals? That was ultimately what the Christian Reformation was about. In the United States, we refer to it as the Protestant Reformation, as though this was some sort of conflict between Protestant reform and Catholic intransigence, and by golly, the Protestants won. But of course, that's not what happened.

Martin Luther's another one who just wanted to be a better Catholic, right?

Right. And by the way, who was absolutely, bloodily unforgiving of any fellow reformer who happened to disagree with his particular interpretation.

Yeah, well, there's that too.

When you say that an individual should be able to interpret a faith however he or she wants to, then of course you are opening up a can of proverbial worms, if you will. What you are saying, then, is that every interpretation is now equally valid, and the result, of course, is not just a cacophony of voices. It's a situation whereby it's usually the loudest and most violent voices that tend to carry the day. That process of reformation, the passing of institutional authority into individual hands, has been taking place in Islam for a century, really since the twilight of the colonial era.

Authority began to crumble as we saw widespread access to new and novel sources of information, dramatic increases in literacy and education across the Middle East and the larger Muslim world. And, of course, a heightening sense of individualism, which was a direct result of the colonial experience. And, of course, as what necessarily happens in this kind of situation, what you have as a result are individualistic interpretations that promote peace, and tolerance, and feminism, and democracy. And you have individualistic interpretations that promote violence, and misogyny, and hatred, and terror. And because Islam, a religion of 1.6 billion people, the second largest religion in the world, has no centralized religious authority—there is no Muslim pope, there is no Muslim Vatican—no one can say who is and who is not a proper Muslim, what is and what is not proper Islamic behavior. What you have is just a shouting match between all of these individualized interpretations fighting amongst each other while also fighting amongst the institutions of the Muslim world. Violence is a direct result of the reformation, not proof that one is needed. We're watching this incredibly transformational moment in what will soon be the largest religion in the world, right before our eyes. We have to remember that fundamentalism is a reactionary phenomenon, not an independent one. It is a reaction to the natural progress of society. And so when I see fundamentalism surge, I know that what is really happening is that the natural progress of society is surging. And fundamentalism is reacting to it. I choose to focus on the progress, not the reaction.

Sylvia Boorstein

Sylvia Boorstein was one of those young Jewish seekers of the 1960s and 1970s who helped to bring Buddhism to mainstream culture in the west.

And she's another twenty-first-century hybrid spiritual being. Over the years, she's reintegrated Jewish teachings and rituals in an enlivening, organic interplay with Buddhist teachings and practice.

> You have to know that I grew up in a post-Depression household. Both my parents had jobs and I'm an only child. And my parents went off to work, so my grandmother did a great deal of the mothering, and she was very, very solicitous, so that I remember her bathing and washing and dressing me and making braids and preparing the kinds of foods that I liked. The only thing that she was not moved to respond to was the coming and going of childhood bouts of "I'm not happy." I'd say, "But I'm not happy." And she'd say, "Where is it written"— my grandmother was not a learned woman in that sense, but it's an ethnic thing to use that Talmudic turn of phrase— "Where is it written that you're supposed to be happy all the time?" And I actually think it was the beginning of my spiritual practice—that life is difficult. Then 40 years later, I learned that the Buddhists said the same thing, that life is inevitably challenging and how are we going to do it in a way that's wise and doesn't complicate it more than it is just by itself?

To the question of raising children as human beings who are kind, who have a heart for the world, in a world that's troubled—when you and I met on a panel in Southern California two years ago, you told a story about leading mindfulness teaching sessions. You told a story about a man who at the end of it said, "I'm frightened to go back out into the world. I feel so vulnerable. In here I'm safe, but I don't know how I can be out in the world and be vulnerable." As a parent, a version of that goes through my mind. How much do I expose my children to? How do I teach them to be kind and open to the world's pain and vulnerability?

I want them to be safe, and yet I actually want them to be tough out in that scary world at the same time.

I don't remember exactly that moment, but I'm sure it happened because it comes up often. People will come and spend a week at a retreat center or a weekend or however many days, and then they do say, here everyone is safe and it's quiet and to go out I feel too vulnerable. It gives me a chance to say, really, I don't think we can become too vulnerable. I'm waiting for the time that the whole world is suddenly too vulnerable. Then we all look around and say, we all have to stop. We have to share. We have to make sure there is enough to eat all over the world. We can teach each other our ways and tell each other our hopes and dreams, but we can't kill each other. That doesn't work. And we can't despoil the earth as we are doing. So in a sense that's a half of an answer, Krista. That's what I'd say to an adult who's leaving a retreat.

To a parent I say, as a child is growing up, inevitably they live in the world. We only have a certain amount of control as parents about how much the TV is on and what's on the TV and how much they are confronted by the pain of the world. Sometimes the pain of the world seems incomprehensible and unbearable to me. And I think if there's anything that balances it, it's wonder at the world, the amazingness of people, how resilient they are, how people will take care of others they don't know. If somebody falls or someone's in trouble in a public place, people take care of them. Human beings have that ability. I don't think they have to learn it. They don't have to have lessons. I think we're a companionable species, for the most part.

So to be able to look at human beings and say, life is amazing. The sun came up in the exact right place this morning. Celebrate seasons and birthdays and holy days. Here we are again, at another time in another season, and there's that great cosmos out there to look at. Our ancestors looked at the same stars. I keep in myself a sense of amazement. I tell my grandchildren, "Look at this moon. It's a three-day moon. It's the best moon. It's better than a two-day moon. It's my favorite moon." And if I show that to them, they begin to think, "Oh, it's my favorite moon, a three-day moon." These are balances. When the Buddha taught about needing to see the suffering in the world so that we could respond with compassion, he also talked about the preciousness of life and the need to take care of it.

This is also making me think about how we need to be attentive to what our children can teach us, as well as what we want to impart to them because some of this they know and they actually know more immediately than we do. We lose it. I remember watching something terrible on the news the other day. And my daughter said, "So many beautiful lives in the world, and this is what they focus on."

They don't make good headlines. You know, it would be wonderful—I don't know if it would be commercially viable—if there were a channel that had all wonderful things in the news.

I don't know. It's hard to make good news sexy. It is. I think about this a lot as a journalist. But maybe it's like kindness. Kindness is the stuff of moments, but it can be absolutely transformative in moments. Beautiful lives are transformative in moments. But we have to train ourselves to look for them.

There are two things that you just said. One of them is that when we are really paying attention—which is what mindfulness is—we really connect with other people. Lots of times, for reasons of rush or whatever, even with our own children, we're not completely there. There is something about really paying attention.

What seems most clear to me is that children pick up what their parents live. My friend Jim Finley, who's a Christian contemplative psychotherapist, said, "I learned to pray sitting next to my mother in church." And what I understood from him is that he didn't learn the words of the prayer; he learned the feelings out of her body as she sat there.

Spirituality doesn't look like sitting down and meditating. Spirituality looks like folding the towels in a sweet way and talking kindly to the people in the family even though you've had a long day. Or even saying to them, "Listen, I've had such a long day, but it would be really wonderful if I could just fold these—I'd really love folding these towels quietly if you all are ready to go to bed without me," or whatever it is. People often say to me, "I have so many things that take up my day. I don't have time to take up a spiritual practice." And the thing is, being a wise parent or a spiritual parent doesn't take extra time. It's enfolded into the act of parenting.

Shane Claiborne

Do you think of yourself as being part of a revolution, a kind of revolution? That's a word you've used.

And you can hear my hesitation.

Yes.

I'm careful because I don't ever want to fall in love with a movement or a revolution. I think that Jesus's life shows me that revolution is not a big thing, it's a very small thing. We've got to live it in small ways out of little communities. Dietrich Bonhoeffer has been a good teacher for us on community. . . .

The German theologian who died in a Nazi prison.

Yes. One of the things that Dietrich Bonhoeffer says is, "The person who's in love with their vision of community will destroy community. But the person who loves the people around them will create community everywhere they go." Something that's held us together is not just to fall in love with a movement or a revolution, but to try to live in radical ways and in simple ways. I think that the world right now is undergoing a beautiful transition of thought. And in young people within the church, there's so much that's hopeful.

Talk to me about some of the people in the communities who, for you, are defining the present or, you know, participating in this new imagination that you describe.

Boy, there's so many different communities that give me a lot of hope. I met a suburban family that said, "We're trying to figure out what it means to love our neighbor as our self. And for us, it means that for every biological child that we send to college, we're creating a scholarship fund and making sure that an at-risk youth can go to college. And we get to know their family and interact with them and help make that happen." Then I met a bunch of kids that said, "You know, we're trying to figure out how to find the Calcutta around us." As Mother Teresa said, "Calcuttas are everywhere, if we only have eyes to see." And they said, "So we started looking around and we found this old folks' home and we went in." I should say, they're kind of preppy teenage girls, cheerleaders and stuff. They tell me, "We went in and we asked for all of the women who don't have any visitors or family. And so we go and we visit them and we paint their fingernails and toenails and we just listen to their story."

There are all kinds of expressions of people who are beginning to experience life outside of the detached nuclear family, and who are seeing that bring themselves to life. There was a married couple I stayed with who told me they were unable to have children. "But then we were walking through our neighborhood, and we met this woman who had found herself homeless and she was six months pregnant." They brought her back to their house and said, we'll figure this out as we go. And they really hit it off together. She had her kid there, living in their home. It was so amazing that they continued to live together and raise the child. I just went back to visit them and they've lived together for over 10 years. The woman who's formerly homeless is a nurse. That little girl that she had is almost a teenager now. And the amazing thing is that the woman of that married couple now has multiple sclerosis and she's dying, but she's got a nurse living in her home with her, taking care of her as she dies. Those expressions are all over the place.

How would you respond to someone who said that these stories you tell about good things happening are beautiful in these communities, but it's anecdotal and it's just one person here, one person there, one small group of people here, one small group of people there. You're not going to really change the world.

Well, I'd say if we looked a little closer at history, we see that that's the only way it's ever been done. These groups of people begin to come together and ripple new imagination and ideas that are very contagious.

In the south, where I'm from, you know, we have a saying that you're "the spittin' image" of somebody. You know, I got told I'm the spittin' image of my grandfather all the time, and it's shorthand for "the spirit and image," you know. And it doesn't just mean you look like them but that you have the character of them.

In a lot of ways, I guess what I hope that we are seeing Christians who are beginning to be, again, the spitting image of Christ, you know, that are starting to look like and do the things that Jesus did and not be totally distracted by those which have proclaimed the name of Christ and done so many other things. You have folks that I think are asking great questions, not just about what they're going to do when they grow up, but about who they are becoming. And I think that's a much more important question.

Christian Wiman

Christian Wiman is a poet and essayist who has come to give voice, to his own surprise, to the hunger for faith and the challenge of faith. His Texas upbringing was soaked in both a history of violence and a charismatic Christian culture. He wasn't formally religious for years after he left home, lived all over the world, and became a poet. Then when he was in his late thirties, he married the love of his life, found God again, and was diagnosed with an incurable, unpredictable cancer.

I've heard and read a lot of stories about the interesting ways religion and spirituality get communicated to us as children. I have to say, Christian, that your story, of all of them that I've heard all these years, is the most familiar to me. Growing up absolutely immersed in this religious universe, which meant everything, right?

Right.

But then when I left that place—and, like you, I went far, far away—the religious piece stopped making sense as well, because it was the whole package.

Yes. I think for me it was a big loss. I didn't realize exactly how large a loss for years because I, like so many people, dispensed with it and became an agnostic or whatever you want to call it. But I wonder. I've got little kids now and I do think about what I should teach them and how I should teach them in terms of their spiritual lives, because I greatly value the way I was raised, which was completely immersed in that culture.

Did you go to church twice a week, on Sunday and Wednesday night?

Yep, yep, sometimes even more. We had to learn Bible verses and save them.

And the hymns, the singing.

Knew the hymns and had the singing. And there was no possibility of puncture to that world. You know, I never met anybody who didn't believe until I went off to college. Never met a soul. And I value the coherence of it and I value the intensity of it and the momentum that it's given my life. But it's also created all kinds of difficulties, as I'm sure you know. I have discovered that there is an enormous number of people in this country who have some kind of religious language that they're just unhappy with. It doesn't accord with their feelings of the sacred or their feelings of what spirituality means and they're casting about for some way of believing. Yet you can't just jettison everything that you have.

Recently I was talking to a physicist, a string theorist, who's working with a new kind of mathematical language. And the analogy we were talking about is the difference between poetry and prose. So the fact that there are truths you simply can't convey in a factual sentence, right? And it seems there are physical realities that you can't convey with an equation, but that more visual mathematics might be able to convey.

Gosh, that's interesting. I think that's why physics is so fascinating to so many of the poets. You know, to contemporary poets these days, there is some kind of reality that's being revealed that we can only reach through oblique ways. It's why I'm drawn to mystics like Meister Eckhart and more contemporary ones like Simone Weil and the language of *apophasis*, where you state something, but the statement sort of unstates itself. Meister Eckhart said, "We pray to God to be free of God." We ask God to be free of God. I don't think he wanted to give up his religion. The idea wouldn't have occurred to him, but he wanted to give up that idea of God as being this thing outside of our consciousness. And I think one thing poetry can do is take us to those places where reality slips a bit, like those equations in physics, and suddenly we're perceiving something differently than before. And it's not all airy-fairy mysticism either. It's quite angular and hard-edged and that's what I think the analogy is with physics and with physical science.

You've written "Faith is not a state of mind, but an action in the world, a movement towards the world."

The way I've defined it to myself is that I think of belief as having objects. Faith doesn't have objects. Faith is an orientation of your life or it's an energy of your life or however you want to define it. But I think it is objectless.

It doesn't have to be faith in something?

Right. And that has helped me to understand those terms somewhat and to explain to myself why I do need some sort of structures in my life. I do need to go to church. I need specifically religious elements in my life. I'm comfortable sitting reading books and trying to pray and meditating—but inevitably, if that energy is not focused outward, it becomes despairing. I will look up in a couple of months and I find that I'm in despair. So I think that one of the ways that we know that our spiritual inclinations are valid is that they lead us out of ourselves.

I think it's a perilously difficult situation for everyone to be left on their own trying to choose their spiritual life. I really feel that a whole new language is being created and there are too many people who are struggling with this. Traditional religious language is part of it and will be part of it, but a whole new thing is being created. And it's going to involve other religions, and it's going to involve other practices.

I think a lot about Dietrich Bonhoeffer, in prison before he died, in the extreme situation of having seen the church and orthodoxy and religious language be completely co-opted by evil. And starting to talk about what "religionless Christianity" would look like—but also saying that he thought that even as the language and the ideas might cease to be relevant, the truths behind them would persist—and kind of what you just said, that new language and new forms would continually be recreated to express those truths.

I love Bonhoeffer, and I'm struck by something else he said in a letter: that he was often more drawn to atheists. He felt more fellow feeling with atheists than he did with his fellow believers. He was trying to understand that in himself. I find Bonhoeffer an incredible figure not simply because he returned to Germany when he could have had a safe life in the United States. He returned and he felt like if he didn't share in the destruction of Germany, then he couldn't credibly participate in its restoration. And he also simply felt that he had a call. You know, we wait and wait and wait for the right thing to do in our lives, but he says, no, no, no. You've got to obey, follow that impulse, as hazy as it is, and then your faith will come. You don't get it first. So he lost his life in that. He also said at one point, God has called us to be in a world without God. "Before God and without God, we stand with God." Some of his statements have the feeling of poetry. They seem so wonderfully suggestive.

There is some combination of austerity and clarity that I think we as a whole culture are grasping toward. And the main movement of the culture is against it. All the political language, all that is just rot. But I do think there's this huge cultural grasping toward something that won't be so froufrou and slip out of our grasp and just make us think it's ridiculous, and yet also something that is open enough to engage those parts of us that we don't understand.

Doubt is so woven in with what I think of as faith that it can't be separated. I am convinced that the same God that might call me to sing of God at one time might call me at another to sing of godlessness. Sometimes when I think of all of this energy that's going on, all of what we've talked about, these different people trying to find some way of naming and sharing their belief, I think it may be the case that God calls some people to unbelief in order that faith can take new forms.

SIX

HOPE
Reimagined

W e are flesh and blood and bone. There are those for whom this reality is not a homecoming but a matter of day-to-day survival. Mystics and monastics pray on embodied behalf of those who can't. In a century of staggering open questions, hope becomes a calling for those of us who can hold it, for the sake of the world. Hope is distinct, in my mind, from optimism or idealism. It has nothing to do with wishing. It references reality at every turn and reveres truth. It lives open eyed and wholehearted with the darkness that is woven ineluctably into the light of life and sometimes seems to overcome it. Hope, like every virtue, is a choice that becomes a practice that becomes spiritual muscle memory. It's a renewable resource for moving through life as it is, not as we wish it to be.

In the summer of 2015, the L'Arche movement celebrated the fiftieth anniversary of the day Jean Vanier invited Raphael and Phillippe, two men with Down syndrome from an asylum in Paris, to share life with him. It was such an honor and pleasure to gather with members of the communities around the United States, disabled core members, able-bodied assistants, all beloved and wearing the beauty that beloved-ness imparts.

Still, it took my eyes a little time to adjust. It's unsettling and unfa-miliar, such an uncommon cross section of humanity. Pairs of people led the various parts of the liturgy, including one strapping six-foot-tall twentysomething assistant and a core member, a little person at least three feet shorter and with a different skin color, both of them beaming, their friendship manifest. The entire service ended in a joyful chaos with the passing of the peace, the most raucous passing of the peace I've ever experienced. We never made it to the planned recessional. There was cake downstairs, and everyone headed straight to the party.

I ask a young man of magnetic warmth, Tim Stone of the Chicago community, how he understands Jean Vanier's statement that L'Arche is not a solution but a sign. "Hope," he says: "L'Arche is a sign of hope." Tim is a core member. He is disabled. I understand the usefulness of such a descriptor, but it is also limiting. Tim loves his friends and family. He is passionate about cooking. He creates abstract art. He radiates a tender, profound emotional intelligence and a store of knowledge about the world. L'Arche, like Tim, is a sign of hope in the quietest, most un-assuming way.

The cartography of emerging wisdom about our world is largely like this: quiet. It's animated by projects and people you didn't know to look for. It's joined by points in space and time that have no obvious reason to be important. That language of "signs, not solutions" recurs in my life of conversation, shape shifting and vivid, insisting I take it seriously. These are not the apocalyptic signs and wonders of the religion of my childhood. Those I took seriously too, but they were always beyond holding in one's hand. They were about flashes of vision, not the gran-ular, embodied work of redeeming, one life at a time. The civil rights elder Vincent Harding told me about being with young African American men and women in an inner city, telling him they would like to have "live human sign posts" to help them see and trust in changed possibilities for themselves.

> I've always felt that one of the things that we do badly in our educational process, especially working with so-called marginalized young people, is that we educate them to figure out how quickly they can get out of the darkness and get into some much more pleasant situation. When what is needed, again and again, are more and more people who will stand in that darkness, who will not run away from those deeply hurt communities, and will open up possibilities that other people can't see in any other way except through human beings who care about them.

Once upon a time, maps that revealed the edges and frontiers of the known world were tools of the few, wielded as power, locked away in secret. But we live in a world whose contours are formed by story, not conquest, and shaped and reshaped continuously by connection. We are the points on the map. Our imaginations haven't caught up with this world we inhabit yet. Our eyes can't quite focus on the new human-driven frontiers. And so we're still a bit captive, each of us in different ways, to old arbiters of importance—to the proverbial radar. Almost everything and everyone changing the world now is what we've forever referred to as "under the radar." The radar is broken.

Maybe it's always been this way. As the great Benedictine nun Joan Chittister reminds me, the *New York Times* equivalent of sixth-century Rome never carried the headline BENEDICT WRITES RULE! Benedict of Nursia had a quiet idea: to create a livable rhythm of life that could bring together both hermits—the familiar monastic model of that time—and people joining from the world, and replace the inconsistencies of scattered, competing religious authorities. It did not go that well at first. An early community that called him as their leader tried to poison him. In his lifetime, he started twelve monasteries, each with only twelve men. But he set something in motion that gathered heft over the long arc of history. Benedict could not know in his lifetime, nor could anyone else near or far, that he was fashioning a crucible of resilience that a thousand years later would literally keep Western civilization alive.

I take courage in this story. Even with all of my resources as a journalist, and my efforts to focus on what is good and wise and nourishing, I probably do not see the small bands of inventive people, the blips of action setting something in motion that will save the world a hundred or a thousand years from now.

Still, I am dazzled by the great good I can discern everywhere out there. I've shared a sliver in these pages, just a sliver. I have a heart full, arms full, a mind brimful and bursting with a sense of what is healing us even as I write, even when we don't know it and haven't asked for it. And I do mean healing: not curing, not solving, not fixing, but creating the opportunity for deepened life together, for growing more wise and more whole, not just older, not just smarter.

I've traveled a long way since my early life in Oklahoma—far enough to know that I might be accused of taking this virtue of hope too far. So be it. My mind inclines now, more than ever, towards hope. I'm consciously shedding the assumption that a skeptical point of view is the most intellectually credible. Intellect does not function in opposition to mystery; tolerance is not more pragmatic than love; and cynicism is not more reasonable than hope. Unlike almost every worthwhile thing in life, cynicism is easy. It's never proven wrong by the corruption or the catastrophe. It's not generative. It judges things as they are, but does not lift a finger to try to shift them.

I experience the soul of this moment—in people young and old—to be aspirational. This is something distinct from ambitious, though the two may overlap. I'd say it this way: we want to be called to our best selves. We long to figure out what that would look like. And we are figuring out that we need each other to do so. This listening for the calling, and the shining, fragile figuring out, are tucked inside the musings I hear from young people as much about *how* they want to be and *who* they want to be as about *what* they want to be. Our children don't always listen to what we say, as Sylvia Boorstein points out, but they are always watching us. *Lonely* is one of the adjectives people like Shane Claiborne use, alongside *unsustainable*, to describe the culture of adulthood they grew up watching.

I worry, perhaps too late, about the earnestness of my reflections, the seriousness of this writing. For there is in me, and in this world of burgeoning wisdom I spend my life watching, a newfound ease in play and pleasure and joy. Hope is not all heavy with meaning. Wisdom is not all apparently purposeful. It wouldn't be progress if it were. Novelists have long been some of our best behavioral psychologists and neuroscientists and cosmologists. We've never outgrown the fireside beside which we thrill and scare each other and spin tales of imagined wonder and horror so that we may walk more ably into the real wonders and horrors of life. Our firesides happen on screens large and small, as well as in old-fashioned storytelling and poetry slams. I read fiction in my spare time, not philosophical tracts, and I watch lots of TV, little of it objectively good for me. I want a world free of murder, but not free of murder mysteries. There's an entirely new field of the study of play that has found that it is essential to what makes us human. One of its founders, a physician named Stuart Brown, first found his way into the field through studying the minds of murderers. He found that a common denominator in their childhoods was a dearth of play. The rough and tumble play of childhood, it turns out, is one way we learn compassion.

We are fabulous and contradictory through and through, living breathing both/ands. We're products of our time and its ever more addictive toys and its alluring images of success and its terrifying chasms for failure. Yet there is room in our minds and hearts and lives—a space more and more of us are honoring and protecting and cultivating—for what is nourishing and aspirational and fun. Hope is an orientation, an insistence on wresting wisdom and joy from the endlessly fickle fabric of space and time.

Teilhard de Chardin's first love was geology. He grew up in a volcanic, mountainous region of France and was captivated by rocks—matter in the most literal sense of the word. He was passionate spiritually and scientifically, as far as I can tell, with less time for people—until he became a stretcher-bearer amid the unimaginable carnage of World War I. Writing from there, he described humanity as "matter at its most incendiary stage."

Teilhard was a contemplative, a Jesuit, and so both his spiritual and his scientific worldviews inclined him to a broad and generous view of time. He unearthed fossils that showed how far humanity had come, physiologically, over millions of years. He became persuaded that evolution proceeds toward consciousness and spirit. This was an orientation of hope rooted in scientific observation. "My starting point," he wrote, with a sensibility more at home in our time than in his, "is the fundamental initial fact that each one of us is perforce linked by all the material, organic and psychic strands of his being to all that surrounds him." As I've mentioned, Teilhard believed that human artifacts and invention would overlay the *biosphere*—a newly coined term in his day—with the *noosphere*, a word crafted from the Greek *noos,* mind. He portended the way geologists of our time have decreed a new epoch—the Anthropocene—an acknowledgment that humanity has made an imprint on the biosphere that is geological in scope. Just as our individual behaviors change our bodies, so our collective behaviors have remolded the planet.

Teilhard de Chardin died on Easter day in 1955. His Jesuit superiors had forbidden him to publish on anything other than paleontology in his lifetime. When his spiritual books—*The Phenomenon of Man, The Divine Milieu*—were finally released in the 1960s, they became bestsellers. His ideas are rolling around the world now, with a new energy.

Teilhard's vision calls us to join a long view of time with a commitment to evolving human consciousness and agency. We scarcely possess the vocabulary for this calling. The scenarios we spin most vigorously are about artificial intelligence, computers grown sentient, seductive, evil, in charge. I've wondered why we aren't also pondering, with any sophistication, what the point of consciousness might be. Where is it taking us? Where do we choose to take it? What might *spiritual* evolution look like, in the most expansive sense of that phrase?

Then I peered below the radar and found this very conversation taking place, drawing directly on Teilhard's ideas and questions and adapting them productively for now. The evolutionary biologist David Sloan Wilson had never read Teilhard de Chardin until he was invited to attend a conference at the Vatican in 2009, when the world of science celebrated the Year of Darwin the 150th anniversary of the publication of *On the Origin of Species* and the 200th anniversary of Darwin's birth.

Of course, I'd heard of him. Most people who become evolutionists have heard of him. But have they read him? Would they regard his ideas as current? The answers to those questions are, for the most part, no. What I discovered to my amazement really was that Teilhard was ahead of his time scientifically, that much of what he was saying actually passed muster from a modern evolutionary perspective.

And the main thing he said, which is only now coming back into vogue, is that in one sense the origin of man was just another species. We were just another primate. But in another sense, we were an entirely new evolutionary process and that made us in some ways as significant as the evolution of life. Symbolic thought as a mechanism of inheritance—and the enormous diversity of what we do as cultures—really is a new evolutionary process. Teilhard was correct about that and that amazed me.

Unlike Teilhard de Chardin, David Sloan Wilson is an atheist. But he has studied religions appreciatively from the standpoint of evolutionary biology, as highly effective adaptive groups. Evolution, he points out, is not always tantamount to progress; it can also move in the direction of decline. He's passionate about applying the insights of evolutionary biology towards social good. He's working on urban renewal in this spirit in his city of Binghamton, New York. The book he wrote about that project has a chapter in honor of Teilhard de Chardin called "We Are Now Entering the Noosphere."

Another thing he talked about was what he called grains of thought. What he meant by that is that at first, of course, humans existed in tiny groups and they each had their separate symbolic systems, which were disconnected from each other. Then he imagined these grains of thought coalescing. That corresponds to increasing the scale of society. Indeed, that has happened. He thought that this would result in a single global consciousness. That he called the Omega Point.

The process of evolution reflecting back on itself.

Right. Now it is true that we have the increasing scale of society all the way to the mega societies of today. But the idea that this was going to result in a single global brain—and especially that there is some inevitability about this—is within the realm of possibility. But it is by no means certain. There is such a thing as collapse. I think the real situation is that, yes, there's an Omega Point. But we have to work very hard to get there. And if we don't get there, then woe is us.

And when we think of what it means for spirituality to be the leading edge of evolution, we need to understand what spirituality means, what words such as *spirit* and *soul* actually mean and why we're impelled to use them in everyday life.

When we do that, I think we can come up with a very satisfying meaning for them, which need not require a belief in supernatural agents. And so we can speak frankly about having a soul and even our groups having a soul, our cities having a soul, and even the planet having a soul. That actually can have a straightforward meaning.

It seems to me that one of the points Teilhard was making was that spirit, as he envisioned it, the spirit that evolution is driving towards, wasn't spirituality as a state of comfort. It was about being able to galvanize for something, as you say, to work for the greater good. And in that sense, when I look at what you're doing in Binghamton, it seems to me that this thinking is supporting you.

It definitely is. The way to state that in modern evolutionary terms is that evolution only sees action. Whatever goes on in the head is invisible to evolution, unless it is manifested in terms of what people do. So if what's inside your head, if your meaning system, does not cause you to act in the right way, then it is not very good as a meaning system.

We want a meaning system that causes us to be highly motivated to act and, of course, do the right thing. And in modern life, that needs to be highly respectful of the facts of the world. And then we also need to have values that we're more aware of than ever before, and we must then use those values to consult those facts in order to plan our actions—in a world that's increasingly complex and which requires management at a planetary scale.

A phrase like "management at a planetary scale" strikes me as beyond aspirational. It's wildly out of sync with the present global order or anything transpiring in space and time imagined through the lens of now. So I'm intrigued when the journalist and environmental blogger Andrew Revkin poses an analogy between the turbulence on the planet now, and the picture we're forming of the teenage brain. Both are marked by volatility and unevenness. Areas of fantastic advance cohabit with areas of fantastic recklessness, of enhanced potential, all at once, for creativity and destructiveness.

So you look at anything from stock markets to the way the Tahrir Square events unfolded and then refolded and modulated themselves through Twitter and Facebook. To me, it's as if we're test driving new wiring and we definitely have not figured out how it's all going to work. As a blogger, I live in this arena. It can flame up a lie instantaneously, but then the reality becomes exposed equally—though not maybe as instantaneously.

This leads to some interesting questions. You know, there are the Kurzweils of the world, who see the potential for this system to become more powerful than we are. But I think what's actually much more powerful right now is this growing capacity for this system to help us collaboratively create things, and collaboratively feel things, and experience things as well in ways that weren't possible before. It's actually this capacity to share and shape ideas that's just mind-boggling. It's not just a function of computing power; there's something else going on.

Andrew Revkin coined the word *knowosphere* from Teilhard's *noosphere.*

Here's some language from you again, that whatever term you use— and you were referring to the knowosphere idea—"it's clear that the world is quickly being knitted by new ways to share observations and shape ideas that are bound to have impact on the quality of the human journey." That is spiritual language.

Well, sure. And this gets back to another ugly reality of issues like climate change, which is that they're always cast as scientific. When you actually examine rigorously the human decision-making process, you realize it quickly moves from the realm of science into the realm of values. How much warming is too much? It's not a scientific question. There are all these trade-offs. It's going to cost poor people more money to have energy if we shift away from fossil fuels. So how do we weigh the benefits there versus the benefits of slowing sea level rise, or reducing the risk of crop failure? None of those are really scientific questions. They get into the realm of economics and very quickly into the realm of values.

And I suppose we can get pretty tangled up when we're speaking in the realm of fact, but when you start talking about values, it becomes very fraught in another way.

Yes. This era has been increasingly called the *anthropocene*, the era of the human-managed planet. I think that we need to have a little of what I call *anthropophilia* if we're going to have a smooth ride in the *anthropocene,* which means we have to get more comfortable with our differences.

Within any population, you're going to have people who will have different judgments about the same body of science. And it's only by having a sense of connectedness that when you go onto the Web, you're not staying in your own little bubble, whether it's a green bubble or a Libertarian bubble, but willing to reach out to understand other peoples' views. That's also part of the *knowosphere*: finding places where you can get people who have maybe fundamentally different views of a certain energy choice, but might have the same view on energy efficiency. Then you say, oh, there's the place we can work together. That's all part of this too.

None of the issues that we face on the internet are unique to the internet. They're all part of who we are. In a crowded room, the loudest, angriest people, whatever their ideology, tend to get the most airtime. So one thing I try to do on my blog is try to build tools to foster some input from the quieter people.

I'm fascinated by the transfigurative synergy, where the quieter people find their voices and their callings, between old truths and new. So much of what we discover, when we aspire to be wise, are things human beings have known forever but then forgot.

In Detroit, as the economy changed centuries and people lost their livelihoods, the inner contradictions of the value of convenience were laid bare. Entire city blocks emptied. Some who were left began to plant their own food in vacant lots, at first for survival. But then, they rediscovered real food. Some of these Detroit experiments have emerged and spawned urban gardens around the United States. I spend time with a couple named Myrtle Thompson and Wayne Curtis. I ask them what they grow, and receive a litany of wonder:

> Kale—three types of kale—collard greens, tomatoes, bell peppers, hot peppers, eggplant, squash, strawberries, raspberries, watermelon, onions, potatoes, herbs like cilantro, basil, parsley. We grow sunflowers, some corn last season. Let's see, okra brings people from all over. Our eggplant brings people from Indian culture into the garden, and we get recipes. Watching the kids respond, and our response when you see something grow, I didn't know it'd look like that.

Myrtle and Wayne speak with every bit as much savvy and science as Dan Barber or Michael Pollan about nutrient density. They also talk to me about consciousness.

> Along with growing food, we're growing culture, we're growing community, we're growing ideology, we're growing a lot of things to make sure that our existence is no longer threatened. Developing consciousness is very important. This is not just a warm and fuzzy garden. We're not just growing food, we're becoming part of this process of existence in the whole ecological system that exists not just in the garden, but has existed since the beginning. We're developing a humanistic practice. Our identity is no longer connected to Del Monte.
>
> This also changes your culture when you rediscover what can be eaten that's been there all along. You realize you've

been driving over things that are valuable. You look at what is growing under a pallet where someone is changing oil, and say, "You know, you could eat that." So that changes your relationship with the earth, but it also changes your relationship with another person—because you have to find a way to explain it to them.

In Louisville, I spend a mind-stretching, heart-opening evening with the mayor and the chief of the police, the superintendent of schools, leaders of the faith community, union organizers, members of the city's historic families. We have a lovely dinner in a tiny "country club" that is elegantly informal, more like someone's beloved grandma's home: musty basement, good china. This is where, someone tells me, the 1 percent of the 1 percent has always gathered. The Ohio River runs beyond the windows; its banks are a historic schism of class and wealth. But tonight, this cross section of the city is present. They talk to each other. They listen to each other. This mayor, once he was elected, announced that he wanted Louisville to become a city of compassion, through and through in granular ways that would challenge their civic life together at every level. It's an experiment, but one they are taking very seriously. They're past the romance now and in the weeds of social change, planting long-term projects in schools whose results will not be in until long after this mayor leaves office. In some ways, one son of a leading house told me, it's "just an aspiration." But a civic aspiration is a powerful thing—it gives moral imagination someplace to go.

Most stunning of all is the hard-won sense of trust in that room: of fears calmed, and vulnerabilities laid bare and safe to be so. An African American pastor tells me that the greatest breakthrough was having a politician who was willing to sit with people's pain—just that. Not, in the first instance, to present a policy or a fix—but to acknowledge that damage has been done and dwell with it, let it be in the room, accompanied, grieved—lamented, in the ancient language of the prophets. We know in life that taking in our losses and grieving them is a step that is not in itself productive or effective—all those ways we measure what matters. But it's an opening without which only limited growth, movement out and forward, is possible.

This is more knowledge that is a form of power, if we choose to take it up together in this spirit. It sits uneasily with instincts we honed in the twentieth century to wage war on our problems. This attitude seeped into our ways of creating our professional lives, our foreign and domestic policies, the raising of our children. War takes anger and ambition as its fuel, deferring lamentations, sidelining grief along with compassion. Its calculus counts winning and deplores losing. After 9/11 in America, we had a robust vocabulary of revenge and enemies, and we acted on it. We didn't summon the words to help us dwell with the shattering experience of vulnerability in our strongest fortresses. That vulnerability brought Americans into a new point of kinship with far-flung strangers around the world, who live this way much of the time. But our response drew us apart again.

Now, from business to education to psychology, we are remembering that failure has always been part of every human story of success. I'd extend that in more meaningful and less triumphalist terms: failure and vulnerability are the very elements of spiritual growth and personal wisdom. What goes wrong for us as much as what goes right—what we know to be our flaws as much as what we know to be our strengths—these make hope reasonable and lived virtue possible. They are part of our gift to the world. Brené Brown has become a sought-out teacher in all kinds of settings, at every level of leadership, on this ancient, basic truth that had been lost from our common vocabulary for generations. It all began with research she did at the University of Houston's Graduate College of Social Work, where she's a professor.

I always ask a very simple question to people. I just say, think of the last time you did something that you thought was really brave or the last time you saw someone do something really brave. And I can tell you as a researcher—11,000 pieces of data—I cannot find a single example of courage, moral courage, spiritual courage, leadership courage, relational courage, I cannot find a single example of courage that was not born completely of vulnerability. We buy into some mythology about vulnerability being weakness and being gullibility and being frailty because it gives us permission not to do it.

Brené Brown's own life—as a self-professed classic perfectionist—was turned inside out by these findings. She went on to share what she was learning at a TEDx talk in her Houston hometown. That has since become one of the most widely viewed TED talks of all time, despite an arguably unappealing title: "Listening to Shame." I love learning that she stumbled on old, new truths that sound negative in modern ears while researching the nature of "wholehearted lives."

I started coding data and looking for patterns and themes in words and they started emerging very quickly. I started to put together lists. Here are the things that wholehearted men and women really consciously choose, and here are the things that they push away from. And I just remember looking up and looking at the kind of do-not-do list. It described my entire life. I'm like, I'm on the wrong list.

So what was on it? Well, let me just ask you this first. Did you think that you were going to find that these people had been better parented or had less trauma or better support systems?

I had a lot of self-righteousness about that. I think I thought, well, these people, you know, the people who believe in their worthiness, their lives probably panned out extremely well. They were dealt a better hand of cards. Their nail polish doesn't chip, no stretch marks, no struggles. But that wasn't the case. There weren't fewer divorces or bankruptcies or history of trauma or addiction. They were just like the general population in terms of those variables. They were just like everyone else.

So what was on the list that described you?

Perfectionism, judgment, exhaustion as a status symbol, productivity as self-worth, cool, what do people think, performing, proving, quest for certainty. Such a pretty picture.

And was vulnerability—the way you use the word now—an underlying quality of these lives of wholeheartedness?

Yes, absolutely. These were folks who show up in their lives without a lot of guarantees. I remember sitting at that table a couple of days later kind of making the decision that I was going to put the data away and get a therapist—and I did.

I remember thinking: Does this mean that our capacity for wholeheartedness can never be greater than our willingness to be brokenhearted?

This gets back to our cultural allergy to vulnerability—what we have done with this primal sense of vulnerability. It's not a bad impulse, our need to protect ourselves and those we love, but we've gone perfectionistic on it.

We have. I think the part that really pushed me to getting help and wanting to live differently was what I was seeing about parenting. Who we are and how we engage with the world is a far more accurate predictor of how our children will do than what we know about parenting. I agree with you. I think we're in a gentle, quiet awakening period right now. But I started my research just very coincidentally six months before 9/11. Over the course of the last 12 years, I have seen fear absolutely run roughshod over our families. And I have seen us go to these crazy lengths to protect ourselves and our children from the uncertainty of the world today. I've not only seen that through my lens as a researcher, but certainly experienced it as a parent, and as a college professor.

I see students come to us who have never had experiences, real experiences, with adversity. And how that shows up is hopelessness. One of the most interesting things I've found in doing this work is that the wholehearted share in common a profound sense of hopefulness. The literature on hope, very specifically C. R. Snyder's work from the University of Kansas at Lawrence, shows that hope is a function of struggle.

I think that's one of the most stunning sentences that I saw in your writing.

And that hope is not an emotion. Hope is a cognitive, behavioral process that we learn when we experience adversity, when we have relationships that are trustworthy, when people have faith in our ability to get out of a jam.

Which is different from this pattern of having faith in our children, which means telling them everything they do is wonderful and shield-

ing them from pain as long as we can. But boy, we know this, don't we,
this desire to create a beautiful world and life and experience for these
people you love?

> But you know what? I think we lose sight of the beauty. The
> most beautiful things I look back on in my life are coming out
> from underneath things I didn't know I could get out from un-
> derneath. The moments I look back in my life and think,
> "God, those are the moments that made me," were moments of
> struggle.

Hope is brokenhearted on the way to becoming wholehearted. Hope
is a function of struggle. I ask the evolutionary biologist David Sloan
Wilson if there's something nonsensical in evolutionary terms about the
way we humans sometimes progress by relearning things we once knew
and forgot. Here's how he answers: a fish can take itself out of water and
no longer be able to survive or thrive. Human invention can do the
equivalent of taking us out of water in a million clever ways. Relearning
the role struggle plays in growing up; rediscovering real food or the
vivifying effect of green spaces in the middle of common life, or the
comfort of knowing our neighbors—these are less reversals than a waking up to what we need in evolutionary as well as human, spiritual terms.
Recovering necessary elements of survival and vitality is a step forward,
a piece of intelligence. This is another way to talk about the move from
intelligence to wisdom—seeing basic realities again, finally, but for the
first time with consciousness: evolution reflecting back on itself.

I'm glad for the language of resilience that has entered the twenty-
first-century lexicon, from urban planning to mental health. Resilience
is a successor to mere progress, a companion to sustainability. It ac-

knowledges from the outset that things will go wrong. All of our solutions will eventually outlive their usefulness. We will make messes, and disruption we do not cause or predict will land on us. This is the drama of being alive. To nurture a resilient human being, or a resilient city, is to build in an expectation of adversity, a capacity for inevitable vulnerability. As a word and as a strategy, resilience honors the unromantic reality of who we are and how we are, and so becomes a refreshingly practical compass for the systems and societies we can craft. It's a shift from wish-based optimism to reality-based hope. It is akin to meaningful, sustained happiness—not dependent on a state of perfection or permanent satisfaction, not an emotional response to circumstances of the moment, but a way of being that can meet the range of emotions and experiences, light and dark, that add up to a life. Resilience is at once proactive, pragmatic, and humble. It knows it needs others. It doesn't overcome failure so much as transmute it, integrating it into the reality that evolves.

Such language itself, and the orientation to service it engenders, is an axial move. Andrew Zolli is one of the people who has brought this term into entrepreneurial parlance. He led a renaissance of the PopTech community of social entrepreneurs for a decade. He's now advising inquiries into the human condition in places like Facebook. He has his finger on the pulse of our collective awakening to the implications of new scientific as well as cultural understandings of reality between the last century and this one.

Something you've said that is so striking is that we need systems that "fail gracefully," that don't bring down everything else around them. I think about the economic downturn of 2008, or Hurricane Katrina. This makes so much sense. And this notion of failing gracefully—it's true in life as well. Yet we haven't wanted to think it would be true in our institutions, in the way we manage and organize our common life.

It's true. And part of the reason is, we believed that we could essentially out-engineer failure. That we could inoculate ourselves from it. I'll speak about my own personal journey. My first independent decade as an adult was in the '90s. It's interesting to reflect on what was going on then. The Soviet Union had collapsed. We weren't at war. The Internet was ascendant. People were publishing books with titles like *The End of History*. It was over. It was like a party that I just arrived at and everyone was going home, which is not the last time that would happen in my life. And the idea was that it was going to be clear and easy sailing. Our fights were going to be about economics and creativity and they weren't going to be over physical resources. And they weren't going to be real wars; we were moving past that.

There was going to be nothing that went downward; everything would go upward.

That's right. The laws of physics had been repealed. And we were busy spending our peace dividend. Contrast that to the decade that came right after—which in many people's minds began with a spectacularly successful global act of terrorism. Proceeded through huge, expensive, complicated, painful, shocking wars and natural disasters. And concluded with a huge economic crisis. I believe that historians years from now will find that this decade is going to replace the '70s as the suckiest decade in American history. It's not the one that we're all going to love. But the most important thing is that we moved from a period of relative tranquility to real disruption in basically the blink of an eye. That fact has begun to permeate our culture. So you ask about graceful failure. I think the first premise is that all things fail. In fact, not only do all things fail, but failure is intrinsic, healthy, normal, and necessary to most complex systems.

Over-reach and failure are inevitable too, and alas, in problem solving and service. Innovators and activists across the ages have been as prone to burnout and excess as the nuclear arms experts with whom I spent my 20s. There is a fine line between saving the world and manipulating other lives, however well-meaningly, in our own image. The dark side of entrepreneurialism, even social entrepreneurialism, is that it can draw instinctively on that old trope of the self-made man, the noble but distracting impulse to save the world by my best ideas and efforts alone. But my own hope rests, as much as anything else, on my experience of so many of the young among us. A self-aware core of them is poised to do change differently, resiliently. Courtney Martin, an admirable and delightful thirtysomething thought leader and activist, diagnosed the problem with "saving the world" with profound sophistication in her 20s, rejecting its implied logic that there are savers and those who need to be saved, that the world could be divided up this way. "Our charge is not to 'save the world' after all," she's written. "It is to live in it, flawed and fierce, loving and humble." Everywhere I turn, I see Courtney and her compatriots learning to be reflective and activist at once, to be in service as much as in charge, and to learn from history and elders while bringing very new realities into being.

When Einstein praised spiritual genius in his age, he saw it as a counterbalance to technological advance—to a destructive, unreflective application of the fruits of science. This generation's wisdom is being spun in concert with technology. The Internet is our version of splitting the atom. It holds immense powers, both perilous and promising, as it upends the meaning of ancient, elemental human things like making and leading and belonging and learning. A concern I live with, and which complicates my sense of the transformative possibilities of the age in which we live, is how much the digital world disperses the very energies and initiatives it makes possible. My favorite wise man about the Internet, Seth Godin, is attentive to this danger too. But looking at life writ large through the lens of the Internet, he also sees that the digital world hands us a power to take the axial move farther than humanity could previously envision. We know ourselves not only to be connecting to others beyond kin and tribe. We have the means and the freedom to create our own tribes bound by passion and service, quite apart from bloodline or geography. These are digital analogs to John Paul Lederach's notion of "critical yeast." They can catalyze what the iconic anthropologist Margaret Mead, who studied old-fashioned flesh and blood tribes, called "evolutionary clusters."

There are so many digital tribes joining intelligence to wisdom across space, cyberspace, and time. Nathan Schneider's hackers of the Rule of Benedict is just one story; so is the story of Maria Popova's Internet phenomenon, *Brain Pickings*.

> I spend most of my days sort of buried in book piles and letters and diaries and old philosophy books and what not. There's this term in kind of new-agey circles, spiritual re-parenting, which is a bit too new-agey even for my taste. And I can be quite the hippie sometimes. But there's an aspect of it that I like. It's led me to think about what I do as a kind of two-way generational re-parenting—on the one hand caring for these bygone thinkers, while at the same time imbuing the present generation with their hand-me-down wisdom and their most enduring ideas.

Maria Popova was born in Bulgaria when it was behind the Iron Curtain. The notion of the "soul" had been banished in that world. But she was raised by her grandparents in a book-lined apartment, and she still to this day studies the marginalia in the books of her grandfather, for whom intellectual life was a form of spiritual survival. In a changed post–cold war world, she came to study in America. And while working in an office to pay for college, in the early days of e-mail, she started a weekly e-mail newsletter, about ideas, for a few colleagues. I think Maria's central European background gives her an audacious, somewhat un-American faith in the power of ideas. And somehow she manages to use technological tools in service of old-fashioned wisdom. When I speak with Maria at thirty, she's already been at this for a decade. *Brain Pickings* is a labor of love with a vast following now, and it points at technology's redemptive potentials. She, like Brené Brown, has stumbled on a robust vocabulary of hope while pursuing seemingly unrelated questions.

I think the magnetism of your work, the appeal of it for people, is that it's aspirational. Which is a contrast to "disruptive." We have all these assumptions we walk around with and lay over new generations, that there's no place for depth, that you can only take things in bite-sized pieces. And yet, you present this discovery to people that we want our brains to be stretched. I feel that there's a real quality in you as a human being, which comes through in your work, of intellectual confidence and generosity. Is there a philosophy in you about that?

Well, there are certain core beliefs, I guess. I think a lot about the relationship between cynicism and hope. Critical thinking without hope is cynicism. But hope without critical thinking is naïveté. I try to live in this place between the two, to try to build a life there. Because finding fault and feeling hopeless about improving our situation produces resignation, of which cynicism is a symptom, a sort of futile self-protection mechanism.

But on the other hand, believing blindly that everything will work out just fine also produces a kind of resignation, because we have no motive to apply ourselves toward making things better. I think in order to survive, both as individuals and as a civilization, but especially in order to thrive, we need to bridge critical thinking with hope.

You often say that one of the things you're looking for in content for Brain Pickings *is something that contains "both timeliness and timelessness."*

So much of culture deals with what is urgent right now and not what is important in the grand scheme of things. And there is this sort of time bias or presentism bias that happens.

Presentism. I like that.

Which is in part because of the way that the Internet is structured. So when you think of anything from a Twitter feed or a Facebook feed to a news Web site, the most recent floats to the top always. And it's always in reverse chronology. And I think that's conditioning us to believe rather falsely that the most recent is the most important. And that the older matters less or just exists less to a point where we really have come to believe that things that are not on Google or on the news never happened, never existed, or don't matter.

The Internet—its beauty is that it's a self-perfecting organism, right? But as long as it's an ad-supported medium, the motive will be to perfect commercial interest, to perfect the art of the listicle, the endless slideshow, the infinitely paginated oracle, and not to perfect the human spirit of the reader or the writer.

You've quoted Anne Lamott—she's actually talking about something Emily Dickinson said—that, "hope inspires the good to reveal itself." When you say that the Internet is a self-perfecting organism—do you have hope and confidence in the Internet, in our technology as a place where the human spirit can be cultivated and deepened? That's not language people often use when they're speaking of our lives with technology.

Well, the thing to keep in mind is that this is such a young medium, you know? We have not even had a full generation live and die with it. And I think, like any territory to which we bring the pioneer spirit, it is bound to have both the good and the evil. And we're not going to know how it turns out until much, much, much later. But in the meantime, the decisions we make, the microscopic decisions that we make daily, shape it. And I am not so foolish as to make predictions, but I can tell you my hope, which is that I do think that people will come to rebel against the things that just don't work for us spiritually, intellectually, creatively.

And we're seeing this to some degree. I think the younger generations—and I don't mean this by age, but I mean people who are more recently coming onto the scene of the Internet—are more willing to, for example, pay for ad-free versions of publications or to limit what they engage with and recognize that, actually, it takes time and thought and effort and resources to produce a publication that is nourishing as opposed to a cat listicle, and to make decisions according to how something makes you feel in the end, and what kind of contribution it's making to the common record.

I was listening to an interview with Jimmy Wales, the founder of Wikipedia, and he said that people contribute to Wikipedia for free because they want to do something useful with their time. I agree. I think people hunger to do something useful with their time in our age of uselessness, time uselessly spent. But also to do something ennobling with their time— and this can't quite be quantified. There's no utilitarian value to it the way that there is with usefulness. I deeply believe that people want to be good, that more than that, we want to be better, to grow, to ennoble our souls. And I have hope for this medium with that lens.

We never see the world exactly as it is because we are how the world is. I think it was William James who said, "My experience is what I agree to attend to, and only those things which I notice shaped my mind." And so in choosing how we are in the world, we shape our experience of that world, our contribution to it. We shape our world, our inner world, our outer world, which is really the only one we'll ever know. And to me, that's the substance of the spiritual journey. It's not an exasperating idea but an infinitely emboldening one, and it's taken me many years to come to that without resistance.

Hope inspires goodness to reveal itself. Hope takes goodness seriously, treats it as a data point, takes it in. This is a virtue for living in and of itself: taking in the good. That phrase first entered my imagination by way of a slightly tongue-in-cheek *New York Times* article one Thanksgiving a few years ago. A scientific study had demonstrated health benefits from a simple exercise of gratitude, which was all about registering the good in the course of one's days, including the bad days. It yielded a remarkable list of measurable outcomes: sounder sleep, a sense of peace of mind, less anxiety and depression, kinder behavior and higher long-term satisfaction with life. The tongue-in-cheek spin: "A new study shows that feeling grateful makes people less likely to turn aggressive when provoked, which helps explain why so many brothers-in-law survive Thanksgiving without serious injury."

Like hope, like goodness, gratitude can appear a bit innocent, lacking in gravitas. Like happiness, it's too often presented one dimensionally, as an orientation you are either born with or not, graced with the good fortune to muster or not. It's not a word that trips lightly off my tongue. But deciding to honor it as a piece of wisdom returns me to the vocabulary of spiritual traditions where it is a vivid and developed choice, just like the scientists found, but wrapped in meatier language—the habit of rejoicing, a calling to gladness. Praise functions as a habit in the psalms of the Hebrew Bible, which gives voice to every human experience from humiliated disappointment to murderous rage. Nevertheless, the psalmist insists, "This is the day that the Lord has made, let us rejoice and be glad in it."

I'm not a person with a deep well of comforting childhood memories. But I can still see myself communing, with something like rejoicing and relief, with certain passages of the Bible amidst the intense, unacknowledged despair that was in my family when I was growing up. I memorized beautiful, poetic lines of the Apostle Paul, written to the struggling young church of the Philippians: "Finally, Beloved, whatever is true, whatever is honorable, whatever is just, whatever is pure, whatever is pleasing, whatever is commendable, if there is any excellence and if there is anything worthy of praise, think about these things. Keep on doing the things you have heard and seen from me, and the God of peace will be with you." This is a prescription for mental and spiritual resilience.

This peace of God is what scientists are taking into a laboratory two millennia later and offering up to us as secular spiritual technology.

Still, all of this begs the question of why a simple, natural, refreshing thing like taking in goodness, wherever and whenever we see it, requires any effort at all—why it needs all these words. There's a telling social scientific term for people who defy the "realistic" expectations of a simplistic "survival of the fittest" understanding of evolved humanity: "positive deviance." My profession of journalism, which I love, too often covers whatever is true, honorable, just, pure, pleasing, commendable, excellent, and worthy of praise as positive deviance. This is a form of reverse moral imagination. Everyone I've cited in this book is a positive deviant, easily written off by portenders of doom as an exception to the distasteful human rule. I can hear the criticism now, of singling out *Brain Pickings* as an example of what the Internet makes possible, when cyberspace's fecundity of pornography, violence, and trivialization is so clear.

Reality is a both/and. More to the point, as Maria Popova says, the Internet is in its infancy. It is at a fundamental level a new canvas for the old human condition, salvation and sin, at digital speed and with viral replication. It is a magnifying glass on every human inclination, beautiful and terrible, trivial and mean, generous and curious.

Take note of how this realization puts the power back with us. We can choose how our technology will change us. See how even the Internet's most grandiose amplification of evil yields, at times, a chastening, a mirror at which we recoil. Cyberspace is forcing us to reckon with bullying, something that has long flourished in the flesh and blood spaces in which we rear our young. Western civilization at the highest levels has colluded for centuries, by participation or silence, tolerating bullying as an unavoidable rite of passage for the unfortunate few. Seeing bullying and following its effects on the Internet's oversized, public canvas has made it suddenly intolerable. We are finally developing a new consciousness around bullying, teaching children to overturn it, launching campaigns to end it for the first time. This is a moral watershed.

In the particular span of time in which I am finishing this writing, a handful of months carry a precious cargo of faces and lives brought into relief by the dark side of human reality and technology's capacity to bring it to us immediate and raw. Some of their names are Kayla Mueller, Deah Shaddy Barakat, Yusor Mohammad Abu-Salha, Razan Mohammad Abu-Salha, and Clementa Pinckney. I want to remember them in these pages because such lives tell a larger redemptive story about who we can be, if we choose it.

Kayla was taken hostage by ISIS militants when she was stepping out of a Doctors Without Borders clinic in Syria. She died eighteen months later. Deah and Yusor were husband and wife, dentistry students at the University of North Carolina. Razan was a student too, an aspiring filmmaker, and Yusor's sister. They were shot by a neighbor in their apartment in North Carolina. These four young Americans were ordinary people—neighbors any of us might have found ourselves living near, and members of a young generation we often blithely dismiss as self-absorbed.

I routinely reflexively turn away from such terrible news stories. I shield myself from their images with a sense that there is nothing I could possibly do to help. But I was captured by a gorgeous meditation on the lives of Deah, Yusor, and Razan, which my wonderful friend and colleague the Muslim scholar Omid Safi lovingly pulled together. It brought them to life for me: a photo of Yusor dancing, radiant in her wedding dress, just weeks before her death; an account of how Deah and Yusor were using their vocation of dentistry to provide relief to refugees in Turkey and to neighbors in North Carolina. It took me to a haunting, profoundly nourishing video created by Razan, featuring the smiles, courage, and hard-won hope of dozens of other young Muslim Americans, students at UNC who are still with us now. In one frame after the other, they hold up statements that radiate in their stances, their faces:

"It would be absurd to believe that my generation is apathetic and lethargic."

"In the future I will be part of a community that is of my own making."

Kayla Mueller's letters home to her parents, which brought her to life for me, were likewise testaments to wisdom and grace beyond her years. On her blog she'd written: "This really is my life's work, to go where there is suffering. I suppose, like us all, I'm learning how to deal with the suffering of the world inside myself . . . to deal with my own pain and most importantly to still have the ability to be proactive." Following this calling, she'd started a local chapter of Amnesty International and volunteered with Big Brothers and Big Sisters and a women's shelter in her hometown. She'd served in places of desperation from India to Guatemala before she landed in Syria. A letter to her parents, sent while in captivity, reminds me of my reading of mystics and saints across the ages, figures like Julian of Norwich and Mother Teresa:

"I have come to a place in experience where, in every sense of the word, I have surrendered myself to our creator b/c literally there was no else . . . + by God + by your prayers I have felt tenderly cradled in freefall."

"I have been shown in darkness, light + have learned that even in prison, one can be free. I am grateful."

To be clear, Kayla's letters home would never have been published in the *Guardian* and the *Washington Post* had she not died in captivity. We would not be watching YouTube videos of Yusor, Razan, and Deah had they not been murdered in their apartment in North Carolina. And I would not have had the possibility of this deep introduction to them without the technology I often experience as a distraction from what matters in life.

So how, I begin to ask myself, can I honor more than their memory? How can I take in my knowledge of such lives in the world as a gift, and let it speak to the life I'm privileged to continue? How can we—and I use this "we" lavishly and presumptuously—be present to and supportive of all the beautiful lives that have not been extinguished as a way of honoring those we have lost and found at the same time?

Clementa Pinckney died in a year that saw the heartbreaking deaths of one black man (and woman) after another in the United States, often at the hands of police. He may in fact go down in history as a person whose death at forty-one brought the Confederate flag to rest from the state capitols of South Carolina and Alabama, 150 years after the Civil War ended. Looking at Clementa Pinckney's life after the fact, it's almost as though he knew he had to be in a hurry. He was ordained at eighteen, and he became a state senator in the South Carolina House of Representatives at twenty-three, the youngest person ever to hold that office. He was a public servant while a full-time minister at Emanuel AME Church in Charleston, a spiritual heart of that city. It was in his church that he was gunned down, along with eight radiant members of his congregation, by a young white man they'd all welcomed in for a Wednesday night Bible study.

"The most irritating thing about Senator Pinckney," a journalist quoted one of Clementa Pinckney's fellow legislators as saying, "is that when you had a debate he would just come over and pat you on the back and say, 'Maybe tomorrow you'll be thinking right.' He was full of love and full of respect." Like the prophets, Clementa Pinckney used language that shimmers and elevates, to open possibilities for action. He used poetic words when he argued for measures for transparency of po-

lice action after the death of a South Carolina man, Walter Scott, in police custody, in what would turn out to be the year of his own murder:

*"We have a great opportunity to allow sunshine into this process, to at
least give us new eyes for seeing."*

Our world is abundant with quiet, hidden lives of beauty and courage and goodness. There are millions of people at any given moment,
young and old, giving themselves over to service, risking hope, and all
the while ennobling us all. To take such goodness in and let it matter—
to let it define our take on reality as much as headlines of violence—is a
choice we can make to live by the light in the darkness, to be brave and
free like Razan, Deah, Yusor, Kayla, Clementa, and all their kindred
spirits. Taking in the good, whenever and wherever we find it, gives us
new eyes for seeing and living.

In Youngstown, Ohio, I'm invited to share what I've learned about
opening new conversational spaces, new relationships, amidst the challenges we need to approach anew and those we've not yet figured out
how to name. This city grew up as a steel town, an industrial power-
house in an economic landscape that has well and truly vanished. Generations of livelihood and self-respect withered with it. Over half of
Youngstown's children are now living under the poverty line. My talk is
in an Episcopal church on a muggy, stormy Friday night in June, but the
sanctuary is packed. I speak, and I listen to their questions and their
stories and wisdom, that night and the next day. Person after person puts
flesh on the bones of what I feel in that room before someone says it like
this: "This is a community that is dying and being reborn at the same
time."

Their story is our story, over and over and over again—the story of
each and every one of our communities of family and place and chosen
kinship. We often don't quite trust that rebirth will follow the deaths of

what we thought we knew. We sense that somehow what comes next is up to us, but we're not sure where to begin. Yet it's precisely in these moments when we let our truest, hardest questions rise up in our midst, allow their place among us, that we become able to live into them rather than away and to do so together. We are so achingly frail and powerful all at once, in this adolescence of our species. But I have seen that wisdom emerges precisely through those moments when we have to hold seemingly opposing realities in a creative tension and interplay: power and frailty, birth and death, pain and hope, beauty and brokenness, mystery and conviction, calm and buoyancy, mine and yours.

The kind of conversation I spend my life in is, like poetry, a tribute to the human capacity to articulate truth at the edges of what words can touch. I reach the end of this writing in fear and trembling, to use Kierkegaard's phrase, at all I haven't said and can't articulate or begin to tie up—at the limits of my words, acknowledging their necessary humility.

Humility is a final virtue to name and beckon here. It is woven through lives of wisdom and resilience. It's another word that has acquired a taint of ineffectuality. But my life of conversation has reintroduced it to me as a companion to curiosity and delight. Like humor, it softens us for hospitality and beauty and questioning and all the other virtues I've named in these pages. Spiritual humility is not about getting small, not about debasing oneself, but about approaching everything and everyone else with a readiness to see goodness and to be surprised. This is the humility of a child, which Jesus lauded. It is the humility of the scientist and the mystic. It has a lightness of step, not a heaviness of heart.

That lightness is the surest litmus test I know for recognizing wisdom when you see it in the world or feel its stirrings in yourself. The questions that can lead us are already alive in our midst, waiting to be summoned and made real. It is a joy to name them. It is a gift to plant them in our senses, our bodies, the places we inhabit, the part of the world we can see and touch and help to heal. It is a relief to claim our love of each other and take that on as an adventure, a calling. It is a pleasure to wonder at the mystery we are and find delight in the vastness of reality that is embedded in our beings. It is a privilege to hold something robust and resilient called hope, which has the power to shift the world on its axis.

The mystery and art of living are as grand as the sweep of a lifetime and the lifetime of a species. And they are as close as beginning, quietly, to mine whatever grace and beauty, whatever healing and attentiveness, are possible in this moment and the next and the next one after that.

CONVERSATION PARTNERS, 2003–2015

You can listen to every interview in its entirety at http://onbeing.org

Mohammed Abu-Nimer

Sami Adwan

Leila Ahmed

Mustafa Akyol

Ilana Alazzeh

Elizabeth Alexander

Kecia Ali

Wajahat Ali

Alberto Ambrosio

Bonnie Amesquita

Maya Angelou

Kwame Anthony Appiah

Karen Armstrong

Reza Aslan

Scott Atran

Ali Abu Awwad

Nidal Al-Azraq

Michele Balamani

Nadia Sheikh Bandukda

Dan Barber

Anita Barrows

Basil Brave Heart

Natalie Batalha

Stephen Batchelor

Mary Catherine Bateson

Whitney Battle-Baptiste

Patrick Bellegarde-Smith

Peter Berger

Wendell Berry

Amahl Bishara

Cheryl Blake

David Blankenhorn

Jelle de Boer

Grace Lee Boggs

Nadia Bolz-Weber

Roberta Bondi

Sylvia Boorstein

Alain de Botton

danah boyd

Greg Boyd

Greg Boyle

Jim Bradley

Kate Braestrup

David Brooks

Joanna Brooks

Bernadette Brooten

Sharon Brous

Brené Brown

Stuart Brown

Michael Dennis Browne

Walter Brueggemann

Mirabai Bush

Anthea Butler

Ira Byock

Joseph A. Califano, Jr.

Joan Brown Campbell

Simone Campbell

Nancy Cantor

Jimmy Carter

Joe Carter

Majora Carter

Rosanne Cash

Bernard Chazelle

Susan Cheever

Cheryl Crazy Bull

Joan Chittister

Rebecca Chopp

Richard Cizik

Shane Claiborne

Lynn Schofield Clark

Paulo Coelho

Robert Coles

Paul Collins

Charles Colson

Guy Consolmagno

Seane Corn

Vincent Cornell

Harvey Cox, Jr.

George Coyne

Donald Cozzens

Michael Cromartie

Mario Cuomo

Wayne Curtis

Barry Cytron

Thupten Dadak

Jim Daly

Robi Damelin

John Danforth

Mohammad Darawshe

Richard Davidson

Paul Davies

Ellen Davis

Joan Dehzad

Anita Desai

Keith Devlin

Calvin DeWitt

Adele Diamond

Alan Dienstag

E. J. Dionne

Carol Dittberner

David Dixon

Martin Doblmeier

Pete Domenici

Phil Donahue

Mercedes Doretti

Elliot Dorff

Rod Dreher

Joshua DuBois

Nathan Dungan

Freeman Dyson

Sylvia Earle

Lindon Eaves

Arnold Eisen

Jennifer Elder

Paul Elie

George F. R. Ellis

Jean Bethke Elshtain

Eve Ensler

Greg Epstein

Cynthia Eriksson

Khaled Abou El Fadl

Mohammed Fairouz

Feruze Faison

Margaret A. Farley

Tom Faulkner

Bruce Feiler

Carl Feit

Richard Feldman

Malka Haya Fenyvesi

Helen Fisher

Béla Fleck

Anne Foerst

Edward Foley

David Fox

Robert M. Franklin, Jr.

Andrew Freear

Sylvester James Gates, Jr.

Bill George

Penny George

Seemi Bushra Ghazi

Amitav Ghosh

Jean Berko Gleason

Marcelo Gleiser

Pumla Gobodo-Madikizela

Seth Godin

Natalie Gold

Peter J. Gomes

Ursula Goodenough

Cedric Good House

Adam Gopnik

James S. Gordon

Adam Grant

Jonathan Greenblatt

Brian Greene

Kevin Griffin

Dan Grigassy

Jane Gross

Prabhu Guptara

Vigen Guroian

David P. Gushee

Lia Hadley

Debra Haffner

Jonathan Haidt

Getatchew Haile

Yossi Klein Halevi

Joan Halifax

Philip Hamburger

Ann Hamilton

Patricia Hampl

Thích Nhất Hạnh

Dan Hanson

Sue Hanson

Vincent Harding

David Hartman

Aziza Hasan

Charles C. Haynes

Richard Hays

Jennifer Michael Hecht

Chris Hedges

Gordon Hempton

Joe Henry

Hendrik Hertzberg

David Hilfiker

Imelda Hinojosa

His Holiness the XIV Dalai Lama

Jo Anne Horstmann

Christopher Howard

Marie Howe

Thomas Hoyt, Jr.

Ed Husain

Mark Hyman

David Isay

Adrian Ivakhiv

Pico Iyer

Samar Jarrah

Thupten Jinpa

Lucas Johnson

Luke Timothy Johnson

Douglas Johnston

Serene Jones

Ingrid Jordt

Rex Jung

Jon Kabat-Zinn

Khalid Kamau

Rosabeth Moss Kanter

Sarah Kay

Fatemeh Keshavarz

Muqtedar Khan

Jim King

Ursula King

Barbara Kingsolver

Frances Kissling

Kevin Kling

Diane Komp

Scott-Martin Kosofsky

Bruce Kramer

Lawrence Krauss

Nicholas Kristof

Lawrence Kushner

Joy Ladin

Elpidophoros Lambriniadis

Anne Lamott

Lisa Lampman

Ellen Langer

Ernie LaPointe

John Paul Lederach

Thomas Levenson

Janna Levin

John Lewis

John Lipscomb

Mario Livio

Steven Longden

Robin Lovin

Linda Loving

Gloria Lowe

Gabe Lyons

Yo-Yo Ma

Wangari Maathai

Joanna Macy

Cheri Maples

Ibrahim Al-Marashi

Joel Marcus

Oana Marian

Courtney E. Martin

James Martin

Michel Martin

Martin E. Marty

Ingrid Mattson

Michael McCullough

Bobby McFerrin

Tim McGuire

Vashti McKenzie

Bill McKibben

Brian McLaren

Tiya Miles

B. J. Miller

E. Ethelbert Miller

Robert Millet

Anchee Min

Pankaj Mishra

Stephen Mitchell

Leonard Mlodinow

Virginia Ramey Mollenkott

Meredith Monk

David R. Montgomery

James Moore

Thomas Moore

Debbie Morris

John Morris

Richard Mouw

Abdul-Rasheed Muhammad

Precious Rasheeda Muhammad

Isabel Mukonyora

Paul Muldoon

Marc Mullinax

Nancey Murphy

Jef Murray

Lorraine Murray

Emily Muschinske

Rami Nashashibi

Seyyed Hossein Nasr

Vali Nasr

Jacob Needleman

Carrie Newcomer

Louis Newman

Jacqueline Novogratz

Sherwin Nuland

Sari Nusseibeh

John O'Donohue

Mary Oliver

Adnan Onart

Michael Orange

Mehmet Oz

Parker Palmer

Eboo Patel

Katy Payne

Mariane Pearl

M. Scott Peck

Jaroslav Pelikan

Imani Perry

Xavier Le Pichon

Gregory Plotnikoff

Sylvia Poggioli

Rachel Pokora

John Polkinghorne

Robert Pollack

Margaret M. Poloma

Maria Popova

john a. powell

Helen Prejean

Joseph L. Price

James Prosek

Nicole Queen

Abeer Raazi

Alan Rabinowitz

Ahmed H. al-Rahim

Allee A. Ramadhan, Sr.

Varadaraja V. Raman

Arnold Rampersad

Lisa Randall

Jonathan Rauch

Paul Raushenbush

Amy Ray

Martin Rees

Darius Rejali

Rachel Naomi Remen

Andrew Revkin

Matthieu Ricard

Alice Rivlin

Cecil M. Robeck, Jr.

Andrew Robinson

Marilynne Robinson

Dario Robleto

Richard Rodriguez

Maria Romero

Mike Rose

Catherine Roskam

Coleen Rowley

Michael Ruse

Mary Doria Russell

Jonathan Sacks	Sherry Turkle
Omid Safi	Desmond Tutu
Don Saliers	Anthony Ugolnik
Emily Saliers	Sahar Ullah
Sharon Salzberg	Bessel van der Kolk
Cheryl Sanders	Mary Stewart Van Leeuwen
Matthew Sanford	Jean Vanier
Gustavo Santaolalla	Yanina Vaschenko
Sandy Eisenberg Sasso	Manuel Vásquez
Nathan Schneider	Charles Villa-Vicencio
Katharine Jefferts Schori	Miroslav Volf
Harold M. Schulweis	Binyavanga Wainaina
Mary Hope Schwoebel	Steven Waldman
Anoushka Shankar	Jim Wallis
Sabiha Shariff	Arlene Sanchez Walsh
Martin Sheen	Larry Ward
Gwendolyn Zoharah Simmons	Kay Warren
Tami Simon	Rick Warren
Steve Skojec	Abigail Washburn
James K. A. Smith	Bruce Weigl
Andrew Solomon	Leon Weinstein
Mark Souder	Margaret Wertheim
Elie Spitz	Elie Wiesel
David Steindl-Rast	Ellen Williams
Esther Sternberg	Terry Tempest Williams
Columba Stewart	David Sloan Wilson
Amy Sullivan	Christian Wiman
Tayyaba Syed	Diane Winston
Maria Tatar	Michael Wolfe
Doris Taylor	Robert Wright
Studs Terkel	Mayfair Yang
Myrtle Thompson	Rachel Yehuda
Robert Thurman	Arthur Zajonc
Phyllis Tickle	Paul Zak
Eckhart Tolle	Andrew Zolli
David Treuer	Laurie Zoloth
Pádraig Ó Tuama	Avivah Zornberg

INDEX